TUNNELLERS

Photo, F. C. Inglis

"THE TUNNELLERS' FRIENDS"—THE SCOTTISH WAR MEMORIAL,
EDINBURGH

TUNNELLERS

The Story of the Tunnelling Companies,
Royal Engineers, during the World War

BY

Captain W. GRANT GRIEVE

AND

BERNARD NEWMAN

ILLUSTRATED

HERBERT JENKINS LIMITED
3 YORK STREET · ST. JAMES'S
LONDON S.W.1 ✿ ✿ ✿ ✿ ✿

A HERBERT JENKINS' BOOK

First printing 1936

Printed and bound by Antony Rowe Ltd, Eastbourne

TO THOSE WHO
STAYED UNDERGROUND

CONTENTS

CHAPTER   PAGE

        FOREWORD   -   -   -   -   -   -   11

        INTRODUCTION -   -   -   -   -   -   17

   I.   THE BIRTH OF THE TUNNELLING COMPANIES   23

  II.   1915   -   -   -   -   -   -   -   37

 III.   GALLIPOLI   -   -   -   -   -   - 77

  IV.   SPRING, 1916 -   -   -   -   -   -   87

   V.   THE SOMME, 1916   -   -   -   -   -   112

  VI.   ARRAS, 1917 -   -   -   -   -   -   139

 VII.   GIVENCHY, THE BLUFF——AND ELSEWHERE   -   163

VIII.   FOSSE 8 -   -   -   -   -   -   -   191

  IX.   NIEUPORT, 1917   -   -   -   -   -   199

   X.   MESSINES, 1917   -   -   -   -   -   204

  XI.   PASSCHENDAELE   -   -   -   -   -   248

 XII.   THE MARCH RETREAT, 1918   -   -   -   256

XIII.   GIVENCHY AND THE LYS, 1918 -   -   -   275

 XIV.   THE TURN OF THE TIDE   -   -   -   -   292

  XV.   THE TUNNELLERS' FRIENDS -   -   -   -   311

        CONCLUSION   -   -   -   -   -   -   316

        INDEX   -   -   -   -   -   -   -   325

ILLUSTRATIONS

" The Tunnellers' Friends," The Scottish War Memorial,
  Edinburgh -   -   -   -   -   -   - *Frontispiece*

FACING PAGE

The Late Lieut.-Col. Sir John Norton Griffiths, Bart.,
  D.S.O., M.P. -   -   -   -   -   -   -   38

Major-General R. Napier Harvey, C.B., C.M.G., D.S.O. -   74

Mine Crater at La Boisselle -   -   -   -   -   -   130

Interior of Mine Crater in High Wood -   -   -   -   130

Rescue of Trapped Miner by Sapper wearing Proto Set -   -   186

Australian Tunnellers Constructing Dugout -   -   -   250

Havrincourt Bridge -   -   -   -   -   -   -   300

FOREWORD

BY

MAJOR-GENERAL R. NAPIER HARVEY, C.B., C.M.G., D.S.O.

IT was a great pleasure to be asked to write a foreword to this volume ; for it gives me the opportunity to add something to impress the mind of the reading public with the real character of the work which these very gallant gentlemen, " the Tunnellers," were called upon to perform in France and elsewhere during the War. I was associated with them from the very inception of the scheme for the formation of special mining companies and left them at the end of 1917. I accompanied Major Norton Griffiths on his memorable trip from G.H.Q., St. Omer, to the front line at Givenchy, when he inter-viewed every Head-quarters formation *en route*, and explained the science of " clay-kicking " before the aston-ished members of each successive Staff which he met, and I was again with him on his way back after he had satisfactorily proved to himself and his colleague, Foreman Miles, that mining operations were feasible, and pro-claiming that the nature of the clay made his mouth water.

Once started, the formation of the Tunnelling Companies wanted no " boosting," for Norton Griffiths, armed with the Adjutant-General's authority, brooked no delay, and cadres of Companies sprang up as fast as he called for them.

After officers and men came the provision of suitable tools and materials. These were collected at home and sent out to France. The tools demanded were almost unknown to Ordnance officers ; but nothing that was not familiar to miners was accepted. They wanted Hardy picks, miners' shovels, timber sets of miners' dimensions, surveying instruments to suit work in galleries—away with five-feet dumpy levels and theodolites, bring up those on dwarf legs for use in galleries not more than four feet high. Miners' dials appeared in numbers, to the confusion of the A.O.D., who had never seen this type before. Ventilation ! The army type of blower, *last used in the Crimean War*, made a noise like a traction engine, and always drew fire. These were speedily replaced by blacksmith's bellows, and later by Holman's air pumps, in order to save unnecessary casualties among ventilator men. Power pumps of a special design for evacuating water, not liable to be choked by the threads of hairy jute of which sandbags, which were used for carrying spoil from mine face to dump, were made, were obtained from home under some difficulty. Listening apparatus was painfully evolved from the stethoscopes borrowed by Norton Griffiths from the London Water Board via French soldiers' water-bottles fitted with medical stethoscope tubes, and finally to Geophones. This French invention may safely be called the greatest discovery in mine warfare—with a pair of geophones and a compass a good listener could tell you all about the activities of an enemy miner almost as well as if he saw the man face to face.

Again, a suitable explosive for mining use had to be found. By the end of 1914 no cordite was available ; nor was guncotton ; the whole supply of both was reserved, the former for gun and rifle ammunition, and the latter for naval purposes, mines and torpedoes. Fortunately, an inventor suggested that ammonal was plentiful, safe and effective. Finally, large numbers of canaries and white mice were required, the humble friends of the miner, to warn him of the presence of deadly gases.

It may be stated generally that during the year 1915 most of the preliminaries for the work of the Tunnelling Companies had been tried out.

With the exception of the operations round Hill 60, in April, there had been no very extensive mining operations in 1915, but there had been a great deal of sporadic work at shallow levels, not more than twenty to thirty feet depth ; there was very little to show for it, however, though nearly thirty companies had been formed and launched at their local objective, which was the protection of our infantry in the front line trenches. During 1915 theories were formed that something better than unco-ordinated local efforts should be attempted—why not a combined offensive by two or more companies ?

Again it was Norton Griffiths' brain which, far away in August, 1915, sowed the seed of " Messines." The seed fell apparently unheeded ; but, like other seeds, it germinated in secret, and by January, 1916, the seedling plant was approved by the Commander-in-Chief, and eventually grew to fabulous size.

It was now, in the latter part of 1915, that the authorities at home suggested the concentration of the control of the mining under one head at G.H.Q., with a representative at every Army Headquarters. The proposal was approved by G.H.Q., and the necessary appointments were made of an Inspector of Mines at G.H.Q. and four Controllers, one for each Army. Thus, 1916 saw the systematic control of mining operations in co-operation with surface attacks. Every battle overground had its mining counterpart below.

Now that the mining personnel in the front line had their own representatives at G.H.Q., their requirements and views as to shortage in equipment, change in pattern of any instrument or scientific plant, and matters affecting personnel could be represented direct. Once a control office at G.H.Q. had been formed, records could be carefully compiled, important information and data were circulated to the companies, notes of everything of importance or interest collected. Thus, for instance, when it came to drawing up regulations to prevent any risk to our own men from debris blown by our mines at Messines, the whole of the data for the purpose were at hand, and the regulations drawn up and issued resulted in there being no case of failure.

Special mention must be made of mine rescue work, which was organised under Lieut.-Colonel Dale-Logan, one of the devoted band of medical officers attached to the miners. To him was entrusted the whole of the mine rescue organisation and the training of the rescue crews. All the great success which attended the work is due to him.

The story here told is how the Imperial miners from all over the world, after a bad start in December, 1914, fought the German miners, and had finally beaten them at every point of the game by the time the mines of Messines had been fired in 1917.

The following pages are crowded with stories describing the gallantry of Tunnellers in every field in France. Can you beat the following examples ?   The calm self-sacrifice of Lieutenant Hansen at Givenchy ; the patient waiting and hoping of Sapper Bedson at Peckham for ten days, and his ultimate release ; the cool courage of Stokes and Hill, who waited and watched below a German gallery at Armentiêres for ten days until zero, and then " blew " while the enemy was working ; of heroes like Brisco at the Bluff, and Beasley at La Cordonnier, who fought the enemy hand-to-hand with electric torch in one hand and revolver in the other ; of Spencer, at the Bluff, who scouted out in No Man's Land, geophone in hand, dodging about from shell hole to shell hole till he located the enemy working in his gallery, and then bored down and blew him from the surface ; again, the patient waiting for zero hour while the enemy was heard approaching, and the skilful listening of the Australian miners at Hill 60, who predicted that the enemy gallery would pass clear of theirs, and were calmly working when the time came for the Hill 60 mine to play its appointed part in the Messines victory.

Details of all these exploits, and many other similar, can be read in " TUNNELLERS," and are taken from records left by this band of heroes, whose footsteps I was privileged to follow and on some few occasions to direct.

Never before had such a colossal amount of explosive been concentrated in one area as on one section of the Messines front—two hundred and fifty tons on a front of four thousand five hundred yards.   And this without a single failure, in spite of the constant efforts of the Germans to find their opponents.

I was once asked how it was that the secret of the mines was never given away.   The answer was : " The miners didn't talk, and no one else knew."   Even when the

German mining had ceased and our miners took to other work, they were constantly exposed to dangers in searching for and removing booby traps, concealed charges, delay-action mines, etc., left behind by the Germans in their retreat.   The amount of explosive thus collected amounted to no less than two and a half million pounds.

In addition to this second main branch of work, the Tunnelling Companies proved their general usefulness by taking on every form of engineering work as it came to hand ;   construction of deep dugouts, repairs to roads, bridge building, water supply, drainage ;   and in times of stress they fought in the line with rifles, fully proving the claim of their originators that the Tunnelling Companies as organised for the Great War were the most valuable engineering units in France, and the most highly-prized by the commander of any formation who managed to get possession of even one company of them.

R. N. HARVEY

INTRODUCTION

THIS is really Captain Grieve's book. Himself a Tunneller, he has spent nearly three years among the overwhelming mass of archives covering the mining part of the War. In due course he produced a detailed history of the Tunnelling Companies.

His manuscript was submitted to several eminent authorities, and also to me. Now, Captain Grieve had, of course, written as a Tunneller for Tunnellers, but we came to the unanimous conclusion that the story deserved a far wider public. It is a story which ought to be told to the world ; reading it, my first impression was that Tunnellers had been absurdly modest ; I myself, with four years' service in France, had only the haziest idea of the value of their contribution.

In my partial redrafting of the book I have left almost untouched the interesting fact and detail which Grieve has collected. I have simplified his account so as to make it more readily intelligible to the lay reader ; I have added an occasional setting and frequent comments. I tried to avoid excess in simplification ; the exploits of the Tunnellers belong to history, and deserve a detailed telling.

Theirs is a grand story to tell. I do not pretend that some sections are easy reading, and the book is necessarily episodic. But there can scarcely be an ex-serviceman who will not thrill time and time again at recollections aroused by a tale of those stern days from a new angle. Many Tunnellers, in fact, will themselves be surprised at the magnitude of the mining effort. And non-service readers will surely be filled with admiration for the men whose lives often depended on the length of a canary's claws.

BERNARD NEWMAN

HARROW,

January, 1936.

ACKNOWLEDGMENTS

THIS record of the activities of the Tunnellers has been made possible by the courtesy of Brigadier-General Sir James Edmonds, C.B., C.M.G., R.E., Director of the Historical Section (Military Branch) of the Committee of Imperial Defence. General Edmonds has on many occasions given me invaluable personal assistance, and at all times his staff has been most helpful. Major A. F. Becke, R.A., has aided me in the compilation of some of the maps, which have been drawn from information supplied by the Historical Section. The text includes several quotations from the Official History of the War, which are gratefully acknowledged.

Major-General R. Napier Harvey, C.B., C.M.G., D.S.O., Inspector of Mines at G.H.Q., 1916–17, has been most helpful in supplying data. I have also to thank the Institution of Royal Engineers, Chatham, for permission to reproduce plans and sketches as published in " Military Mining."

My grateful thanks are also tendered to Lieut.-Colonel L. G. D. Hutchinson, M.C., who has arranged the drawing of the bulk of the sketches included in the book ; to the staffs of the Imperial War Museum Library and Photographic Sections, for willing and valuable help ; to Captain T. H. Smith, late Honorary Secretary to the Tunnellers Old Comrades' Association ; and to all those Tunneller officers who, by supplying me with information, have contributed to the compilation of the volume.

I want also to acknowledge my debt to Mr. Bernard Newman, whose knowledge of the War and ability as a writer made him an invaluable collaborator.

W. GRANT GRIEVE

TUNNELLERS

TUNNELLERS

CHAPTER I

THE BIRTH OF THE TUNNELLING COMPANIES

I

THE war of movement in the West was over. The greatest armies known in history had met at the frontiers in heroic yet confused clash ; on both sides commanders entered the campaign with exuberant expectations—and within a few days all hopes were sadly diminished. The Schlieffen plan, grandly conceived but inadequately executed, failed not less certainly if more spectacularly than Plan XVII, inadequately conceived but gallantly executed. There followed the turning point of the Marne, when far-sighted men began to prepare for a long war : not so the rival commanders ; after a vain clash on the Aisne, each endeavoured to outflank the other in the mis-named " Race to the Sea." So battle was joined from Switzerland to the North Sea—four hundred miles of mortal combat. The great " sweeps," the " masses of manœuvre," the outflankings, the counter-marchings, the cavalry charges—all these were compulsorily discarded, most of them for the duration of the War. Mobile warfare gave place to siege tactics.

This highly significant fact was realised by the fighting men weeks (sometimes years !) before his commanders. At a very early stage he found that the costly and complicated machinery of modern warfare was totally inadequate, particularly to the offensive. Once the war of manœuvre was over, the dominant weapon was not the howitzer, the machine-gun, or the rifle, but the humble spade. Ingenious men bent their energies to the harassing

23

of an enemy roughly entrenched behind a barrier of barbed wire. It was remarkable that some of their happiest efforts were based on ancient ideas—adaptations of the weapons of the days when a war was little more than a succession of skirmishes and sieges. The grenade, the sling, the mortar, the catapult—all these were revived from the realm of the museum. Due perhaps to the haste of their improvisation, many of the weapons were almost as dangerous to friend as to foe. But valuable weeks passed before anyone in authority gave any consideration to the most obvious and one of the most effective forms of siege warfare—the mine

At this time the British Army—almost exclusively trained for mobile warfare—had no special organisation capable of conducting mining effectively, although some instruction had been given to the Field and Fortress Companies of the Royal Engineers. This training consisted of sinking a small shaft and driving a short gallery, both lined with the standard R.E. casing, in which a charge was placed and exploded. But as this work was rather hurried and crowded into a few days, the site chosen for these operations was naturally selected with an eye to easy working, so that the experience thus gained was totally inadequate as a guide to mining in bad ground.

Some very useful data were, however, obtained at Chatham in 1907, when more elaborate experimental work was carried out ; this consisted of attacking one of the forts by driving galleries in chalk, firing large charges in them, and also firing charges in the counter-mines— a series of permanent galleries or listening posts around the forts. It was unfortunate that the valuable experience gained in these operations was not available to the Tunnelling Companies in their early days, for undoubtedly it would have been of great assistance to them.

A little desultory sapping undertaken by the Sappers and Miners of the Indian Corps appears to be the first attempt at mining on the part of the British. As early as November, 1914, attempts had been made with " placed " mines. Actually, these " mines " were little more than portable charges, placed in position near the German trenches by men crawling out between the lines at night, and fired from our trenches. These " mines," however, were not very successful.

The first official move in mine warfare on the British side was made by General Sir Henry Rawlinson, commanding the IV corps, who wrote on 3rd December, 1914, to Army headquarters suggesting the formation of a special battalion of sappers and miners to undertake such work. This idea was received with approval, and forwarded to G.H.Q., with a strong recommendation that it should be adopted.

Coincidently, another British officer of vastly different rank and temperament was considering even more practical propositions. In 2nd King Edward's Horse, a regiment he was largely instrumental in raising, was an officer remarkable for energy and enthusiasm—Major J. Norton Griffiths, M.P., the head of a large firm of Engineering Contractors, who had carried out numerous engineering works in various parts of the world as well as at home. In addition, he had found time to devote some of his boundless activity to politics ; being a keen Imperialist, he was popularly known by the nickname of " Empire Jack."

His active spirit curbed by the boredom of training troops at home, and eager to find some new outlet for his pent-up energies, he conceived the idea that his experience in tunnelling might be of service to the Army in France. He accordingly wrote, on 15th December, 1914, to the War Office, stating that he had an expert lot of underground tunnellers and borers who had experience in driving tunnels under London, Manchester and other large cities. These men were specialists in a class of work known as " working on the cross " or " clay-kicking " ; the chief merits of which are that men can work speedily and noiselessly in a very limited space. Suggesting that as sapping would, in all probability, prove of the utmost importance, he asked permission to collect quietly a certain number of these men, even if for experimental purposes only, and take them to such places along the front where this class of work might prove extremely useful.

At this very moment the first serious British mine was

under construction. The Dehra Dun Brigade of the Indian Corps had been ordered to attack from the Orchard, on the Festubert front. In conjunction with this attack a shallow gallery was run out 70 feet towards the enemy trenches, when it was estimated to be within 13 feet of a German sap. A charge of 45 lbs. of gun-cotton was placed in position, but, before it could be fired, an enemy trench mortar bombardment flattened our parapet to such an extent that the trench had to be evacuated. The sap head was closed and the mine abandoned : this was not a very auspicious augury for Norton Griffiths' campaign.

The first honours of mine warfare very definitely went to the enemy, whose equipment for trench warfare in all its forms was vastly superior to ours. On 20th December, 1914, he launched an attack on the Indian Corps, then holding the Givenchy-Festubert front. Supported by an artillery and trench-mortar bombardment, the infantry advance was preceded by the firing of a series of ten small mines under the fire trenches, east of Le Plantin, occupied by the Sirhind Brigade, which was so completely surprised and shaken that the survivors were incapable of offering any serious resistance to the enemy and were compelled to fall back to the reserve line some 500 yards in rear. These were the first recorded mines fired against the British during the War, and though they were only small charges, their physical and moral effects were considerable.

Subsequently an account of them, prepared by the German VII Corps, was captured by us ; as it gives full details and indicates the careful preparation and carrying out of this attack it is worth quoting fully :

" Sap-heads had been dug out from our line to within three metres of the enemy's position. The enemy, who was very active in throwing hand grenades, had forced us to cover in our sap-heads. He himself had made no saps in the region of the attack. From the ten sap-heads in the zone of the attack, mines were laid under the enemy's trenches, each charged with 50 kilogrammes of explosives.

" To ensure the ignition of the mines, the attack was arranged for 9.0 a.m. so that the leads could be tested by the company commander and his second in command, and that any improvement which appeared necessary could be made by daylight. A mine was also laid under a house, held by the enemy on the right of the front of attack (Quinque Rue), and was charged

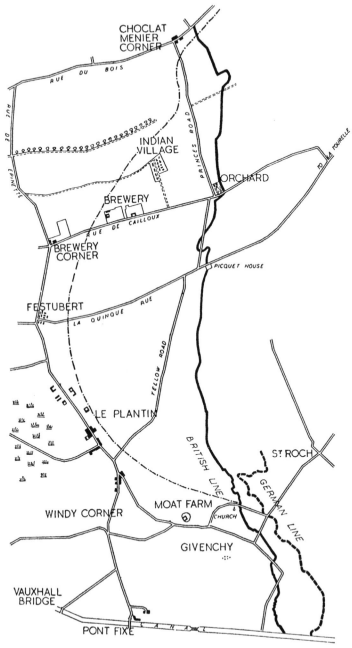

CHOCLAT MENIER CORNER

RUE DU BOIS

RUE DE L'ÉPINETTE

INDIAN VILLAGE

PRINCES ROAD

TO TOURELLE

ORCHARD

BREWERY

RUE DE CAILLOUX

BREWERY CORNER

PICQUET HOUSE

FESTUBERT

LA QUINQUE RUE

YELLOW ROAD

LE PLANTIN

ST ROCH

BRITISH LINE

GERMAN LINE

MOAT FARM

WINDY CORNER

CHURCH

GIVENCHY

VAUXHALL BRIDGE

CANAL

PONT FIXE

SCENE OF THE FIRST MINING ATTACK; THE DOTTED LINE
SHOWS THE FINAL BRITISH POSITION

with 300 kilogrammes (660 lbs.) of explosive. All the telephone communications were manned to ensure the neighbouring sectors commencing
the attack simultaneously in the event of there being any delay in the explosion.
Actually the explosion did not take place till 10.25 in the morning owing
to special difficulties in connection with one of the leads. When it was
reported to the senior pioneer officer on the front of the attack that all the
mines were ready, he had three flare signals fired simultaneously. This
signal was only meant for pioneers, who then fired all the mines, including
the one under the house in Quinque Rue.*

" At the same time a number of *Minenwerfer* directed their fire on to the
cover trench. The explosion was the signal for the attack, which was carried
out as follows by the 2nd and 3rd Battalions, 57 Regt. Infantry, 2nd and
3rd Companies of the 7th Pioneer Battalion (less 2 sections) and the 1st
Battalion, 19th Pioneer Regt. (less 1 Company).

" A storming party of half a section of infantry with 12 pioneers was in
readiness in each of the 10 saps. They rushed into the enemy's trench,
searched it for mines, and cleared it with hand grenades and incendiary
torches.

" A second storming party (in strength, a section of infantry between
every two saps) rushed simultaneously across the open from their own
position on both sides of the sap (sortie steps had been prepared for this),
and reached the cover trench behind the enemy's position.

" A third party—a company from each Battalion—occupied our own
trench in case of a counter-attack.

" A working party in reserve—the remaining sections of the six attacking
companies with pioneer detachments and material for providing cover
(shields, sandbags, etc.)—followed the attacking party into the enemy's
cover trench for the purpose of reconstructing this into a new position facing
West. Every Battalion had therefore sent forward 3 companies in echelon
for the attack, and retained one in rear for holding the original position against
counter-attacks.

" Up to the moment of the explosion, the allotment of targets and task
of the artillery remained the same as they had been on the previous days,
so as not to excite the attention of the enemy.

" Not until the mines were fired were the neighbouring sectors to engage
the enemy by increased fire action.

" The whole operation was carried out according to plan. The 10 mines
exploded simultaneously. With the aid of the overpowering effect produced by them, our attacking parties, who had immediately rushed forward,
succeeded in getting into the enemy's cover trench with few losses, and took
up their position there. The enemy, English and Indians, who fled from
the position, suffered heavy losses.

" The effect of this attack on the enemy was such that he immediately
brought up the 9th Indian Cavalry Brigade which was in reserve at Béthune,
and part of the 142nd French Territorial Regt., and 'alarmed' the 1st
Infantry Division (English) which belonged to his army reserve and was

* This mine failed to explode.

in the vicinity of Hazebrouck. This division was brought up by rail and motor to Béthune and used for heavy counter-attacks on the 20th, 21st and 22nd, all of which were repulsed with heavy losses.

" There are many indications that the enemy suffered great loss, both moral and physical, through the explosion of the mines.

" Six machine guns and eleven small trench mortars were captured and 19 officers and 815 men taken prisoners. According to a reliable estimate 3,000 of the enemy lay dead upon the battle-field.

" In dugouts of the trenches which were destroyed by the mines, a large number of Indian corpses were found still sitting; they had apparently been suffocated. In view of the success we obtained, our own losses in the attack (10 officers and 425 men wounded now in the hospitals of the Army Corps, 549 slightly wounded, and about 250 killed) were not great, and in the actual assault itself they were inappreciable. Apart from the bravery of the troops, success was due to the minute and detailed preparation, by both the infantry and the pioneers and to the accurately timed co-ordination of the mines, *Minenwerfer*, infantry assault and artillery fire."

II

As a direct result of this reverse, G.H.Q. instructed Armies to proceed with offensive sapping and mining. But the Field Companies were already overwhelmed with other important duties ; on them fell the brunt of the improvisation necessary in the first unprepared winter of trench warfare, and it was physically impossible for them to undertake the additional duty of conducting mining operations. Moreover, they had not the personnel necessary to give effective supervision to such an undertaking. Nevertheless, a certain amount of casual mining was actually done by some Field Companies, Fortress Companies, Field Squadrons and Divisional Engineers, much of which was taken over by the Tunnelling Companies on their formation.

In order to assist the Field Companies, men with mining experience were collected from units already at the front and formed into *Brigade Mining Sections*, each of which usually consisted of one officer and about fifty other ranks. These formations commenced work at once, though most of the work they did consisted of sinking small shallow shafts and driving galleries for listening posts. Unfortunately, this work was undertaken in too great haste and probably resulted in the spoiling of many good mining sites. For, when the enemy pushed his mines towards our trenches, he was at a much greater depth, and a big charge fired in a shallow gallery would destroy our mines without seriously harming the enemy. This also may be said of much of the work taken over from the French later on, when the British front was extended.

Towards the end of December, 1914, G.H.Q. received from the War Office Major Norton Griffiths' letter, containing suggestions for the use of " clay-kickers," for consideration. As was almost inevitable, the new idea was not received with any great enthusiasm : it was argued that military mining differed considerably from its civilian counterpart in that discipline was of primary importance. Further, owing to the very dangerous nature of this work, it was feared that the men engaged upon it might not be relied upon when working within 20 yards of the enemy, with a good chance of being buried in their own tunnels.

Incidentally, the infantry reinforcements arriving in France at this time were also under suspicion, and it was feared that they would be no match, in close fighting, for the better trained and more experienced German soldiers. Fortunately, in both cases, these doubts proved groundless.

But despite the askant glances of G.H.Q., a series of events, trifling in themselves, were sufficient to force the hands of those commanders who distrusted the civilian soldier. Early in 1915 there were unmistakable signs that the enemy was mining on a definite system, and both First and Second Army made urgent demands for special mining units to protect their front and counter the enemy's efforts, especially at Givenchy and in the vicinity of Ypres. But before any decision had been reached as to the employment of miners, the enemy once again succeeded in mining our front line—this time opposite the Brickstacks on he Cuinchy front.

On 25th January, 1915, at about 6.20 a.m., a deserter came in to our lines and reported that the enemy had mined our trenches, and that an attack would be commenced in about half-an-hour's time. Consequently, all troops were immediately warned. At 7.30 a.m. there was a big explosion south of the La Bassée Canal, followed shortly afterwards by a series of violent explosions, twenty or more in number, along the front line trench.

Under cover of the smoke, dust and confusion caused by these explosions, the enemy launched an attack and, meeting with little opposition, soon overran the first and support lines of trenches, and succeeded in reaching a strong point in rear known as the " Keep," where he was finally held up. The Guards Brigade were holding this part of the front at the time, and though counter attacks were immediately carried out, the original trenches were not recovered from the enemy.

This was the second occasion within a month on which a series of small mines were fired beneath our front line, and each time the enemy had succeeded in making an advance—at a considerable cost to us. Yet even at this stage further persuasion was apparently necessary, and the initiative came, not from G.H.Q., but from the War Office.

Towards the end of January, 1915, the War Office informed G.H.Q. that it was now in a position to obtain a considerable number of specially qualified men, and asked whether they should be enlisted at once, or at some future date. Yet even the War Office appears to have had only a hazy notion of the practicalities of mining, for at the same time it was suggested that the wet sand on the Belgian coast would be a very suitable material for the men to work in ! Mining is not quite the same thing as the making of sand pies : one of the miner's principal difficulties is not the construction of his tunnel, but keeping it intact.

Then followed an immediate request from G.H.Q. for the enlistment of two hundred experts in tunnelling, coupled with the proviso, " if they can be relied upon." It was considered that, " as Scotch miners are notoriously undisciplined people," it would be better not to ask for too large a number at first. But the force of circumstances sidetracked these doubts, for early in February, 1915, subordinate commanders all along the front were making insistent demands for miners ; thus it was decided on reconsidering the matter that the experiment should be tried with more than the two hundred originally asked for, and, if as many as five hundred miners could be secured, they would be taken readily. The proviso had now changed its ground, for G.H.Q. insisted that the men must be sent out " with all possible speed." G.H.Q. even suggested to the First and Second Army Commanders that as one of the French Armies had achieved considerable success by the employment of sapping and mining, particularly in the vital matter of the saving of life and ammunition in minor operations, more use might be made of this form of attack. Attention was drawn to the fact that certain units (e.g. the 8th Royal Scots) consisted almost entirely of miners, and drafts might be requisitioned from their ranks.

On receipt of the somewhat belated request from G.H.Q., the Army Council took immediate action, and, on 13th February, 1915, instructed Major Norton Griffiths to proceed to France to confer with G.H.Q. as to the numbers, equipment and organisation most suitable for the Tunnelling Companies which it was proposed to raise for service with the Expeditionary Force. Leaving London accompanied by two civilians in uniform, Mr. Leeming and Foreman Miles, Norton Griffiths arrived at G.H.Q. the same evening and reported to General Fowke, Engineer-in-Chief, at St. Omer. On the following morning the little party of pioneers accompanied Colonel Harvey to Béthune to I Corps Headquarters, where a discussion on the proposals took place, and later proceeded to the trenches at Givenchy, where the mine at the Orchard was inspected. On the way to Givenchy various headquarters had to be visited, in order to obtain the necessary permission to pass through the area under their control. At each of these Norton Griffiths described the object of his visit and, the more to impress the importance of his claim, surprised and delighted his astonished audience by initiating them into the mysteries of " clay-kicking," going through the motions lying prone on the office floor.

III

As the mysteries of the art of " clay-kicking " will be as unknown to the average reader as they were to the average staff officer, it would be well to interpolate a brief description here. It must be appreciated that military mining bears little relation to civil mining. In mineral mining the galleries are of vital importance, and must be of appropriate size and properly maintained, so as to be adequate to convey the mineral from the working face to the bottom of the shaft—sometimes a distance of miles. In military mining, however, the gallery is only a means to an end—that end being the placing of a charge under the enemy line. Consequently, the gallery is as small as is compatible with efficient working. There is, however, a type of civilian mining almost exactly equivalent to this —the work done by the men who burrow the small tunnels under cities for such purposes as the carrying of electric cables, water pipes, and the like.

This type of mining is popularly known as " clay-kicking "—because the subsoil of a city is often clay, and because the movements of the miner resemble kicks. It is alternatively known as " working on the cross," for a reason which will become immediately apparent.

" Clay-kicking " is a method of driving a heading or a gallery so small that the miner has insufficient room to swing a pick. The necessary energy is supplied by the legs, and not by the arms, as is usually the case in coal mining. Instead of a pick, a grafting tool is used ; this is a special type of spade, with a curved blade, the cutting edge of which is much narrower than the top. Some inches above the heel of the spade are projections on either side of the handle ; these receive the force of the thrust imparted by the " kicker's " legs.

In order to secure the necessary leverage, the " kicker " must have some support for his back. This is provided by a substantial wooden cross (hence the term, " working on the cross "). The cross is set up in the gallery or tunnel at an angle of about 45 degrees, near enough to the working face for the " kicker " to reach it with ease. The " kicker " sits on an improvised seat on the upright of the cross, leans his shoulders against its projecting arms, and stabs the grafting tool into the clay. He then drives the tool home with his legs, and prises the clay down.

C

Once the first " spit " has been removed, usually from the lower half of the face, progress is easier. The lumps of clay are passed back along the tunnel by another man, lying full length alongside the " kicker." They are loaded by other miners into sacks or miniature trucks, and removed from the gallery.

CLAY-KICKER, WITH GRAFTING TOOL (LEFT)
AND " CROSS " (RIGHT)

The sketch inset should make the uncomfortable process quite clear. Readers who knew the army in the early days of 1915 will easily raise a smile at the very thought of Norton Griffiths' performance—giving practical demonstrations of the tactics of the " clay-kicker " at each headquarters before an amused and sophisticated staff.

IV

Norton Griffiths and his advisers, after a close inspection of the ground, came to the conclusion that the district was suitable for " kicking " ; the good news was reported to each headquarters on their return journey.

The next day, the 15th February, the result of the visit was reported to General Fowke, and further discussion took place with General McCready and General Sir William Robertson regarding the organization, transport, pay, etc., of these new units. By this time G.H.Q. was fully convinced that specialized mining formations were essential, and Norton Griffiths was despatched to the War Office with a special letter asking for authority to form these units. The War Office wired approval immediately.

The story of the gestation of the Tunnelling Companies is a familiar one—a few enthusiastic specialists seeking to convince a lukewarm staff, with many disappointments and delays. But now everyone was agreed—every obstacle to the formation of mining units had fallen down or had been removed. The days that followed were days of drama, with the active energy of Norton Griffiths for once unrestricted. His first step was to wire to Mr. Leeming, who had returned to England, to enlist twenty of the most suitable " Kickers " * he could find. Norton Griffiths himself dashed back to London, to find the twenty men already awaiting him. His firm was engaged in a big contract in Manchester, and Leeming had no difficulty in securing the necessary volunteers.

Eighteen of the men succeeded in passing the medical examination, and proceeded to the depot at Chatham forthwith. There they were issued with uniform and kit ; they must have looked a motley collection, apparently confirming the worst suspicions of G.H.Q. Naturally they had no drill, and their first salutes almost induced apoplexy in a passing sergeant-major. They held their rifles gingerly, as if not quite certain which end the bullet came out. But three days later they were at work in France.

General Harvey has described the formation of the first Tunnelling Company as the quickest *intentional* move of the War. On Thursday, February 17th, 1915, these men, as civilians, were burrowing sewers under Manchester : on Monday, 21st February, they were working underground at Givenchy ! Not even the Germans ever surpassed this feat of rapid organization—for tools and equipment had of course to be provided as well as men : the greater part of the credit must go to Norton Griffiths, who was now in his element.

The nucleus party from Manchester had been joined

---

* Norton Griffiths consistently referred to them by the appropriate term of " Moles," but could not persuade the War Office to adopt this term—although it had been used to describe military miners prior to the War.

in France by twelve miners drawn from each of the following regiments :   8th South Wales Borderers, 11th Welsh Regiment, and 8th South Staffs.   Norton Griffiths' subaltern was Second-Lieutenant L. A. Barclay, R.E.   The complete unit was railed to Béthune.   The 11th Field Company, R.E., had a few days previously commenced mining in the 2nd Divisional area, between Givenchy and the La Bassée Canal.   The new-comers, who formed the nucleus of 170th Tunnellers Company, were attached to the 11th Field Company, under Captain Preedy, and immediately on their arrival were set to work underground. The long, painstaking and glorious history of the Tunnellers had begun.

CHAPTER II

1915

I

THE idea once adopted, the War Office pursued it with vigour, and immediately sanctioned the formation of eight Tunnelling Companies, four to be allotted to each Army. Norton Griffiths, the presiding genius of the new arm, found ample scope for his tireless enthusiasm, and with remarkable energy and zeal applied himself to the task of supervising their formation, and starting them to work at the front. For this task Norton Griffiths was attached to G.H.Q. The original proposal was that these new units should be Army Troops, and that each company should consist of six officers and two hundred and twenty-seven men, comprising a headquarters and four sections, each of three reliefs capable of driving twelve headings ; actually this establishment was revised from time to time. The commanding officers were to be regular Royal Engineer Officers ; in the case of the first eight companies this rule prevailed, but later is was found that the regulation was neither desirable nor necessary, as the new formations contained officers with the necessary experience and ability to undertake the command. The junior officers were to be mining or civil engineers.

Armed with a special letter of authority which gave him almost autocratic powers, Norton Griffiths was to be seen almost daily rushing across from G.H.Q. to the War Office, then back again to France with an officer or two and a handful of miners or " kickers," hastily collected and hurried to Chatham, where, in a remarkably short time, they would be transformed into soldiers, and actually served out with rifles and ammunition, the correct use of which still remained a mystery to many of them long after their arrival at the front. Wise officers relieved recruits of their ammunition immediately on their arrival at their units ; this prevented accidents.

These men were a very fine type, though some of them were long past the age usually regarded as suitable for enlistment into H.M. Forces ; but the need of their services was pressing. Regulations sometimes do become elastic, and the official eye is not always too critical. So, with astonishing haste and scant ceremony, they were hurled into the scramble for supremacy underground.

Norton Griffiths did not overlook the potential material already serving with the British Expeditionary Force. He was no slave to official methods, and dashed off in his famous Rolls Royce to all parts of the front in his continuous search for suitable men. Battalions recruited from mining areas were specially paraded, and he often reaped an abundant harvest—much to the wrath and dismay of regimental officers who, themselves demanding reinforcements, saw their best men ruthlessly spirited away. Very few men could have undertaken such a task without incurring serious complaints. Probably the experience of Norton Griffiths as a politician stood him in good stead, for many a depleted battalion ruefully paid tribute to his persuasive ability. In addition he had a thorough knowledge of army psychology. Though he took many badly needed men, he usually left behind him some physical palliative as a peace-offering.

Norton Griffiths thoughtfully carried a few cases of " emergency rations "—usually consisting of whisky or port—obtained from unknown and probably illicit sources —in his car, and found them of the greatest value in consoling resentful Commanding Officers for the loss of their men.

He was aided in his task, too, by the enemy activity in mining. From all parts of the front came reports of enemy mines, and appeals for protection. Norton Griffiths' drafts, whether drawn from civilian or army sources, were hurried into action the moment they were available. Naturally the organization of the new units was scrappy : at first they were in the charge of Field Companies, R.E.,

THE LATE LIEUT.-COL. SIR JOHN NORTON GRIFFITHS, BART., D.S.O., M.P.

but gradually they outgrew their foster parents and became independent units.

Not all the recruits were " clay-kickers "—whose numbers were necessarily limited. But it was argued, justly, that ordinary miners would adapt themselves to the different working conditions. This, however, was no easy task—particularly under the deplorable conditions prevailing at the front, but the men faced it gallantly and successfully. Theirs was no pleasant initiation—a hurried call from civilian work, a scramble into uniform, a Channel crossing which almost took the heart out of them, followed by an appalling rail journey in cattle trucks. Then, within a few hours of reaching the battle area, with not the slightest allowance for acclimatization, they would find themselves underground. But their spirit never faltered : on the contrary, they represented keenness personified, and there was much competition for the honour of firing the first British mine of the War.

Actually, the honour cannot be claimed by the Tunnelling Companies, for on 17th February, 1915, a mine which had been taken over from the French was completed and fired by Lieut. White, R.E., on the front of the 28th Division at Hill 60. Its effect was not very great, and only its sentimental importance calls for notice.

II

In the meantime, however, the enemy had been continuously active. On the morning of the same day—17th February—a small salient in our front line at Zwarteleen was blown up by an enemy mine. The Germans rushed and occupied the position, but were eventually driven out by the 2nd Battalion King's Own East Yorkshire Regiment, who were holding this part of the line at the time. It should be noted that on each occasion when the enemy fired a mine his infantry acted in co-operation with the pioneers and either made a slight advance or, as in this instance, occupied the crater.

A few days later another, a more severe disaster, overtook our troops. To the east of Hill 60 there is a large

wood which was colloquially known as Shrewsbury Forest.
Through this the line ran, and here also the right flank
of the Second Cavalry Division joined up with the French
Army.   The 16th Lancers were holding this part of the
front on 21st February, 1915, when, as if to challenge the
arrival of the first draft of miners, the enemy blew a large
mine, the largest to date in fact, destroying the trenches
and inflicting severe losses on the cavalry.   The enemy,
as usual, occupied the crater.   Immediate counter-attacks
were launched, but were held up by machine-gun fire,
and eventually a new line had to be made on our side of
the crater.

At this stage, before considering the achievements of
the Tunnelling Companies, it is convenient to glance at
the geological formation of the district, the difficulties of
the ground, and the methods by which they were overcome.

The whole of the twenty miles of front held by the
British Army in the early part of 1915 lay in the flat,
water-logged valley of the Lys River, now a comparatively
small stream, but which in bygone ages was in all probability
much wider.   During countless centuries vast deposits of
alluvium were spread over the valley by the flood waters,
and these generally consisted of sandy loam, upon beds
of saturated sand, with occasional pebbles and sometimes
a band of shaly stone above blue clay—identical with the
London clay.   These layers vary in thickness, and in
places it is possible to sink 16 feet to 20 feet before reaching
the wet or running sand.   Mining in the top layers was
simple enough, and it was in these belts that the majority
of the early shallow mines were driven.   Any attempt
at deeper mining invariably met with difficulties, as it was
almost impossible to penetrate the running sand and
slurry * with the means then available.

Shaft-sinking in wet or broken ground is a most difficult
and dangerous operation in civil practice, and calls for the
exercise of extreme caution and the most experienced
workmanship even with adequate material and plant, but

* Slurry—mud, sand or loam, saturated with water until it become semi-liquid
—a hopeless element for a miner to tackle without proper equipment.

the difficulties are increased enormously when it is undertaken under such conditions as prevailed at the front early
in 1915. The difficulty of sinking through these saturated
strata can well be realized when it is recalled that in sinking
some of the shafts in the nearby coal basin, what is known
as the freezing process had to be employed to overcome
the water difficulty.

This is a method sometimes adopted for sinking shafts
in wet ground. Water is perhaps the greatest enemy of
the sinker. If the ground is so wet that it is impossible
to sink a shaft—because the sides cave in at every step—
more elaborate measures are necessary. But if he can
solidify the ground temporarily, it will remain firm long
enough to excavate and timber his shaft. This solidifying
is accomplished by actually freezing the ground about the
site of the shaft. Pipes are inserted into the ground around
but at some distance from the prospective shaft. A freezing
liquid is circulated through the pipes, and when the ground
is thoroughly frozen the shaft is sunk through the hard
ground. After the shaft has been lined, the ground is
allowed to thaw—the lining keeping back the released
water.

It is probable that the enemy did actually employ this
method, for an extract from a letter of a French officer
in the trenches near Soissons states that " if there is no dry
stratum, the enemy freezes the ground." Little wonder
is it, then, that handicapped by the appalling conditions
and particularly the lack of suitable and adequate material,
many of the early attempts at shaft-sinking failed and had
to be abandoned. In fact, so serious did the situation
become at this period, that the confidence of the staff in
the efficacy of mining evaporated, and the question of its
complete abandonment was considered.

Mining engineers, however, were only dismayed by the
almost complete absence of plant. Tubbing,* for example,
was an elementary essential, but whence could it be pro-
cured ? An officer was sent post-haste to search the local

* Tubbing—material used for the lining of a shaft or tunnel for the purpose
of keeping back water. It usually consists of cast iron segments, made so as to
bolt together. Miles of it line the London Underground Railway.

iron works for sheet iron to make improvised tubbing, but the French Government had already been round and collected all such material for munitions.

Eventually one company succeeded in sinking a shaft six feet by six feet through six feet of running sand by means of " piling." * and this fact is recorded by Norton Griffiths in his diary. Then gradually—far too gradually —proper material and plant became available. Even then the rate of supply was wholly inadequate. Once started, mining operations developed so rapidly that it became increasingly difficult to obtained the necessary stores, tools and materials, so that frequently work had to be delayed for want of these essentials. Timber, frames and sets, which were at this period supplied by Field Companies, to which the sections of Tunnelling Companies were attached, could not be turned out in sufficiently large quantities to keep the miners employed. It is doubtful if serious mining has ever been attempted under such conditions as those which prevailed in the early days of 1915.

The explosives used in the early mines were ordinary black powder, packed in 100 lb. sacks, and gun-cotton, in slabs of a couple of pounds. Gun-cotton was in great demand by the Navy and, as it could not be produced in sufficiently large quantities to supply both services, a substitute had to be found.

About this time ammonal came into prominence, and a small parcel of some ten tons, packed in water-tight tins, was despatched to France for experimental purposes. So satisfactory did it prove that it was almost universally adopted for charging mines ; it was safe, easy to handle, and could not be detonated by a bullet ; the resultant gases after a large explosion were not so troublesome as those of gun-cotton ; its detonation was more suitable for mines ; further, it had the added advantage of being some three and a half times as powerful as guncotton. The introduction and use of ammonal is perhaps one of the

---

Piling, or spiling—a method of shaft sinking in wet or sandy ground. Long boards, pointed chisel fashion at one end, are driven down into the ground. When a complete square has been formed, the enclosed earth is removed—i.e. in effect, the walls of the shaft are built before the shaft itself is excavated.

most important events in mine warfare from a Tunneller's point of view.

In spite of every difficulty, however, the work was pressed eagerly forward. The distinction of being the first actually to mine the enemy's trenches fell to the lot of 171st Tunnelling Company. Lieutenant Cloutman and a party of ten miners were attached to the 1st Field Squadron, R.E., which had commenced mining in the 1st Cavalry Division area near Ypres. From a shaft 12 feet deep, sunk by the 1st Field Squadron, a small gallery, 25 feet long, was run out towards the enemy's lines, and a charge of 130 lbs. of gunpowder fired with the object of " rendering the region difficult for the enemy to mine." But evidently this mine destroyed a shaft or deep sap-head, for timber was observed to have been blown into the air by the effect of the explosion, which appeared to be very concentrated.

The same company was then engaged in constructing a listening gallery in the form of a " T," from a shaft 11 feet deep. The gallery was only 31 feet and the " T " 7 feet to the left and 15 feet to the right. This work only occupied forty-eight hours, after which the men were immediately engaged in an offensive mine which had been commenced by the 1st Field Squadron. The gallery had been driven 50 feet when the " kickers " took over ; assisted by the sappers and some miners collected locally, the gallery was pushed out another 70 feet to within 10 feet of the enemy's line. Although hampered and delayed by bad air, lack of lamps, and awkward bands of hard clay—the ground was hard sand and quite dry, requiring no timbering ; consequently the time taken, including charging with 850 lbs. of gunpowder and 38 feet of tamping* with air spaces, was only seventy-two hours. As the enemy

---

* Tamping. It is not enough to fire a charge placed at the end of a gallery. Since the force of the consequent explosion follows the line of least resistance, this force would flow along the uninterrupted gallery, and the earth above would scarcely be disturbed. Consequently, when the charge has been placed in position, the gallery behind it must be filled in *and made stronger than the earth above the charge*. This filling behind the charge is called tamping ; it need not consist of one solid mass of sandbags, as gaps or air spaces between successive masses of sandbags help to withstand the shock of the explosion. Sometimes timbers are strutted across the gallery to stiffen the tamping.

was heard approaching and was believed to be below this gallery, the mine was fired at 7.40 p.m. on the 4th of March, 1915, by electricity.   A crater some 45 feet in diameter was formed and a considerable portion of the trench blown up. The 2nd Dragoon Guards went forward and occupied some 70 yards of the damaged trench, but later were dislodged by means of a bombing attack.

This then is the first occasion on which we succeeded in damaging the enemy's trenches by means of a mine, and also the first occasion on which British " infantry " participated, though on a small scale, in an attack in connection with the firing of a mine.

But, as Mr. Weller would have remarked, these " infantry " were cavalry !

III

During March, mining activity developed considerably, consequent upon the arrival of more miners, and its importance began to be more fully appreciated.

The 173rd Tunnelling Company came into being and commenced work at Fauquissart near Neuve Chapelle under Major G. C. Williams, R.E., in the 7th Division, IV Corps, area ; while in the III Corps area 174th Tunnelling Company commenced mining at Houplines under Major B. W. Y. Danford, R.E. ; in these cases, as with the companies formed earlier, the mining was of a defensive nature, designed to keep German miners at a healthy distance from our own lines.   Thus, within a month of the creation of the Tunnelling Companies, extensive defensive work was in progress at Hill 60, Ploegsteert, Houplines, St. Eloi, Fauquissart, Ypres Salient, Givenchy and Cuinchy.

In most of these areas the trenches were close together, but opposite 174th Company the distance was upwards of 120 yards.   In one case the objective was no less than 540 yards distant, but this difficulty did not seem to deter these hardy pioneers, who gleefully set out to drive that distance without the aid of proper survey instruments or ventilating apparatus.   In the early days of mining many of the objectives scarcely merited the immense labour involved—barricades across roads, behind which probably sheltered small garrisons, suspected machine-gun posts or snipers' lairs were considered suitable ; later on attention was concentrated on targets worthy of the labour of shaft sinking and driving long galleries through such difficult ground. The first mining report by Norton Griffiths concerns the Givenchy and Cuinchy mines at the Brickstacks, and is dated 13th March, 1915. As it is quite brief it is here quoted verbatim.

" Work has been of a defensive character, with a view of checking the mining work of the Germans. The head of No. 3 drive has some 50 yards to go to reach the German trenches. Capt. Preedy states he intended to push this work, but hitherto his instructions were to confine his efforts to *defensive measures* which the accompanying plan proves to be the case. Work well done. Soil, sandy loam, fair amount of water. Depth average 12 to 14 feet.

" Work at Givenchy, protective work of a similar nature, has been stopped on the morning of my visit, the 12th of March, 1915, on account of a general attack. Much energy and good progress has been made by Captain Preedy and the officers under his command."

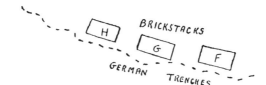

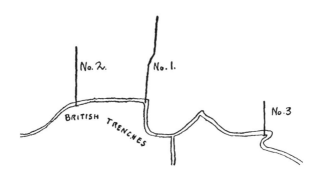

At the request of G.H.Q., the position of shafts was shown in relation to the trenches, and what is probably the first plan showing the locality of the shafts and headings completed at Cuinchy at the 2nd March, 1915, is shown on page 45, a modest enough beginning dwarfed into insignificance by the plan opposite, which shows the condition of the same ground fifteen months later.

IV

To the south of St. Eloi was a well-known feature of the Ypres Salient—a tiny eminence known as the Mound. This was strongly held by British troops, and was highly fortified—as trench fortifications counted in those days. On 14th March, 1915, the Germans exploded mines under, and in the vicinity of, the Mound, and under the protection of a very heavy artillery fire launched a determined attack in which bombing was the chief feature. They succeeded in capturing the Mound and the trenches in the immediate neighbourhood, including one of our shafts. Part of our line was blown up at the same time as part of the Mound, and most of the troops on the Mound, together with two machine guns and their detachments were buried.

A counter-attack met with no more than partial success, as the Germans were able, from their advantageous position on the Mound, to enfilade the trenches which we recaptured so that they became untenable and were evacuated.

Our losses in this engagement were considerable, amounting to some five hundred officers and men killed, wounded and missing. Subsequently the defences at the Mound were strengthened and mining restarted by a Field Company ; eventually this work was taken over by the 172nd Tunnelling Company.

About this time also the enemy fired a large mine at Zwarteleen and made a crater 30 feet deep at the side of the miniature salient there. This effort was not so successful ; either the mine was blown too easily or its position badly calculated, for as much damage was done to the German line as to ours.

More and more reinforcements for the Tunnelling

CRATERS on CUINCHY FRONT.

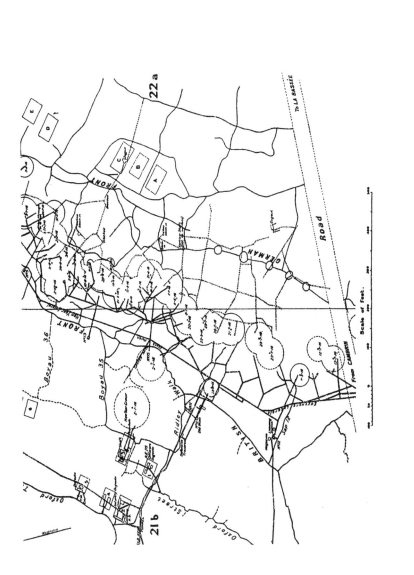

Companies were arriving almost daily, but the constant demands made by the infantry for protection underground were becoming a source of concern to corps commanders ; the moral effect of the enemy mines was beginning to tell on the troops, and they were becoming "jumpy."

Patrick MacGill, in his play "Suspense," accurately caught the atmosphere of alarm impelled by the sounds of mining beneath. The bravest men, who never funked a " show " which involved hand-to-hand fighting, have confessed to nervous fears as they have crouched in a dug-out listening to the monotonous tapping of enemy miners below. So long as the tapping continued there was safety —it was the occasional silences that were terrifying. Then the enemy might be charging his mine—at any moment might come death in its most horrible form. Our infantry had stood the strain of that appalling first winter of the War —deficient in numbers, with utterly inadequate trench equipment, they had held their own against a courageous and persistent enemy. Now a new trial oppressed their harassed nerves ; above, death came suddenly ; below, his approach was slow and stealthy, and the waiting time was enough to shake the stoutest heart.

Hence the persistent demands for counter-mining action —and hence the innumerable false alarms. Any noises which could not be accounted for were attributed to the enemy working in his mines, even when heard in places a very considerable distance from the front line. Nothing would suffice except that a mining officer personally visited the scene of the " scare," as these reports came to be known, and held a thorough investigation into the cause of the suspicious sounds. Not infrequently the result was comic. Two confidently reported cases of enemy mining proved to be inspired by the sound of a batman chopping a wiring picket with an entrenching tool in order to provide fuel for cooking the evening meal, and—infinitely richer— a brood of young mice squeaking in their nest behind the timbers of a dugout. The croaking of frogs in a pond in the garden of a house used as a Brigade Headquarters was thought to be the sound of an enemy boring machine until suspicion was allayed by a Tunnelling Officer.

As time went on the number of these scares increased considerably, and an enormous amount of time was taken up in investigating them which could have been put to better purposes, especially as the number of officers available to supervise mining was all too small.

In the early days of mining, listening—for suspicious sounds which would indicate the approach of enemy galleries—was invariably carried out by the unaided ear, as no suitable apparatus was available. The Metropolitan Water Board was approached, and gave half a dozen listening sticks, such as are used by its officials to detect leaks in water mains, but these proved of little or no value.

An improvised listening instrument frequently used was a French Army pattern water bottle. Suitable on account of its round, flat shape, the bottle was filled with water, and to the stopper was fitted a rubber tube, an ear-piece being attached to the other end. Although somewhat crude in design, this instrument proved fairly reliable, though some experience in its use was necessary to achieve the best results. Coal miners are adept at listening, as they are accustomed to signal to each other, especially when headings driven from opposite directions are approaching, by knocking on the face with the head of a pick. This signal is commonly known as the " miner's knock," and consists of two dashes and three dots repeated several times.

Mining was now developing rapidly, and its earlier improvisations gave place to a more solid organization, especially in the matter of reliefs. In order to achieve success, mining must be carried on continuously throughout the twenty-four hours. This is essential, but obviously an adequate number of men must be available. Some of the earlier parties to arrive remained as long as three weeks in the line before being relieved, although they did not all work continuously. The shortage of officers threw even heavier burdens on the shoulders of the few available. Lieut. Cassels, of 175th Company, remained for six weeks in a dugout in Sanctuary Wood—possibly a record. Such a state of affairs could not continue indefinitely, and the war establishment again came up for revision, and was increased to permit of proper shifts or reliefs being arranged.

V

Early in April the work commenced in February was nearing completion on the Cuinchy front, where one section of 170th Tunnelling Company was at work. Three shafts, each 4 feet by 4 feet, numbered 1, 2 and 3, had been sunk in the front line to 16 feet deep and galleries driven out with about 12 feet of head cover, and connected by a lateral—a gallery running parallel to the front line trench —some 65 feet out from the shafts. These galleries were originally intended for use as listening galleries, but later it was decided to attack two points in the enemy line.

Consequently the galleries from Nos. 2 and 3 shafts were driven out, the former towards " G " brickstack, which had been fortified and used as a machine-gun post

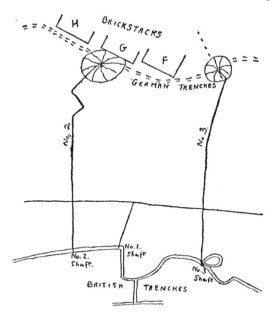

and also as a snipers' lair, while the latter attacked the junction of a communication trench and the front line at a point to the south of " F " brickstack. The formation was described as softish sandstone mixed with loam, which

D

gave off a large amount of water, and "kicking" was impossible. From the listening gallery or lateral, No. 2 gallery (whose dimensions were 2 feet 9 inches at the bottom by 2 feet 6 inches at the top by 3 feet 6 inches high) was driven 170 feet in fifteen days ; No. 3 was 158 feet long, and took the same time. In both cases work was delayed as the pumps were inadequate to deal with the water and also for the want of good blowers or ventilating apparatus. When the two galleries were about 25 feet from their objectives, work was stopped again in order that the necessary three days' notice should be given before firing the mines.

A charge of 1,000 lbs. of gunpowder, contained in ten water-proof bags, was placed in a chamber 3 feet by 3 feet by 3 feet, and both electrical and instantaneous fuses were inserted into the charge. The tamping was of filled sandbags—7 feet solid, then 5 feet air space and a further 1½ feet solid. The tamping was carefully done, but more would have been put in had not the time of firing the mines been advanced by one hour. It was estimated that the charge was 8 feet below the bottom of the enemy's trench.

Fired on 3rd April, 1915, this mine is reported to have destroyed about 80 yards of the enemy trench, and brought down the face of the centre or " G " brickstack.

The mine from No. 3 shaft was similar, the chamber being 2 feet by 3 feet by 3 feet, charged with 650 lbs. of gunpowder and 7 feet solid tamping, 4 feet air space, 5 feet sandbags, 5 feet air space and 5 feet sandbags. The explosion destroyed 30 yards of trench. This work was under the direct supervision of Second-Lieutenant E. P. Lacy, Westmorland and Cumberland Yeomanry, attached R.E.

A few days after the firing of these mines, the sections of the 170th Tunnelling Company, R.E., which had been until now attached to the Field Companies, R.E., in the First and Second Divisions, were brought together and formed into an independent unit under Captain Preedy, R.E., and headquarters were established at the Mayor's house in Cambrin.

From now onwards the firing of mines by both sides

became almost incessant, but by this time the enemy was not having matters all his own way, as he did at first. Nevertheless, he did succeed in getting in another big blow with even more sinister purpose.

At 11.15 p.m. on 14th April, 1915, a German mine was fired at St. Eloi which formed a huge crater some 70 feet in diameter, about 50 feet short of a shaft which 172nd Tunnelling Company had sunk from the cellar of a ruined house—a favourite place for shafts in the early days. The house was shaken down and part of the trench damaged, but only slight damage was done to the shaft. Several days' artillery fire preceded the explosion, but it was not followed by an infantry attack, which, under the circumstances, was most fortunate, as our troops were somewhat demoralized and in confusion, and in no way prepared to resist one had it developed.

It transpired subsequently that the real reason for this bombardment was to detract attention from the vicinity of Ypres, where all was in readiness for the launching of the first gas attack on April 15th ; but, owing to the wind being unfavourable, it had to be postponed.

VI

To the south-east of Ypres, where the Ypres-Commines railway line passes through a cutting in the Ypres Ridge, are to be found three small artificial mounds or spoil-banks, formed by the excavated earth from the cutting. One of these mounds, " Hill 60," became famous throughout the world as the scene of some of the fiercest fighting throughout the war. It received its name from the fact that on certain maps the sixty metre contour line, indicating its height above sea level, encircles the top of the mound enclosing the numerals 60. Many other hills and eminences were distinguished in a similar manner, such as Hill 63 near Messines, and Hill 70 near Lens.

Hill 60, although the slightest of eminences, was of the greatest importance, as it commanded Ypres, gave uninterrupted observation over a large tract of country to the west, and also overlooked our communication

trenches. Covering Hill 60, but on the other side of the
railway line, was another spoil-bank, which, on account
of its peculiar shape, became known as the " Caterpillar."
The third and smaller mound was called the " Dump."

Until the 10th December, 1914, the French had held
Hill 60, but on that date they were driven off by the
German 39th Division.   In order to regain this position,
the French had commenced to mine it, and when eventually
the British 28th Division took over this part of the line,
they continued to use the gallery from which the French
had fired several mines.   The men employed at this point
were miners recruited from the 1st and 3rd Battalions
Monmouthshire Regiment (T.F.), attached to the 1st
Northumbrian Field Company, R.E., working under the
direction of Major D. M. Griffiths, R.E., assistant to the
C.R.E., 28th Division.   Subsequently, when the 5th
Division relieved the 28th Division, this party remained
to carry on and complete the work in the mines, and
eventually it became absorbed in 171st Tunnelling Company, R.E., under the command of Captain Wellesley,
during the early part of April, 1915.

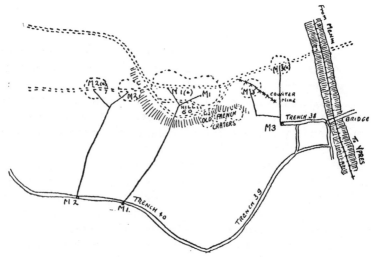

A short month after it had been commenced, the largest
and most ambitious mining scheme of the early days—a

systematic attack on Hill 60—was progressing satisfactorily and rapidly approaching completion. It consisted of three shafts, M.1 and M.2, situated in Trench No. 40, and M.3, in Trench No. 38—the latter being the French shaft in which several small mines had been fired. It was only 3 feet by 2 feet 6 inches in section, with about 60 feet of 3 feet 3 inches by 2 feet 3 inches gallery left intact ; its condition was very bad indeed, as due regard had not been paid either to direction or level. Matters were not improved by the numerous corpses, rifles, and broken timber buried there on account of the " shot-up " nature of the ground.

M.1 and M.2 shafts were both 12 feet deep, and 4 feet 6 inches square in section, and the galleries became smaller in section the nearer they approached the enemy. Commencing at 4 feet by 4 feet 6 inches, they contracted to 2 feet 6 inches top by 3 feet bottom by 4 feet high, and towards the end forked into still more reduced galleries of 2 feet top by 3 feet bottom by 3 feet 3 inches high.

This latter section seemed to be quite sufficient when the galleries were being driven, but when being charged the confined space occasioned great difficulty in handling the bags of gunpowder, which weighed 100 lbs. each. The galleries were chambered to receive 2,700 lbs. of gunpowder in M.1 and M.1A, 2,000 lbs. of gunpowder in M.2 and M.2A, but in M.3 and M.3A only 500 lbs. of gun-cotton were placed in the galleries.

The tamping was 10 feet sandbags, and 10 feet air space, alternatively for 50 feet. Great precautions were taken to provide against the chance of a misfire, and two sets each of electric leads and two powder fuses—that is, four independent means of igniting the charges—were put in. As a further precaution against the risk of misfire, an officer took charge of the placing and testing the leads and detonators, each of which had a separate exploder.

At M.3, in the gallery nearest to the old French craters, the enemy's countermine had been heard approaching the shaft—so close, in fact, that it was thought that at any moment the Germans might break into our gallery, as they could be heard talking distinctly. Accordingly work on this gallery was stopped and a charge of 250 pounds of guncotton placed as a precautionary measure, only to be fired in case of emergency. Great caution was employed in placing this charge, which was subsequently increased to 500 lbs. just before firing, and very little tamping was put in.

The day before the attack, the Germans were again heard working very close to the junction of M.3 and M.3A, their intention being to blow up Trench 38. Fortunately they were forestalled by a couple of days, for on the 17th April, 1915, at 7 p.m., our mines were fired with great effect, "the inside of the hill being literally blown out," resulting in an enormous pit being formed by the craters of the two centre mines, M.1 and M.1A, which in shape resembled the figure "8" on its side, its longer axis measuring about 180 feet, the other 90 feet. At the time these mines were considered to be enormous, but in comparison with some of the subsequent blows they appear very insignificant. At the same time it must be remembered that up till now we had very little practical knowledge on which to base our preparations. The men who did the early work had to buy their own experience—often very dearly—and deserve the highest credit that they accomplished so much under the prevailing conditions.

One of the charges hung fire for two seconds ; then some black substance appeared in the centre of the column of earth which was thrown up. This was possibly damp and unexploded powder. Our trenches were undamaged by the explosions, and the infantry attack which co-operated with the mines was quite successful, and met with only few casualities on the way over No Man's Land ; they were subjected later on to heavy artillery fire and numerous counter attacks, in which they repulsed the enemy with heavy losses : thus Hill 60 again found itself within the Allied line—its aspect almost completely changed by its new scars.

In driving these galleries, trouble was experienced in providing good and ample ventilation. The service blowers were found to be much too noisy, and were discarded in favour of the ordinary blacksmith's bellows, to which rubber hose pipes were attached and led along the galleries. Lighting was by means of candles, but when charges were placed, ordinary electric hand torches were used ; as the batteries soon gave out, these were quite unsuitable.

Flat trollies made to run as silently as possible on wooden rails were used to remove the sandbags filled with spoil ; these were disposed of by building them into the breast-works, and therefore did not disclose the fact that mining was in progress—as the building of a huge spoil dump would inevitably have done.

Our troops were warned to take cover from the debris, some of which flew 200 to 300 feet high, and was scattered over a distance of 250 yards away. The curiosity of one man, who could not resist the very natural impulse to peer over the parapet to watch the effect of the mines exploding, cost him his life.

An examination of the captured enemy trenches disclosed a mine charged, tamped, and complete with leads and an exploder, and one is left to speculate as to what the result would have been had the enemy got his " blow " in first. This charge was subsequently withdrawn at considerable risk by two officers, Lieutenant Dick-Cleland and Second-Lieutenant Gard'ner, of the 172nd Tunnelling Company, R.E.

Warnings had been issued to the troops against entering the mines until they had been reported free from gas, and also not to enter the craters for at least half an hour after their capture. Unfortunately, these warnings were disregarded by two sappers, who entered M.3 shaft thirty-six hours after the explosion of the mine and were asphyxiated, probably because of the large amount of gun-cotton used in the charge in these mines, and also to the small amount of tamping put in, owing to lack of time.

VII

It is common knowledge that the miner's greatest enemy is gas. As our operations became more ambitious, difficulties in countering gas increased. Curiously enough, two companies (170th and 172nd) had their first experience of the deadly effect of mine gases within a day of each other. As our mines progressed it was only natural that, sooner or later, opposing galleries would approach each other somewhere under No Man's Land. This happened at the Orchard Mine, Givenchy, where an enemy gallery was heard approaching—so near, in fact, that conversation was audible. It was decided to get our blow in first. A barricade was built in the face, and four feet back from it a second was in course of erection. Between these a charge was to be placed, a space being left at the top of the second barricade over which the charge was to be passed.

While Lieutenant Barclay and Lance-Corporal Bishop were actually engaged in this work, however, the enemy fired a mine. Sergeant Ford, who entered the mine shortly after the explosion, found that both had been killed instantly.

Next morning Captain Preedy went to the face of the gallery to investigate, and decided that a second attempt should be made to place the charge immediately. Lieutenant Torin was accordingly instructed to undertake this work, having had considerable experience in handling high explosives. Lieutenant Boardall and Second-Lieutenant Martin were detailed to accompany this officer for instruction. About noon, Private Bishop, who went down the mine, was overcome by gas resulting from the explosion of the German mine ; he was brought out by Sapper Smith, R.E., and Private Hesson.

The shift to which these men belonged was relieved at 2 p.m. The oncoming shift had not been informed of the presence of gas, possibly because the stoppage of the air pump was only temporary, and may have allowed a little gas to collect, which could be cleared easily when the pump began again. But a bombardment of the German trenches, during which our men were withdrawn from the saps, according to the practice prevailing at this period, caused further stoppage of the fan ; and, when this was concluded, Lieutenant Torin decided to visit the gallery and inspect the position before commencing work.

Followed by Sergeant Ford, Second-Lieutenant Martin

and Lieutenant Boardall, he proceeded along the gallery, pausing to light a candle, which burnt with a bright flame. There were no indications of the presence of gas, but all were overcome except Lieutenant Boardall, who managed to scramble out and raise the alarm. Corporal Hutchinson went down and brought out Second-Lieutenant Martin before he himself was overcome. Lieutenant G. Whidbone, 3rd Coldstream Guards, then organized a rescue party, and eventually all were brought out, but Lieutenant Torin was dead before being brought to the surface. On the 27th, Private Hall, 1st Black Watch, twice went down into the gallery with a rope tied round his waist, an exploit for which he volunteered. Not content with this, he again came up on the afternoon shift, after his shift had been relieved, and assisted in placing a charge, which was successfully fired on the 29th.

On 27th April, 1915, 172nd Tunnelling Company also had its first experience of gas—in this case from one of our own mines. In a gallery in the Kemmel sector a small charge of 100 lbs. of ammonal had been fired, as the enemy was known to be quite close. Four hours after the blow, Lieutenant Daniels and Sergeant Harper entered the gallery to examine the effect of the blow, and were overcome by gas. The alarm was raised and an officer from the trench with ten sappers formed a rescue party and went in and brought out the men. All the party were more or less badly gassed, and Sergeant Harper died from the effects.

Eventually the gallery was " bratticed " and cleared of gas. This process, commonly employed in coal mining, involves the use of brattice cloth, a heavy type of sacking or hessian, specially treated to render it impenetrable to air, and also to withstand damp. It is placed in position so as to divide a shaft or gallery into the unequal compartments. Good air is driven forcibly into one compartment, and carries the gas with it round the end of the brattice cloth along the length of the other compartment, thus completing its circulation and gradually clearing the gallery of gas. In the case of a shaft, the brattice cloth is hung down one side. A brazier is lighted at the bottom of the

smaller compartment formed, and the rising hot air is
assisted in its ascent by the heavier column of fresh air
and induces a current to circulate.

Gas sometimes had the most extraordinary effects.   One
tunnelling officer (Lieutenant Stafford Hill, of 185th Company) had the misfortune to be underground at the time
of a secondary gas explosion and was badly burned all
over.   The most inflammable part of his body—his hair—
completely vanished !   At the dressing station he received
a liberal anointing with picric acid and was swathed in
bandages.   It was some time before he recovered from the
shock of his gassing—only to receive another.   When
the bandages were removed, a wonderful crop of *bright
green hair* was revealed !   This so thrilled the local M.O.
that he invited his fellow medical cronies for miles around
to come and view his museum piece.   However, the
unnatural shade of hair soon disappeared.   But out of evil
cometh good ; the victim was at least spared any future
necessity of shaving or visiting a tonsorial artist.

VIII

Week by week the strength of the Tunnellers increased.
Towards the end of April 175th Company was formed at
Terdeghem under Major S. H. Cowan, R.E., and 176th
Company at Lestrem under Captain Momber, R.E.
Unlike the first five companies, these two were not rushed
into action with such haste.   As officers and men arrived,
they were attached to one or other of the older companies
for a short period to gain experience, and in one case an
experimental mine was constructed near the billet.   This
training seems to have been regarded with tedium, and
it was with pride that the O.C. made this important entry
in his diary.   " Orders received for 175th Company to
commence independent work at once."   Railway Wood,
Hooge, and Armagh Wood became the scene of its activities.
176th Company began to mine near the Orchard at Bois
du Biez, where suspicious sounds, of supposed enemy
mining, had been reported.

" Mine warfare commences when the attack and defence meet under-ground," according to instructions issued by the Germans in 1915. If that is so, then that state existed when the Germans broke into No. 2 mine level crossing, to the surprise of the men of 174th Company, who were working there. Contact was made at a point 70 feet in from the shaft, and after a fight, the enemy fired a small mobile charge, killing one of our men. A few days after this incident 172nd Company had a somewhat similar experience at G.I. mine. The enemy mined right up to the timber in our gallery, but we succeeded in firing a charge of 100 lbs., which made a crater and destroyed 10 yards of the German parapet, and also shook down part of the Peckham House. The gallery was again " picked up " and driven round the blown ground.

On account of the increasing number of mines and camouflets fired by both sides, the number of casualties from mine gases steadily increased, and several companies made urgent demands for modern rescue apparatus, to replace the antique smoke helmets, *actually relics of the Crimean War!* These resembled divers' helmets, cloth hanging down to be tucked inside the tunic. A hose pipe connected the helmet with a small hand bellows, by means of which the wearer was supplied with air ! The demand for twentieth century apparatus met a ready response, and six " Proto " sets, such as were in use at the mine rescue stations in the home coalfields, were sent to First and Second Army R.E. Parks ; Corporal Ellison and Lance-Corporal Clifford, both of whom had experience in the use and care of such apparatus, were detailed to take charge of them, and also to instruct others in their use. The following day twelve men from 171st Company arrived at Strazeele for a short course, followed by parties from other companies. From this beginning a Mine Rescue School was formed later at Armentières.

Two long drives which 173rd Company had pushed out with difficulty, on account of slurry and bad ventilation, under the enemy's trenches in the Cordonnerie Farm sector, were charged with 2,000 lbs. of gunpowder, and success-fully exploded. These mines were a preliminary to the attack on Aubers Ridge, and 50 feet of trench on each side of the craters were captured with little loss, but later had to be abandoned on account of the failure of the infantry attack elsewhere.

These headings were driven in the blue clay, though at times they ran out of it into the green sand immediately above, owing to the undulating nature of the top clay deposit. From one account of these mines, it is inferred that the Germans were not aware that it was possible to reach the clay, and they only attempted to do so after this blow. The opinion is contradicted by the fact that blue clay—a certain indication of mining in the vicinity— had previously been definitely identified in sandbags in the enemy parapet at Ploegsteert.

So far, it will have been noticed, the efforts of the Tunnelling Companies had been desultory, although individually successful. They were, of course, under the orders of army, corps, and divisional commanders, whose ideas naturally varied. Some looked upon the tunnellers as purely defensive fighters : others pitted them against appalling difficulties for most trivial objectives : some considered them quite useless. Except for the organized attack on Hill 60, all offensive tunnelling work had been entirely disconnected, and one company knew nothing of what its neighbour was doing. Through a complete lack of appreciation of tunnelling potentialities, valuable weeks of work were often wasted on the most trifling tactical advantage.

All this was very galling to Major Norton Griffiths, to whom the Tunnelling Companies owed their existence. His dream had come true—his tunnellers were growing daily in strength and experience. But he had never imagined that they would be used merely to put in defensive systems and occasionally to harass the enemy ; he took a longer view—the war on the Western Front had become a vast siege operation, whose problems should be tackled by appropriate siege methods. A definite policy was essential, not a series of isolated and detached attacks on enemy strong points. Accordingly, he worked out a preliminary scheme, involving the concentration of 172nd

and 174th Companies on the front between St. Eloi and
Wulverghem. Here was an awkward salient, and a well-
planned mining programme would make it possible to
flatten it out. But G.H.Q. frowned on his scheme—at
that time G.H.Q. was far from convinced that the front *was*
in a state of siege. Colonel Harvey, however, recognized
the potentialities of Norton Griffiths' plan. In it is the germ
of the great mining offensive which became known as the
Battle of Messines. But this was not fought until two
years later.

IX

The formation of 177th Tunnelling Company early in
June at Terdeghem under Captain P. W. Bliss, R.E.,
completed the eight companies originally authorized, and
a fortnight later it had commenced sinking two shafts
designated by the titles Buckingham Palace and Windsor
Castle. Little wonder then that, labouring under the
burden of such imposing designations, the ground was
unable to support them, and the latter collapsed and had
to be abandoned.

In our record of the progress of the Tunnelling Companies, the individual side must not be overlooked. No
great imagination is necessary to picture the miner at work
in a low, narrow tunnel under No Man's Land or even
under the German lines. The ordinary perils of mining
under such conditions and with inadequate equipment
would be quite enough for the ordinary man, but the
tunneller had to face the opposition of the enemy as well
as nature. A chance shell on the mouth of the shaft
might arrest the flow of precious air, or mean condemnation
to an indescribable death in a living tomb. More exciting
if no less unpleasant was the prospect of running into an
enemy gallery. War has made strange strides since the
days of chivalry : the knights of old would stare in amazement on a modern battle with the implements of death
miles away. And surely they would refuse to believe the
evidence offered by their own eyes could they have seen
underground combat—men fighting to the death in tiny
tunnels not more than three feet square.

Many were the exciting incidents that enlivened the monotony of the miner's day. Some of them might well be classed as fiction were the stories not fully substantiated. At the Old Monmouth Mine near Le Toquet, for example, was a big gallery, constructed some weeks previously, which was being kept in repair pending future operations. One day the two men engaged on this work were vastly surprised when a light was shone on them *from the direction of the German lines.* They fired several shots, and then advanced to the spot where the light had been seen, but could find no trace of the enemy. They duly reported this to their officer, Lieutenant P. Rought, who made a thorough examination of the gallery without discovering any untoward sign. Work was accordingly resumed, but shortly afterwards the enemy fired a mine which completely wrecked our gallery. Rescue work was quite impossible, and it was regretfully assumed that the two men at work in the gallery must be dead. However, three months later one of them, Private Longstaff, was reported by the Germans as a prisoner of war ! How he escaped the explosion is not known. He may have been overpowered and captured before the charge was fired, or he may have reached the surface through a shell crater. But if a fiction writer attempted to use such an incident, the critics would certainly describe it as " far-fetched."

174th Company had further exciting moments in the Ploegsteert sector. Here again the enemy fired a mine which damaged one of our galleries, cutting off nine men who were working near the face. Rescue work was immediately put in hand, short shifts of men working at top pressure. Fortunately, the armoured hose pipe had not been damaged by the explosion ; this had a double value—not only could a supply of air to the entombed men be maintained, but their morale was kept up by the use of the pipe as a speaking tube telling confidently of the desperate efforts of their comrades to rescue them. Thus encouraged, they themselves worked valiantly from their end.

No harder work was ever accomplished during the War. The gallery was a mass of broken timbers, but in thirty-six hours over 100 feet had been repaired or redriven, while the entombed men themselves, fighting for their very lives, had cleared no less than 30 feet. Hungry, but otherwise unhurt, all the nine men were liberated—and after a night's rest took up their normal place in the next shift !

x

A few days later the same company carried out a very enterprising scheme at Houplines. Six adits,* which had been commenced by the infantry as listening posts prior to the formation of the Tunnelling Companies, had been taken over in March, but as they had only about 8 feet of head cover, were not of much practical use as offensive galleries. Shaft chambers were constructed in some of them and shafts put down about 20 feet, and then galleries driven out to attack the enemy strong point colloquially known as the " Chicken Run." One of these galleries was over 100 yards long and had penetrated 100 feet beyond the enemy'a trenches, and branched. Each of its ends was charged with 600 lbs. of gunpowder. Three other headings had smaller charges.

Before these mines were quite ready an hostile gallery was detected approaching one of our galleries. A hasty blow would undoubtedly ruin all our plans and much labour would be wasted. By dint of restraint, and careful listening, continually carried out by two officers, Stokes and Hill, it was calculated that if the enemy gallery were allowed to advance, it would pass over the top of our own. The tenseness of the situation can well be imagined, but the opinion was justified—the German gallery literally scraped over the top of ours. So close was it that for two days the enemy could be heard talking loudly. The next day all was silence, which is usually a danger signal. Accordingly a camouflet † of 50 lbs. of ammonal was placed in the gallery, immediately beneath the German gallery, and this

---

* An adit is a horizontal drive into the side of a hill or cliff face.

† Camouflet—a small mine which expends all its force underground and does not break the surface. Used extensively in counter-mining.

was fired at 7 p.m. Twenty minutes later the two large
charges were fired, followed fifteen minutes afterwards by
the three smaller charges. Two days later the enemy
gallery was broken into from No. 4 heading, and much
useful information obtained.

Although Norton Griffiths's scheme for a deep level
attack, at least 60 feet deep, on a wide front, was at first
rejected, mainly on account of its lack of detail, it was not
abandoned entirely ; by order of General Allenby, 171st
Company commenced an incline shaft from the north side
of the railway cutting, referred to previously, the objectives
being Hill 60 and the Caterpillar, both some considerable
distance away. By way of an experiment, Lieutenant
Nicol of 174th Company designed an improvised wooden
caisson to sink through the waterlogged greensand beds
to the blue clay. Encouraged by this design, he set to work
to prepare plans for a more ambitious scheme, an iron
caisson, which the Army Workshops at Armentières built
to his specification. As the rings or sections were completed, they were sent to a site at Rue du Bois, and sinking
commenced. All was going well, and the caisson was
down 27 feet in running sand and slurry, when orders
were received that 174th Company were to be moved to
a new part of the front. This was typical of the confusion
of those days ! The caisson was then handed over to
173rd Company, and Lieutenant Cropper took charge,
having been given a special party of forty men to carry
on the sinking operations.*

In the beginning of June, 176th Company took over
the Givenchy sector from 170th Company, who in turn
extended to the right, taking over from the French a new
sector to the south of Cuinchy, and towards the end of
the month succeeded in destroying a small salient and
inflicting heavy losses on the enemy. The tactical method
employed is interesting. Two small mines were first
fired from the Old Mill Mine with the object of drawing
the enemy to occupy the salient in force. As was expected,
when the small mines " went up," the enemy manned
the salient—in anticipation of the customary infantry attack

* The sinking was successfully accomplished.

—and opened a heavy enfilade rifle and machine-gun fire, supported by trench mortars, on to the craters and our parapet. But these small mines were no more than a stratagem, and no sooner had the enemy concentrated his defence than a large charge was exploded, completely destroying the salient and its garrison, and wrecking the defences in the vicinity.

Near the Bluff 172nd Company had the unpleasant experience of running a gallery into the end of an enemy charge, and immediately commenced the ticklish job of removing it. After working two hours as silently as possible, for any sound would betray their presence and mean instant disaster, they discovered two detonators, which were removed with the greatest caution and respect. A party working under the direction of the O.C., Captain Hepburn and Lieutenant Syme, then removed the remainder of the charges, in all about 1,350 lbs. of pebble powder and lignosite. Both officers and several N.C.O.'s and men were suitably decorated for their action. It was ascertained later than the Germans were righteously indignant at this theft of one of their mines literally under their very noses !

XI

On 24th July, 1915, 174th Company moved to the Somme front and established headquarters at Bray. It took over from the French no less than sixty-six shafts at Carnoy, Fricourt, Maricourt and La Boisselle, and received a warm reception from the enemy, who could be heard plainly at work all around. The enemy was particularly active in these sectors and very aggressive, constantly firing camouflets, which usually succeeded in destroying not only our galleries, but the shafts also, just by way of demonstrating his superiority.

Generally speaking, the La Bassée canal forms the line of demarcation between two entirely different geological formations. To the north the country is flat, low-lying and water logged, rising only a few feet above sea level, with certain notable exceptions, while to the south

E

the chalk formation appears close to the surface. In the northern or clay area silent working was imperative, in the south or chalk area it was impossible. Hitherto the greater part of our mining had been in clay or sandy loam, so that this extension of our front marked the commence‑ ment of a new experience ; consequently, the miners had to adapt themselves to entirely new conditions of working.

When the Third Army took over this new front north of the Somme, there were not sufficient Tunnelling Com‑ panies to take over all the mines from the French. A nucleus of two officers and one hundred and twenty other ranks were sent from Rouen to X Corps, and Captain E. V. C. Wellesley, with four lorries laden with stores from the R.E. Park at Bergette, arrived to take command of 178th Company, R.E. Work was commenced at Tambour Duclos, near Fricourt, under the supervision of Commandant Thomas, 6me Gènie. At the same time another party of two officers and eighty other ranks left Rouen for X Corps, Third Army, and remained there until organized under Captain E. O. Alabaster to form 179th Tunnelling Company. Work was commenced at La Boisselle under the direction of Captain Piraud of the French Engineers. A group of Brigade Mining Sections was also formed, but even with their assistance, the French were obliged to leave a large party of about one thousand two hundred Engineers to carry on in the mines for some time after our infantry had taken over the surface.

The newly formed 179th Company provided one of the most piquant incidents of the War. When the orderly officer was inspecting a night shift at its headquarters in Albert, a man reported to him that the " soldier " standing beside him was a woman—and he was right ! " Sapper " Dorothy Lawrence was determined to obtain some first‑ hand information about life at the front. Gaining posses‑ sion of a uniform from some British soldiers she met in Paris, she set out to cycle to Béthune, via Amiens. Here she missed her way and reached Albert ; discarding her woman's clothes, she donned the uniform. She remained in Albert for about ten days before being sent back to Third Army Headquarters, and eventually to England.

The most intriguing part of this true story is
unfortunately missing : *how* did the man discover that his
half-section was a woman ?

XII

In the north, the incessant war against man and nature
continued. Two deep shafts at the Brickstacks, where
the inrush of water was so great that the ordinary lift and
force pumps were unable to cope with it, were causing so
much trouble that it was decided that power pumps were
necessary. Lieutenant Trower was sent to Paris to obtain
a compressor plant, made by the Ingersoll's Rand Company,
complete with pumps, drills and mechanical pick, as supplied
to the French Army. When the plant was installed, it
also was found inadequate to deal with the water, so the
scheme was abandoned and the plant sent to 178th Company.

The introduction of machinery such as the above, the
supply of Barrett forcing jacks and the use of an iron
caisson, indicate the rapid advancement of military mining
in a comparatively short time.

September was a busy month for 173rd Company.
At 2 a.m. on the morning of the 6th, one of their headings
came into contact with the timbers of an enemy gallery.
The men at the face behaved with admirable coolness.
Placing a sandbag into the hole and remaining in the
gallery, they quietly passed out word for the Sergeant.
He in turn sent for the officer on shift, and in the meantime commenced to place sandbags in the face. On the
arrival of the officer, the sandbags were removed in order
to examine the position more freely, taking the greatest
care not to disturb the enemy, who could be heard talking.
The officer decided to place a charge, first placing 3 feet
of tamping in the face and then the charge, through which
a hose pipe was laid. Through this Intelligence Officers
listened for nineteen days, the Tunnellers meanwhile
awaiting orders to fire the charge. No records appear to
have been kept of the results of the listening.

Later the same day, the floor of another gallery collapsed

into a German gallery, which it had struck. The enemy had organized a " reception committee " and were awaiting this event, as they immediately opened rapid fire from a safe distance down their gallery. In spite of this, a small charge of 25 lbs. of blastine was placed and fired. This had the effect of clearing the gallery, and by 10 a.m. it was possible to enter the mine, as the fumes had all cleared. Lieutenant F. Bell advanced a considerable distance along the gallery in the direction of the German shaft, and succeeded in building a barricade against which a 200 lb. charge was placed, tamped and fired at 6.30 p.m.

XIII

Owing to the distinct increase of mining activity on the part of the enemy, and the mining situation on the Somme front, the Engineer-in-Chief asked for authority to raise no less than seven additional Tunnelling Companies, to be formed at the base and brought into the line as complete units.

Meanwhile new companies continued to form. At Labuissiere, Captain W. E. Buckingham, R.E., was busily engaged collecting personnel for the 180th Tunnelling Company, and, in less than a week, commenced preliminary work for shaft sinking at La Philosophe and Vermelles. About the same time, 181st Tunnelling Company was mobilizing at Steenwerck under Captain J. N. Cash, R.E., and its first experience in the line was at Rue du Bois, where it took over the famous caisson, now down 34 feet.

To ensure the best service from a Tunnelling Company, it is necessary to supply it with a large infantry working party to remove the spoil quickly from the mines and dispose of it on the surface, and also to attend to the working of the ventilation fans and water pumps. Consequently it often happened that a Company Commander would be responsible for about one thousand men, and to get the best results more officers were required. To ensure proper supervision the war establishment again came up for revision. The new establishment provided that the officer commanding a Tunnelling Company should hold the rank of Major, and have an assistant or adjutant who would be responsible at headquarters when the O.C. was visiting the various sections—which were not always working in a group. Section Commanders were to be Captains, and the number of officers per section increased to four, and a roster was established. It was discovered that in some cases plans had not been kept, and as it is most essential that accurate plans and records should be kept of all mining work, provision was made for a draughtsman per company.

It was becoming increasingly difficult to provide sufficient reinforcements of the right stamp, and in consequence progress was being retarded. One company commander who had received a draft of thirty miners from England, described them as "an ancient looking lot." The spirit of these veterans, however, was remarkable, but military mining is a young man's job, and few men over fifty were able to stick it for more than six months.

XIV

The story of mine warfare to date has been casual and episodic—apparently disconnected attempts to attach some fragment of the enemy line. This, actually, was typical of the Allied strategy in 1915. There was little trace of a co-ordinated plan ; efforts were spasmodic, and generally the results obtained were out of all proportion to the casualties incurred. Generally, too, the anticipated results were out of all proportion to the resources available. Our attacks at Neuve Chapelle and Aubers Ridge, confidently expected to drive the Germans from their Flanders positions, were almost barren failures. But the autumn campaign promised better things. Here was no casual attack on a narrow front ; the French were to attack in great force in Champagne, while north and south of Lens British and French were to advance side by side.

As news of the impending offensive percolated along the

front—for secrecy was not the Allied strong point in 1915—
Tunnellers naturally began to visualize their share of the
battle. Lens was a mining area; the possibilities were
obvious. Keen company commanders studied maps and made
provisional plans. Some bold spirits went so far as to throw
out hints to the powers above. They discovered to their
dismay, however, that mining was to form no part of the
preparations for battle. The newly-formed 180th Tunnelling Company was indeed ordered to the Loos sector,
but there it found itself engaged in the construction of saps
and communication trenches ; nothing more.

The only active mining participation in the offensive
consisted of a " demonstration " in front of Hooge ; in
front of Sanctuary Wood four large mines were fired, to
attract German attention to this sector and away from
Loos. The mines inflicted considerable damage.

During the battle itself 180th Company rendered valuable
aid to the infantry by bringing up supplies of bombs,
ammunition, and other essentials. After the initial advance
it prepared the defences of the captured trenches and dug
a new line in front of Loos. This work was very important and was willingly performed, but it pertains to
pioneers rather than to skilled tunnellers.

In a battle where everything that could go wrong did so,
the unspoken questionings of Tunneller officers naturally
caused no heart-burnings. Loos was not a battle which
ranks high in the annals of British arms—except in the
valour of the men, mostly civilian soldiers, who fought it.
Yet one more question must be added to the many already
unanswered—why were the possibilities of mine warfare
so completely ignored ? Immediately *after* the battle
tunnellers were given free rein, and for two years this
sector was a hive of mining activity : Hohenzollern
Redoubt, the Quarries, Hulluch, and the Chalk pits are
names which will conjure up vivid memories to thousands
of miners.

In spite of its bungling, the attack at Loos came within
an ace of success. Small parties of troops did actually
penetrate the last German defences ; German headquarters as far back as Douai prepared for hasty departure.

But on the greater part of the front the force of the attack spent itself on the initial enemy defences. Suppose a dozen large mines had been fired at the moment of battle ? It would not have been impossible, and the results might have been far-reaching. Instead, the tunnellers were only flung into the fray after the battle had been fought and lost.

xv

Preparation of the second winter of the War added new tasks for tunnellers, who became responsible for an extensive dug-out system along most of the front. Mining activity continued incessantly, and the increasing number of casualities from gas poisoning in the mines gave rise to a rumour that the Germans were forcing a gas, probably a mixture containing chlorine, into our workings. Careful investigation failed to establish this. In all probability the gas was carbon monoxide, and had been forced into pockets in the clay or blown chalk, especially as the results of camouflets, where it remained until released by the approach of our galleries. Sometimes it came out with such force that it made a hissing sound, similar to a " blower " in a coal mine.

During October, the tunnelling strength was increased by about 50 per cent. by the formation of new companies, the first of which was 183rd. Formed at Rouen, under Captain H. C. B. Hickling, R.E., it immediately proceeded to Fontaine-les-Cappy. Here it took over the mines commenced by the 2nd Wessex Field Company, and was the first Tunnelling Company to be employed south of the River Somme. But its stay in this sector was brief, as the XII Corps, under which it was working, was relieved by the French. 183rd Company remained on under the French Corps, which had no engineers available to relieve it, for about a month, when it took over part of the 174th Company line.

At Rouen Base Depot also, 184th Tunnelling Company formed under Captain J. R. Gwyther, proceeded to Souzanne on the Somme and went into the line at Maricourt. Captain T. C. Richardson, R.E., took charge of

185th Tunnelling Company, proceeded with it to Albert for work at La Boisselle, and immediately commenced a new shaft in Lochnagar Street. A party of seven second-lieutenants and two hundred and fifty-nine other ranks collected at Rouen, left for Bailleil en route for La Clytte ; this was the nucleus of 250th Tunnelling Company, and a few days later it was joined by Captain C. H. Cropper, R.E., as O.C., and relieved 177th Company in the line, coming under the orders of the Canadian Division ; instructions to proceed at once with offensive mining were immediately received. Deeper shafts were therefore constructed in the support line, as the first line system was too shallow.

251st Tunnelling Company, under Captain F. Bullen, was formed at the Base and took over from 170th Company, which was withdrawn to Noeux-les-Mines, prior to commencing work at Hohenzollern Redoubt, opposite Hulluch. 252nd Tunnelling Company was formed at Rouen under Captain R. G. Trower, and a week later moved to Toutencourt and began to work at the Redan. About the same time 182nd Company, in full strength, was in front of Bailleul.

The situation on the Somme front was far from satisfactory, especially at Duhallow trench, which the French had captured. This was already undermined, as it had been the German first line, and their shafts sunk in the support line had galleries under the old front line, close to our shafts. At Tambour the situation was very precarious. Here the enemy exploded two large mines which wrecked our galleries and two shafts, together with 30 yards of our parapet. Almost in desperation it was decided to retaliate with large charges in the hope of stopping the enemy, even at the expense of destroying our own shafts. Therefore large charges of from 8,000 to 10,000 lbs. of ammonal were put in, in one case the L.L.R.* being 80 feet.

170th Company, on returning to the line, took over the Hohenzollern Redoubt sector. We had not previously mined in this sector, and here too we soon met

* L.L.R.—Line of Least Resistance.

trouble. The first shaft had been sunk 35 feet and two galleries commenced when sounds of hostile mining were heard. Careful listening located the face of the enemy mine some few yards in rear of our front line trench, the Hog's Back, and about 40 feet below it.

But by this time we were familiar with this kind of thing on taking over a new front line, and had no scruples about blowing a few yards of our own unoccupied trench, especially if by so doing we wrecked hostile galleries and delayed the enemy, thereby giving us the valuable time necessary to improve our situation. A large charge was fired ; it made a big crater and destroyed part of the Hog's Back, and no doubt some of the enemy's headings.

XVI

In spite of many local successes, the mining situation at the end of 1915 was far from satisfactory. An immense amount of labour had been expended in spasmodic and disjointed work. Apart from casual offensive work, many miles of shallow shafts and galleries had been constructed to form defensive systems at various strategic points of the line. Unfortunately, however, the Staff Officers who ordered the operations had little or no knowledge of the tactics of mining, and a large proportion of the first year's work must be written off as misspent energy and wasted effort. The pity of it was that at least three first-class engineer officers—General Fowke, Colonel Harvey, and Colonel Edmonds (now Brigadier-General Sir James Edmonds, Official Historian of the War)—were attached to G.H.Q. in various capacities. Had their advice and experience been more fully explored, a different story might have been told.

Nevertheless, 1915 must be looked upon as an experimental period in which many very valuable lessons had been learned—for to the mining officers, no less than the staff, many of the problems involved were completely new. They were vigorously tackled ; equipment was vastly improved, silent double-acting air pumps replacing the

noisy chain driven rotary blowers. Suitable survey instruments were provided—many of the officers were sur-
veyors in civil life—though an officer who had the foresight
to bring his own instruments still received a double welcome.
More up-to-date rescue apparatus became available, with
trained personnel, and was the means of saving many lives,
and listening instruments replaced the primitive water-
bottle. On the whole, responsible mining officers were
not too dissatisfied with the technical prospects. It is
proverbial that England always starts a war with the worst
equipment and finishes with the best, and there seemed no
reason to doubt that the adage would justify itself once again.

Nevertheless, the organization of the Tunnelling Companies—now twenty in number—obviously required
drastic overhaul. G.H.Q. knew practically nothing of
their operations. All mining progress reports were
stamped with a large and impressive SECRET, but they had
to pass through so many hands on their leisurely journey
through divisional, corps and army headquarters, that by
the time they reached G.H.Q. they were hopelessly out of
date. Maybe, owing to the archaic staff machinery, many
highly-placed officers completely failed to recognize the
significance of the miner's contribution to the War.

There were, however, notable exceptions—certain of the
army and corps commanders, actively supported by a small
group of far-sighted staff officers at G.H.Q., and impelled
by the irrepressible Norton Griffiths. His energy was
amazing : he had been not only the chief recruiting
officer for the Tunnelling Companies, but the only connecting link between them and G.H.Q. His reports
made lively reading ; they were not couched in official
language, and were always awaited at G.H.Q. with great
glee. At that august and dignified preserve Norton
Griffiths' reports were known as " Punch," and it was,
maybe, their refreshing unconventionality which impelled
a far lighter reception than they deserved. Had Norton
Griffiths written in a formal and precise military English
instead of his own pungent style, he might have achieved
greater results. Other enthusiasts during the War found
that it did not pay to be original.

MAJOR-GENERAL R. NAPIER HARVEY, C.B., C.M.G., D.S.O.

But with the rapid and unexpected development of mining—for the Tunnelling Companies had " just growed " in typical British style—a more efficient administration and direction of all personnel, material and equipment were essential. At the request of G.H.Q., on January 1st, 1916, the War Office approved the formation of a new staff post, that of Inspector of Mines, and Colonel Harvey, R.E., who was then the assistant to the Engineer-in-Chief, was given the appointment. At each Army Headquarters, and directly responsible to the Inspector of Mines, was to be a Controller of Mines ; Lieutenant-Colonel G. C. Williams, R.E., Lieutenant-Colonel A. G. Stevenson, R.E., and Lieutenant-Colonel W. B. Y. Danford, R.E., were appointed to the First, Second and Third Armies respectively. These appointments, involving as they did a recognition of the work of the Tunnellers, were of tremendous importance. The occupants of the posts, too, were admirably chosen.

One of the first actions of the new administration was the formation of Army Mining Schools, which were of very great value, particularly to new arrivals. Suitable medical arrangements were also organized. Lieutenant-Colonel Dale-Logan took charge ; he, too, was an excellent choice, for he had a special and wide experience of miners' diseases and mine rescue work. He became responsible for the organization of medical services in every mining sector, and enlisted the services of doctors from mining areas in England. In his own sphere, Dale-Logan was a veritable Dr. Thorndyke ; after an examination of the body of a dead miner, he would reconstruct a picture of the responsible explosion with uncanny accuracy.

With adequate staff organization added to technical efficiency, tunnellers could look ahead with confidence. Although it was already proving difficult to obtain a sufficient flow of reinforcements of the right type, the men were tackling the most difficult jobs with keen enthusiasm. They seldom became smart parade-ground soldiers, and more than one man who actually fought the Germans underground earned reprimands from officious superiors because of slackness in saluting. At the end of the War there were dozens of tunnellers who had put in four years' service, a considerable part actually under the German lines, who still did not know how to form fours. But it did not effect their military value. Long before the end of the War infantrymen found that in battle they had to forget their parade-ground tricks ; tunnellers never learned them.

CHAPTER III

I

MINING warfare at Gallipoli developed in a somewhat similar way to that on the Western Front. Following desperate and confused fighting, British and Dominion troops—most of whom had never previously been under fire—established a precarious footing on the peninsula. Little further progress was made, and rough lines were established at Anzac and Helles. Owing to the peculiar topographical formation, as at Anzac for example, it was almost impossible to make a continuous line of trenches, although at Helles, later on, this was accomplished. Isolated posts and barricades were established therefore at strategic points on spurs and ridges overlooking gulleys and ravines. The Turks were not slow to appreciate the value of mining to attack these posts ; the first underground attack was made on Quinn's Post on the Anzac front.

Early in May, 1915, Turkish mining was suspected, and the Australians hurriedly put down three " rabbit holes " as listening posts. Soon their suspicions were confirmed, the approach of a Turkish mine could be heard. Small charges were exploded in the " rabbit holes," but were too small and failed to destroy the Turkish gallery. Early in the morning of the day following, the 29th May, 1915, the Turks fired their mine, which formed a crater in our lines and blew up the garrison, a platoon of the 13th Battalion, A.I.F. Rushing forward, the Turks captured the crater and penetrated to the second line. They were unable to hold their gains, and soon were expelled with heavy losses. And so a new terror was added to the already almost unbearable life on the peninsula.

The Australians were not the kind of men who would
take a challenge of this kind lying down, and straightway
took measures to counter this new offensive.   Within a
few hours of the Turkish mine going up, a force of over
two hundred miners had been collected.   Mining engineers
already serving as officers were placed in charge, and *the
same evening* mining had commenced at Quinn's, Pope's

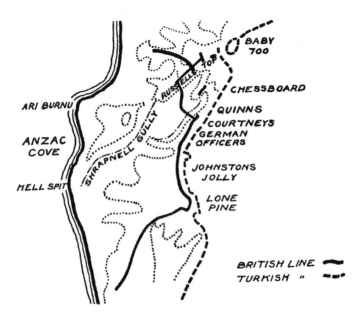

and Courtney's Posts, and very soon the more exposed
parts of the line were adequately protected underground.
As in France, where the miners had already established a
reputation for immediate action, so in Gallipoli.
   On the Helles front a line was established stretching
across the southern end of the peninsula at right angles
from Gurkha Bluff on the Ægean coast to where Kereves
Dere entered the Dardanelles, midway between Cape Helles
and Achi Baba.   It was the first, and for some time, the
only continuous trench line to be established on the
peninsula.   The distance between the opposing trenches,
though at first considerable, was reduced gradually by local

attacks, and by stealthy advances and digging in under
cover of darkness, until only a few yards separated them.

During May, mining squads working under the direction
of the 29th Divisional Engineers, threw down the gauntlet
by blowing a small mine against the Turks. The Turks
readily accepted the challenge and, by way of retaliation,
exploded a mine at Krithia Nullah, causing some damage
to our trenches.

It was soon found that a more systematic policy was
essential, and the mining squads were organized by Captain
H. W. Laws of the Royal Naval Division, a mining engineer
of considerable experience, into the VIII Corps Mining
Company, with headquarters at Pink Farm.

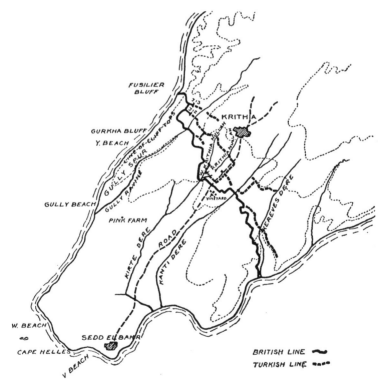

During June and July our line was advanced again.
In the centre, after the Third Battle of Krithia, we occupied

some of the Turkish trenches near the Vineyard and Fusilier
Bluff. Mining began at once from these newly-won
trenches, barricades and bombing posts being the chief
objectives, although heavy charges could not be fired owing
to the shallow depth of the saps and the nearness of the
trenches.

At Fusilier Bluff the formation was sandstone, the first
fifteen feet being soft and easily mined. Here, after the
main protective gallery had been completed, the main
listening gallery was driven out to the cliff face. Owing
to the configuration of the cliff at this point, it was found
to command a considerable stretch of Turkish trenches.
At the request of the infantry, galleries were branched
right and left and driven parallel to the cliff face, and from
them loop holes were made, forming a kind of underground
fort.

At J.13 the Turks could be heard working close to one
of our listening posts, and were allowed to continue undisturbed. On they came until it was evident that they were
about to hole into our gallery. Men were posted to receive
them. They actually broke through at 3 a.m. on 14th
September ; Private Wilkinson opened a lively fire, and
the Turks rapidly retreated. Lieutenant Boyes, coming
up and using his revolver freely, completed their discom-
fiture. But they were not easily disposed of. Returning
with reinforcements and a supply of bombs, they commenced to make themselves unpleasant. So many bombs
were fired that the smoke fumes extinguished Lance-
Corporal Parker's light and almost choked him. Getting
his second wind, he returned and succeeded in blocking
the hole with sandbags. It was then possible to complete
the tamping of a charge which had previously been commenced, but had been interrupted by the enemy breaking
in. The mine was fired at 5.30 a.m. while the Turks
were still throwing bombs. It destroyed about 40 feet
of our gallery and, it is presumed, a similar amount of
Turkish gallery—together with, of course, a number of
Turks.

On 29th September, 1915, a gallery from No. 3 shaft
at the Gridiron holed into a Turkish gallery at a point

where it had been hastily tamped. In place of sandbags, old clothing had been used to hold the soil—evidence that the Turk suffered equally with us from a shortage of mining material. A party of six men were engaged in removing this unconventional barricade when a heavily charged Turkish mine exploded, destroying No. 3 shaft and a portion of our trench near the Western Birdcage. There was a considerable difference of opinion as to what actually happened. Some reports mention two distinct explosions, but whether the Turks had two mines close together and one detonated the other, or whether there was a secondary gas explosion, is not quite clear. Our miners seemed to be firmly convinced that the explosion was caused by our men engaged in removing the tamping, who may have pulled out the leads by force. Fortunately, this part of the line had been regarded as unsafe—the infantry had been withdrawn previously on the advice of the Tunnellers and so suffered no losses from the explosions. Among Tunnellers it was considered a reflection on a company if it allowed the enemy to blow our line and inflict losses on the infantry garrison.

By this time both sides had developed protective systems to such an extent that it was practically impossible to advance without meeting an enemy gallery. This was especially the case in the clay formation at the Gridiron and also at the Vineyard. At the former a charge had been placed in the main gallery to the left of No. 1 Shaft, as the Turks were known to be very close. Before it could be fired, however, the Turks broke in and removed it. It was here, too, on the 13th October, 1915, that the Turks fired a heavy charge, forming a crater abutting on " Cawley's " Crater, damaging our workings beneath the crater, and cutting off three tunnellers working in the face of the left gallery from No. 2 Shaft. The trench parapet was also damaged for some distance, and the sap leading to Cawley's closed in.

Sergeant-Major Dean, rushing to the mine as soon as the explosion gave the alarm, was informed by the local infantry commander that several of his bombers had been buried in their post by debris. Going down No. 2 mine,

F

Dean found it badly damaged and full of gas : there was
no trace of the face men. Crawling out over the top to
examine the new crater, he heard cries for help coming
from beneath him. Flashing, his torch down a crevice
between two lumps of earth, he saw a man's head about
three feet down. Clearing away some of the dirt as best
he could, Dean took hold of the man's equipment and
tried to drag him free. The victim, however, was firmly
held fast by sandbags across his back ; the body of another
man appeared to be entangled with his legs. This second
man, although completely buried, appeared to be still
alive. A journey back to the trench to seek assistance met
with no response, although there were about a dozen
bombers and R.A.M.C. men about. Returning to the
buried men, Dean tried again to free them. Soon, however,
he was joined by two men from the trench, and, leaving
them to carry on, he went forward into the new crater to
investigate, moving lumps of earth and listening here and
there. At one place he heard distinct sounds of picking,
and fancied he heard voices coming from below. Again
he sought assistance from the trench, but even the relief
shift refused to volunteer for the task, so he returned alone
to the two partly buried bombers. His two helpers had
almost cleared the debris. At last their efforts freed them,
and the bombers returned to the trench little the worse
for their unpleasant experience.

Sixty-five hours after the Turkish mine went off, Privates
J. Grimes, P. Dennis and a third man, name unknown,
haggard, begrimed and dazed, crawled out to freedom
through a small hole in the bottom of the crater. They
had been buried by the effects of the explosion in one of
our galleries. Not knowing that a rescue party was working
from the crater towards them, but never giving up hope,
they commenced to dig their way into the crater ; their
tools hopelessly buried, they used jack knives and finger-
nails in their desperate effort for freedom. Spurred on
by the sound of the Turks working so close that they could
be heard speaking, haunted by the ever-present dread of
another explosion before they could escape, they suffered
acute mental anguish and physical pain, until finally their

grit and determination carried them through to safety.
They received a congratulatory message from the G.O.C.
VIII Corps on their safe return.

So much mining and counter-mining had been done
that it was considered advisable to commence a deeper
system. Consequently, towards the end of October,
vertical shafts were sunk from the foot of several of
the inclines at Fusilier Bluff. Four weeks later three
tunnels were driven from the cliff's face, connecting
with these shafts, forming a good backing-up system
at 40 feet deep. In some cases the ground was very
hard, and boulders were frequently met with, so that
extensive blasting was necessary, which naturally delayed
progress.

On completion of a defensive system at the Vineyard,
five offensive galleries were run out. Three mines were
fired in quick succession, in conjunction with infantry
attacks. One of them is known to have destroyed two
Turkish mine galleries. There was also a deep system at
the Gridiron. Here the boring apparatus, which had at
last arrived from Mudros after repeated urgent requests,
was used to good advantage. Bore holes were kept about
25–30 feet in advance of the face, spread out fanwise,
and in them small charges were fired every 15 feet advanced.
This method of progress was slow, but it had the advantage
of being comparatively safe.

November 25th, 1915, saw a new terror added to underground warfare. In the early hours of morning the
Turks, who had previously been heard working nearby,
broke into a recess near Fusilier Bluff. A shot was fired,
and sound of Turks retreating down their gallery were
heard. But the enemy soon returned, and our listeners
reported sounds as of tamping being put in : actually
the Turks did erect a barricade in their gallery. Instead
of following the conventional method of blowing in our
gallery, however, *they began to force gas through a hole in
this barricade into our workings.* Fortunately this gas was
not very strong—it was of lachrymatory type—and we
were able to seal the recess with a stopping. A fire built
at the top of the nearest incline helped to clear out the gas.

Nevertheless, the new method aroused all kinds of anxious and uncomfortable suggestions.

Three days later we struck back, by firing a mine from a borehole under the Turkish gallery. A few minutes later Second-Lieutenant Macnamara and Lance-Corporal Greenhalgh went down to investigate the results. Unfortunately, no precautions were taken to guard against gas from the explosion. On reaching the stopping, Macnamara was affected by gas and, falling, became wedged against the sandbags. Greenhalgh tried to drag him away but failed and, on feeling himself being affected by the gas, staggered to the foot of the shaft and called for help. Then followed a confused series of rescues and counter-rescues. Greenhalgh's cries brought Second-Lieutenant Bernard to the scene, but he, on going to rescue Macnamara, was himself overcome. Two privates, Robertson and Morton, succeeded in bringing out Greenhalgh. In the meantime, Private Brown rushed in and brought out Bernard. Morton again went into the mine with another man, Gibson, and both were gassed. These two men became separated ; Morton lost his way, and was later found and brought out at another shaft. Gibson was found by Brown and brought out by him, assisted by Private Bannerman. Brown had then rescued two men. Privates Steward and Begg then went down No. 3 shaft, where there was less gas, and succeeded in bringing out Lieutenant Macnamara. Greenhalgh and Gibson had by this time recovered from the gas, and immediately tried to revive Macnamara by artificial respiration, but though they persisted for a long time, their efforts were in vain. All the others recovered.

II

On the peninsula December was a strenuous and anxious month for all concerned. The VIII Corps Mining Company, which had struggled on for months, handicapped in many ways but especially by the limited number of officers and N.C.O.'s at its disposal, had done good work. None the less, the strain of the arduous and continuous

task was beginning to tell. The arrival from England
of the 254th Tunnelling Company, consisting of eight
officers and eighty-six other ranks came as a great relief,
and enthused new life into the veterans. The old title
was dropped, and the old unit merged into the new ; its
commander was Major Laws, D.S.O., R.N.D., who had
been in charge of mining on the peninsula since its
beginning. Then the front was rearranged into two
sectors, these again being divided into sub-sectors. Captain
Edwards was placed in charge of the right and Captain
Chambers on the left, each having the assistance of at
least five other officers. This was a decided improvement and allowed for proper relief. With the extra
labour and adequate supervision, mining activity greatly
increased.

Unfortunately, it was all too late. After bitter dis-
cussions, the Cabinet in London had decided to withdraw
from the peninsula. But, if the landings had been bungled,
the plans for evacuation were very carefully thought out.
Anzac and Suvla were the first points to be evacuated :
to distract the attention of the Turks from these sectors,
offensive operations were hurriedly improvised at Helles.
The greater part of the preparation fell on the newly-
formed mining company. Points in the Turkish lines
were singled out for attack, and work was rushed ahead,
double shifts being put on.

Interference by the Turks was highly probable, as their
galleries were close to ours at several points. Fortunately
there was only one collision, and the dangers attending this
were averted by the presence of mind of a non-commissioned
officer, Corporal Nixon. A charge had been laid in the
Gridiron mine, and Nixon remained on guard. Suddenly
he saw a light shining near the charge ; putting out his
own, he advanced down the gallery, when he distinctly saw a
hand thrust through a hole in the side of the gallery. He
acted with cool decision. Clearing out his own men from
the mine and the infantry out of the trenches up above,
he fired the charge at once.

Five days later, on December 19th, more than twenty
of our mines were successfully exploded, followed by

infantry attack. As this was intended only as a demonstration, it was not seriously pressed. Nevertheless, it did reveal the possibilities of the mining method of attack : a staff officer, watching the operation, exclaimed : " Why on earth didn't we think of this before ? "

Gallipoli is an endless field for speculation, mostly profitable. *If* the expedition had not been so widely advertised, *if* a few of the mud-locked troops in France could have been borrowed—there is an unending series of ifs, but no serious critic doubts that we could have carried the peninsula with very little additional effort. Here is another speculation to add to the rest. In France an advance of a mile or so meant nothing ; at Gallipoli it meant victory. Once the backbone ridge was reached we could have commanded the Narrows—this, indeed, was the object of our attacks. It was not a question of time— not necessarily a hurried operation. Once we held the heights the Turk was bound to go. Suppose then, our " surprise " landings having failed, we had concentrated on mine warfare, driving the Turk back yard by yard ? It is not an impossible dream.

Yet no more than a dream : evacuation was real. The last scene at Anzac was dramatic. Lieutenant J. P. Caddy sat alone in the front line ; all the troops had been withdrawn—most of them were already embarked. At a given signal Caddy fired the last mine of the sector—at Russell's Top. It certainly served its purpose, for the Turks got the surprise of their lives when, the following morning, they found our trenches unoccupied.

A considerable force was still maintained on the Helles front, and here the Turk had the last word. On 7th January, 1916, he fired two mines in Gully Spur, accompanied by the heaviest barrage yet experienced on the peninsula. By this time the greater part of our troops had been withdrawn, and for a moment the situation was serious—it appeared that the disaster so confidently predicted was at hand. But fortunately the Turkish infantry attack lacked vigour, and was easily repulsed by our skeleton forces. That same night Helles was evacuated.

CHAPTER IV

SPRING, 1916

I

THE story of 1916 begins as that of 1915 closed—with a record of constant activity, entirely of a local character. Feeling in tunnelling circles was very confident ; many officers and men had almost completed a year's service in France—which classed them as veterans in those short days : the number and strength of Tunnelling Companies was increasing almost weekly, an efficient administration was organizing, and our equipment improving out of all knowledge. In short, we were now moving steadily but surely towards the happy state of being well on top of the enemy—except that the phrase should be reversed, since a tunneller always aims at getting *under* his enemy.

First honours of 1916, however, went to the enemy ; displaying great activity south of the La Bassée Canal, he succeeded in evading our vigilance, slipped through our defensive system before it had been completed and, by way of celebrating the New Year, fired two large mines, one under and the other behind our front line at the Brickstacks. It was the custom to name all craters for identification purposes, and these received the appropriate title of New Year craters.

About this time several new companies were formed. The mining sections which had been formed in the First and Second Canadian Divisions were gradually withdrawn from the line south of Ypres and assembled at St. Marie Cappel, where, under Captain A. W. Davis, late of 177th Tunnelling Company, they were organized into the 3rd Canadian Company. Returning to the line, this new unit took over some of the mines of the 182nd Tunnelling

Company, and later some from the 250th Tunnelling Company, all of which were in the Canadian Corps area. This gave 250th Company the opportunity to concentrate on the deep level mines to attack Petit Bois, Peckham and Spanbroekmolen.

The 253rd Tunnelling Company, newly formed under Major E. B. Currie, R.E., established its headquarters at Sailly Labourse. It was allotted a new front and commenced mining at Cité St. Elie, Hulluch, Hairpin, and the Quarries. Before its arrival at the Hairpin, two hostile mines had already been fired under our front line, and it was not long before two more were fired, destroying two of our shafts.

In January, 1916, the 255th Tunnelling Company was formed, receiving some of its officers and men from 173rd Company and going into the line between 181st and 173rd Companies ; gradually it took over the Red Lamp—Neuve Chapelle Sector. 173rd Company was eventually withdrawn and, handing over its headquarter billets at La Drumez, together with much plant it proceeded to Noeux-les-Mines, and entered a new sector, Hulluch-Double Crassier.

II

This sector, part of the area of the Loos battle, was a scene of incessant conflict.

It will be recalled that in December, 1915, 170th Company had to blow in our front line at the Hohenzollern Redoubt, as the enemy had been located behind it. By March, 1916, the tables had been turned, and we now had three large mines of 7,000, 8,000 and 10,000 lbs., mostly ammonal, and two smaller mines, under and near the Chord held by the enemy. These were fired with good effect on the morning of 2nd March, the craters having high lips from which the German trenches could be overlooked, and an infantry attack was launched to consolidate the new position.

A party of tunnellers, consisting of one officer, two N.C.O.'s and eight others, accompanied the infantry, each

man carrying a small mobile charge to destroy hostile
mine entrances. On entering Triangle Crater (No. 3), an old
one, an incline gallery (A) was found and entered. Two

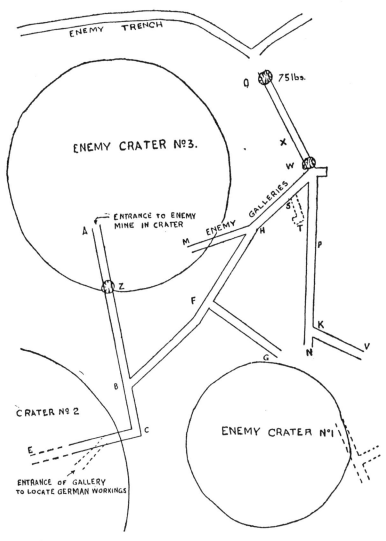

sentries were posted at a branch to the left (B) and the
party proceeded to (C) where, to the right, they found a
gallery (CE) which had been damaged by our mine which

formed No. 2 crater. Returning to (B) and proceeding along the lateral to (W), a working face to the right (FG) and at (H), a wrecked gallery to the left, were examined and surveyed. At (W) the main drive was reached, the gallery inclining towards (O) in the direction of occupied German line, a strong draught coming down. Further investigation revealed what was estimated to be 120 feet of tamping and leads from the German mine which formed No. 1 crater at (N). Clay in sandbags had been mixed with the chalk tamping, no doubt to "seal" the drive and prevent gas coming through. A branch to the left (KV) had been commenced, no doubt to flank No. 1 crater. To close the entrance (O) a barricade was built, against which 75 lbs. of guncotton was placed, tamped with sandbags of chalk, and fired. The gallery at this point was not so close timbered and the ground was a mixture of chalk and clay. A good deal of ground was shaken down by the explosion, but the gallery was not closed—a way still remained over the top of the debris.

A series of desperate counter-attacks by the enemy at last succeeded in driving our infantry from Triangle Crater. This was serious, as the garrison in No. 2 crater was now exposed to mine attack. An incline was begun in No. 2 Crater to intersect the (CE) gallery which was soon reached, and an officer and an N.C.O. entered. None of the enemy was encountered, though there were indications that he had visited the gallery during the interval, as the damage caused by the explosion at (X) had been repaired.

An untamped charge of gun-cotton was placed at (Z), where the ground was disturbed by previous explosions, with the result that 50 feet of timbering was displaced and the gallery completely closed. A futile effort to close the main gallery at (W) where an untamped charge of gun-cotton merely enlarged the gallery to about 7 feet, was followed by a fourth attempt, which had the desired effect. A gallery (ST), driven from the lateral into the V formed by it and the main drive, was chambered, and 300 lbs. of ammonal, well tamped, broke the surface and completely closed the gallery. This gave us control of part of the

enemy system, which could be turned into a valuable
protection to our right flank underground.

III

At Cordonnerie, north of Neuve Chapelle, in February,
181st Company had a very interesting experience. A
charge of 600 lbs. had been fired in No. 7 mine on the
22nd of January, 1916. As the enemy had been located
very near, a new gallery was begun from the lateral to
skirt the blown ground ; this encountered a damaged
German gallery, which was discovered later to be the head
of a " T," at the end of a long gallery, and almost parallel
to our lateral. Our new gallery was continued on towards
the enemy lines for some distance and then branched to
the left, in order to try and locate the stem of the T. On
the 8th of March, 1916, the " kicker " in the face broke
into the top of a gallery. Immediately plugging the hole
according to instructions, the incident was then reported to
Second-Lieutenant S. Wright at the top of No. 7 shaft.
Second-Lieutenant L. T. Grace, who was listening in
another section, was also informed. Both officers immediately proceeded to the underground magazine, where
they met, and a small mobile charge was prepared. While
so engaged, they were informed that the enemy had discovered the hole and had shone a light through it. Returning with the charge, a 15 lb. box of guncotton, it was
placed on top of the German gallery and tamped with about
fifteen sandbags. While lighting the fuse, the enemy was
heard trying apparently to enlarge the hole. The charge
detonated at 12.45 p.m. Entering the gallery equipped
with " Proto " sets and taking a canary with them, Second-
Lieutenant Trounce and Sapper Docherty tested the air
and reported the gallery clear of gas, air good, and it was
thought our gallery was closed at (B). Orders were given
for a charge of 200 lbs. to be placed at this point.
    At 4.30 p.m. Captain Beasley, Second-Lieutenant
Grace and Sergeant Whittaker went below to lay this
charge, and to their surprise found that our gallery had

not been closed at (B), but had merely been enlarged, making a cavity about 7 feet in diameter, through which

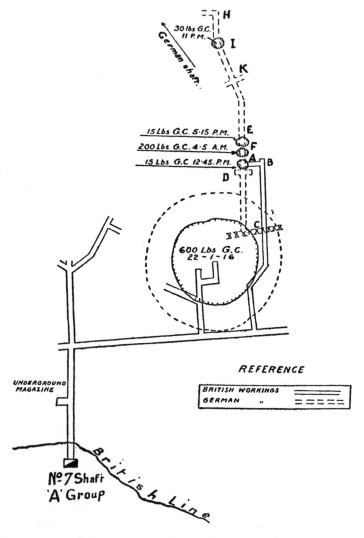

they passed into the German gallery. Proceeding, they discovered signs that the mobile charge had caused several casualties to the Germans. Entering the dead end at (D),

Captain Beasley was affected by gas and was compelled to return. Leaving Second-Lieutenant Grace and Sergeant Whittaker to cover the gallery, raiding parties were organized under Second-Lieutenants Wright and Trounce, working without boots and carrying 15 lb. boxes of guncotton as mobile charges. Second-Lieutenant Wright's party went to the right in the direction of the enemy's shaft, Second-Lieutenant Grace to the left, and Second-Lieutenant Trounce stood by. Lieutenant Wright's party had proceeded as far as (E) when the enemy turned on the electric light in front of him. This officer, with great foresight, had taken the precaution of cutting the leads as he advanced, and as they were wired in parallel, the portion occupied by the enemy remained in full view, while he was in darkness. Two Germans were seen to come round a bend towards him and were fired at, and one was seen to fall. The parties were then recalled by a prearranged signal, Second-Lieutenant Wright leaving his charge at (F). Second-Lieutenants Grace and Wright then returned to fire the charge left at (F), the fuse being ignited by Lieutenant Wright, while Lieutenant Grace, firing over Lieutenant Wright, kept up a fusillade of revolver shots to prevent the enemy approaching from round the bend in the gallery.

At 7 p.m., some time after the charge had exploded, Second-Lieutenant Trounce and Sapper Docherty again went down in " Proto " sets to investigate, and reported all clear of gas. At 8.30 p.m., Second-Lieutenant Brown and Sergeant Whittaker and two riflemen went down. Posting the men at (C) and (B), Second-Lieutenant Brown went to (F) and found all clear and a strong draught coming through from the enemy side. The second mobile charge had failed to close the gallery and had formed a large cavity.

On receiving this report, Second-Lieutenant Grace resolved to make a further attempt to close the gallery. Accompanied by Second-Lieutenants Trounce and Brown and two sappers, each carrying a box of guncotton, the party proceeded as far as (H), where, round the bend, the lights were still on, and men could be seen moving about.

The charge was placed at (I) tamped with all the German sandbags available, and fired at 11.30 p.m.

At 1.15 a.m. on the 9th of March, 1916, after the gallery had been examined and again reported clear of gas as far as (A), Second-Lieutenants Grace, Brown and Morris, with six volunteers, proceeded to (B) with sixteen cases of gun-cotton, and with some difficulty these were got through the broken gallery. The officers went along the gallery as far as (K), where they were met by rifle fire, and after exchanging a few shots, returned to the point where the gun-cotton had been left.

A German then appeared at (A) and, on seeing our party, bolted. Second-Lieutenant Grace then covered the gallery at (E), while the charge was being placed at (F), a small amount of loose clay thrown on as tamping, and the charge at once fired at 4.5 a.m. This was the third and largest charge, and the workings were filled with gas, which was so strong that four canaries at the top of No. 7 shaft were killed. Gas was also seen to be issuing from the German shaft, and an alert Forward Observation Officer immediately brought his guns to bear upon the locality with good effect.

A number of tools and a mobile charge were found in the German gallery, together with a quantity of small sandbags made from all kinds of coloured materials, similar to drapers' remnants. No listening instruments of any sort could be found, and the fact that our miners had worked for several days within a few feet of the German gallery and had not been detected, seems to indicate that the enemy's listening patrol was not alert. Further, our successive attempts proved that small untamped mobile charges merely enlarge a gallery, and do not close it.

IV

On leaving the Red Lamp sector, 173rd Company went to the Double Crassier, south of Loos, where the situation was unique. Here, two long parallel heaps of waste from the nearby coal mine lay in a N.W.—S.E. direction. A section through these heaps resembled the letter M with its " legs " spread out, about 50 feet high and 25 feet across the flat tops.

The German trenches cut the Crassier at right angles, about 500 yards from its northern end, by means of a tunnel, and continuing for about 200 yards, turned and ran parallel to the Southern Crassier for 400 yards before turning away again. The Germans had run out saps to this Crassier, and along its foot and on top of it had built a forward line.

Our trenches followed much the same course except that they did not cut across the Crassier, and 300 yards of our front line ran along the top of the Northern Crassier, at the foot of which ran a communication trench. From this trench our mine entrances ran in beneath the Crassier, with only about a foot of natural ground above. Here for once the enemy had been caught napping, and we commenced to mine it before he did ; but the advantage was short-lived and soon rendered nugatory, for the enemy maintained a continuous rain of heavy shells with delay action fuses on the exposed side of the Crassier, constantly closing the mine entrances and damaging the trench to such an extent that it could not be kept open ; the reliefs and material had to run the gauntlet over the top at night. The temperature, too, generated by the " heating " of these slag heaps, greatly added to the discomfort of the men underground ; on occasions, when entrances were closed for several days and casualties had occurred, the air became so foul that it was impossible to enter the mines. Hampered in this way as we were, the enemy was able to work up to and beyond the end of one of our drives, missing it by only a few feet, and could be heard working away on our side of it. Our mines had been begun as part of an offensive action, but the idea had been abandoned, and, as the enemy was approaching, it became impossible to delay for long their firing.

It was a particularly difficult matter to arrive at the size of charges to be used, for several reasons. The mines were at different levels, from 55 feet to 120 feet deep, and the close proximity of our own trenches and the loose nature of the material in the heaps added to the difficulty.

However, at 6 a.m. on the 16th of March, 1916, seven mines in two groups, with charges varying from 1,000 lbs. to 4,000 lbs., were fired with success. A mass of debris was hurled over on to the German trenches at the foot of the Crassier, while those on the top were completely destroyed, together with machine-gun posts and dugouts, and a view was opened up, through the gaps, to the enemy's lines beyond the Southern Crassier. Considering the fact that premature action was forced upon us by the enemy, the operation was remarkably successful.

v

As hinted in the introduction, the story of the Tunnelling Companies is necessarily episodic. Were the subject being treated for a book of fiction or for a newspaper, then details and accuracy would be subordinated ; instead, one or two outstanding episodes would be selected and dramatized. As reading matter they would be more gripping and interesting ; but this method of approach has been rigidly excluded. Nevertheless, it is realized that by this time the casual reader—though not the ex-service man—may be temporarily satiated with accounts of individual counter-mines. As a change, therefore, let him follow for a moment the extraordinary adventures of a Tunnelling Officer who temporarily left his burrows.

The collar badge worn by R.E. Officers bears the legend " Ubique." On the authority of Mr. Rudyard Kipling, whose knowledge of these matters was probably unique, Tommy had several original variations of the pronunciation of this word. He also gives us some idea of its meaning by enumerating some of the outlandish tasks R.E.'s are called upon to perform, to live up to their motto. As an example of the ubiquitous nature of the work undertaken by Tunnelling Officers, a daring reconnaissance, carried out behind the German lines, is perhaps worthy of note.

With the object—or, may be, excuse—of ascertaining if and to what extent the Germans were mining in the sector Péronne Road—Chapeau de Gendarme, Lieutenant A. E. Eaton, of 184th Tunnelling Company, with remarkable audacity, penetrated the German lines to a point some 800 yards behind the front line ; this was on the night of January 4–5th, 1916.

The Germans occupied the high ground on the north of the Somme which overlooked the marshy ground in the bend of the river near Souzanne. At one time the French held this pocket with some of their best troops, but they were caught napping and badly cut up, after which it was left unoccupied. It was believed that agents used the marshes regularly, though this is doubtful. However, German patrols frequently examined the marshes, and by following one of them Eaton found a path through the marshes and the enemy line.

Coming upon a dump, Eaton attacked the sentry with a life-preserver, and stunned him ; taking from the dump a flag bearing the emblem of the Iron Cross and the figure twenty-three, he boarded a passing G.S. wagon. Finding the wagon was travelling in the wrong direction he jumped off. Next he came across a field battery. Approaching a dugout, he caused a commotion by hurling a Mills bomb into it. During the confusion he made good his escape and entered " Y " Wood. He examined the wood thoroughly but found nothing of interest, so proceeded south to Chapeau de Gendarme, where he regained our lines.

During a stay of eight hours on hostile territory no sign of mining was found. No excessive amount of spoil was seen, except that taken from the deep dugouts, which were numerous. The wire was in a very bad state, thin and broken for the most part, except behind the second line and in rear of " Y " Wood. Trenches were very deep, but very wet and muddy and held by an extremely weak garrison, only one man to fifty yards or so*. For this

---

* It is interesting to compare this with the condition of the same sector six months later, when, having given the Germans adequate warning, we attacked it.

G

unique exploit Eaton received the D.S.O., and the French were so impressed that they decorated him with the Croix-de-Guerre and palms, together with the Legion d'Honneur.

VI

Along the extensive front from Hill 60 to Wulverghem, where 172nd Company was working, the most important physical features were The Bluff and St. Eloi. By way of retaliation for the mines at The Bluff, an offensive, above and below ground, was planned against St. Eloi. This involved strenuous work on the part of the Tunnellers, as, in addition to maintaining the upper levels which were in contact with the enemy, the secret of the deep levels (as far back as August a shaft was down 55 feet) must not be disclosed by noisy working, premature blows, or the careless disposal of the great mass of spoil the deeper and larger shafts produced. In this case, the spoil was carried well away and dumped in shell holes and camouflaged. An intermediate level at 31 feet was run out, but unluckily approached a defensive mine about 100 feet short of the enemy parapet, and was stopped.

All was going well with the deep galleries, from which it was proposed to fire six large mines. One ran under a hostile gallery and was stopped. A camouflet destroyed 20 feet of it, but the gallery was then repaired as quietly as possible, though not driven farther for fear of giving away our scheme.

The Germans were having difficulty in their mines, owing to water troubles, which they had been unable to overcome. They presumed that we also were suffering from a similar disadvantage, and in consequence were lulled into a false sense of security that there was nothing to fear from our mines. They were alarmed, however, for an incautious conversation, in English, over the telephone, relating to mines at St. Eloi, was picked up and suspicion was aroused. The German command at once ordered expert tunnellers to the scene to investigate, and a special air reconnaissance was ordered to search out for our mine entrances and dumps. So cleverly had these been concealed that the airmen failed to locate them, and after a long inspection, the German mining expert reported " no immediate danger " ; he was very soon disillusioned ! *

The following morning, the 27th March, at 4.15 a.m., the first mine exploded, followed at intervals of a few seconds by five more. In all about 74,000 lbs. of high explosives were used ; the largest single charge contained 31,000 lbs. The effect of this huge explosion was tremendous ; observers stated that the village seemed to be lifted into the air. The front and support German lines were completely destroyed over a large area, while many dugouts at a considerable distance away collapsed, causing many casualties ; the German estimate was three hundred, which figure is probably conservative. Our infantry attack was a complete success ; it met little opposition, and the troops dug in some 250 yards beyond the craters.

Owing to the dreadful state of the ground, described as a " vast sea of sticky mud," it was considered impossible to consolidate the crater position, and ultimately we were forced to give up all the ground we had gained and to retire to our original line. Thence we looked on while the Germans consolidated their line round *our* side of the craters, and the net result of the operation was that their position was even stronger than before the firing of our mines ! This incident provides an excellent instance of the poor use made of mining attack by commanders inexperienced in its use.

Later, 172nd Company moved to the right and took over from 181st Company, which was thus free to move to a new sector. Establishing headquarters at Berles with forward billets at Au Ritz, they took over part of the line from the French 15–3me Génie on Vimy Ridge.

The line at this time was just on the crest of the ridge, in front of Nieuville St. Vaast, and the enemy was determined to divest us of this precarious foothold. Here, too, he had the advantage of a well-developed mining system on two levels, and was able at will to blow mines in rows under our unprotected line. As infantry attack to dislodge the enemy from his trenches and so minimize his

* See *Official History of the War.*

mining advantage, was undesirable, and any idea of a withdrawal on our part could not be entertained, it was indeed an unenviable situation, which must be tackled at once, as delay would mean disaster.   The chalk here was covered by about 20 feet of clay-loam, and in this the enemy had his upper levels, backed up by a deeper system at between 50 and 60 feet in chalk.

Attack is often the surest defence.   Realizing this, 181st Company embarked on a bold plan—nothing less than several Russian saps (shallow underground communication trenches or mine galleries, constructed just below the ground surface, with only a very shallow head cover above : they were extensively used in the Crimean War— hence the name) rushed across in the clay at maximum speed to attack and destroy the enemy shaft-heads.   Dame Fortune once again smiled upon the brave.   One of these saps actually holed into a shaft chamber some 20 feet below the surface, unobserved by the enemy, and another sap was within a few feet of another shaft.

Careful listening led to the discovery that the shaft was over 30 feet deep and that a drive had just been broken out from it.   So long as the enemy remained in ignorance of our presence there was little to fear from a blow, and in turn, if we refrained from blowing, valuable information might be obtained.   This was an opportunity too good to miss, and consequently a pipe was placed hard up against the timbers and 4 feet of tamping put in.   An intelligence officer was sent for, and for two-and-a-half days continuous listening was carried on, details of which are given.

Date and Time. 1916.	Listening Results	Remarks
May 31		
1 p.m.	Holed into German gallery.	
2 p.m.	Listening with Geophone. Loud laughter and talking, then windlass working, and picking. Interpreter sent for.	German shift comes on. Enemy suspects nothing.
7 p.m.	We fix 2 inch pipe against lagging board and 4 feet of tamping put in.	
8.5 p.m.	Four or five men sit down opposite pipe. Loud laughter and talking for 30 minutes. Stopped by N.C.O. and work begins.	German shift comes on.
11 p.m.	Our interpreter arrives. Pickwork and winch 18 turns up and down.	Shaft is about 36 feet deep—a total of 50-60 feet below ground level.
June 1		
12.5 a.m.	Conversation in German—" Who is there ? Who is there ? Is it the relief ? " In English—" Who is there ? "	
12.50 a.m. 1.5 a.m.	Work with pick. 15 minutes of winch.	
1.15 a.m. 1.45 a.m.	Winch at work.	
2.10 a.m.	Winch at work.	
2.20 a.m.	Very loud knock.	Timber falling down shaft.
2.50 a.m.	Loud sounds, as if pipe was being touched.	
3 a.m.	Voices and winch starts.	
3.25 a.m. 4 a.m.	Voices and winch at work.	
4 a.m.	Conversation in German—" That will soon be deep enough, will it not ? " " Yes—I do not know." " I will ask the Sergeant-Major."	
5.15 a.m.	Conversation in very low tones.	
5.30 a.m. 6.15 a.m.	Very loud knocks (12).	Knocking up timber.

Date and Time. 1916.	Listening Results	Remarks
June 1 5.15 a.m.	Continuous work with winch. Very loud voices. Night shift goes off.	Enemy still unsuspicious
6 p.m.	Pipe blocked and charge laid (300 pounds ammonal). Extension fitted to pipe and tamping began.	
9 p.m.	German officer comes down shaft.	
10 p.m.	German conversation—" Quite right, but it is too heavy." " Very well then, you can have some more people."	Enemy laying and tamping charges.
11.15 p.m.	Officer comes down and says that men must work more quickly and finish the job. The Germans are unusually quiet to-night.	
June 2 1.15 a.m.	Neighbouring German mine and camouflet fired. Three men working on tamping partly buried, but dug out, and work continued.	Both in shallow system in the clay. They do not effect the shaft.
1.30 a.m.	German conversation not understood.	Enemy trying to ascertain result of his blow.
2.30 a.m.	German conversation—" Well, Bauer, have you found anything ?" " No, sir, nothing at all so far, but they have come further in this direction than I should have thought. We must wait."	He may have found an old tamped gallery of ours.
2.45 a.m.	Intermittent conversation in low tones.	
4.15 a.m.	German conversation—two men at winch. " Karl, have you heard from your wife lately ? " " No, she had not written for two weeks." " We shall not get any more leave now." " Why ? " " I have heard it said."	Enemy is satisfied with his blows, but less cheerful than before.

Date and Time. 1916.	Listening Results	Remarks
June 2 5 a.m.	Working and talking. Not understood. Tamping continued. Nothing heard.	During the morning 93rd Regt. asks 64th if they have been working on the trenches as something has been heard above the shaft.
9 a.m.	Talking and walking about. Nothing understood. Timber being carried	German shift comes on.
10.30 p.m.	Officer or N.C.O. comes down. All work and talking stopped.	Listening period.
12 midnight.	Tapping all round shaft chamber, end with eight loud knocks.	End of listening. A gallery near shaft head is suspected.
June 3. 12.30 a.m.	Work continues as usual.	End of night shift.
6. a.m. 7.45 a.m.	Pipe stopped and tamping finished. Nothing heard through tamping.	No day shift worked.
8.55 p.m.	Mines fired.	

There were four charges, each of 300 lbs. of ammonal, and the explosions were reported to be unusually violent, men being struck with large clods at a distance of 100 yards. Considerable damage was done to the enemy front line, and two mine shafts and a considerable part of his shallow workings must have been destroyed. No trench-mortars or machine-guns fired from this part of the line during the raid which followed, or in fact during the night. Our workings were undamaged and there was no gas, the workings being entered within half an hour of the explosions.

The report quoted above indicates a great lack of caution on the part of the enemy ; such phrases as " loud talking," " loud laughter " and " loud knocks " frequently occur. Further, the visits of an officer appear to be infrequent. Maybe the Germans had become careless, for it certainly seemed unlikely that their position could be assailed—at all events at that moment.

We are indeed far away from the old-time wars of chivalry. What would have happened had the brave knight, one of the most intelligent of his breed, been told that not for him were cavalry charges and hand to hand fights ; instead, he would have to be for hours in an earthen tunnel, some three feet by two feet, and listen, as it were with an ear to the keyhole, to the private conversation of Karl and his friend. Small wonder that the innumerable and inevitable comparisons of this kind provided Bairns-father with some of his happiest inspirations.

VII

On the Chipgny sector, to the north of Neuve Chapelle, 257th Company had run a long gallery well out towards the German lines. It was known from experience that the German system was at about the same depth as our own, and there was a well-founded anticipation that we should encounter a German gallery, which probably would be flooded. Orders were given, therefore, to keep a borehole—a hole drilled by an earth auger, 4 inches to 8 inches in diameter—about 20 feet in advance of the working face as a precautionary measure. Yet, although special dangers were expected, no one was quite prepared for the thrills which lay ahead !

At about 5.30 a.m. on the 9th April, 1917, Sergeant Young reported to Lieutenant C. E. Bailey, the officer in charge, that water was appearing in the borehole. Lieutenant Bailey at once went to examine the face, and while doing so, a sudden flood of water burst into the gallery with such force that it swept off their feet the men working at the face. Two men managed to make good their escape to No. 17 shaft. A third man, Sapper Law, also could have done so, but he realised that a trolley near the face would hinder the escape of his comrades. Making his way through surging water to the trolley, he strove to move it, but the force of the water had wedged it firmly against the timbers and his frantic efforts to move it were of no avail.

The water was now rising fast in the shaft, and the party below was completely cut off. The two electric pumps and the hand pumps in the shaft were all worked at full capacity. All available men and pumps were rushed to No. 17 shaft head, but they could not cope with the flow, and the water rose higher in the shaft. Still the pumping was continued, although under the circumstances there appeared to be no possibility that anyone underground could have survived.

Several hours later Captain De La Mare, the section commander, regretfully resigning himself to the loss of his men, was informed by his servant that " Mr. Bailey is in the mess, sir." Wondering what on earth had possessed anyone to carry the recovered body of the entombed subaltern into the mess, he was amazed to find Lieutenant Bailey sitting in a chair and able to talk, though in hazy and far-away manner.

After a time he recovered sufficiently to relate what had happened and the remarkable manner in which his party had escaped from the flooded mine. Finding the way to No. 17 shaft cut off by the rising water behind them, and recognising the danger of the imminent collapse of the untimbered gallery, Bailey was forced to take the only other alternative and *find a way out by the way the water came in—that is, through the German workings.* Accompanied by Sergeant Young and Sapper Hartley, the only survivors of the party at the face, Bailey groped his way through slush along the German gallery and into the lateral. At length the three men found their way to the foot of an incline shaft. Very cautiously, as may be guessed, they crept up to meet the unknown. At best they would be made prisoners of war—at worst death, which they had cheated below ground, might yet overtake them on the surface. Maybe safety would lie in the surprise of their sudden and unexpected appearance in the German trenches. Anyway, there could be no turning back—they must go on and risk it.

Stealthily they climbed the incline. All was still as

they paused now and again to listen. Nearing the top
of the shaft, they were relieved to see the first dim sign
of daylight. At last they reached the open trench, and to
their surprise found it unoccupied. So far fate had been
kind. But they were not yet out of danger—they must
run the gauntlet across No Man's Land in daylight.
Delays are dangerous—they must act at once. The very
helplessness of the situation spurred them on. Throwing
all caution to the wind, they dashed over the top and
scrambled through the German wire. As they stumbled
over the wet and broken ground, their breath coming in
choking gasps from sheer excitement and the exertion of
the heavy going, they flung themselves into a shell hole
for a moment's relief. Rising again, they blundered on
across ditches and shell holes until, almost exhausted, they
tumbled into sanctuary—our front line trench.

Sapper Law was one of the four men who perished in
the flooded mine. His gallantry in going to the assistance
of his less fortunate mates cost him his own life : regardless
of his own safety, he sought to aid others.

VIII

On another sector—near Cambrin, in front of Béthune,
other tunnellers encountered excitements. At Mad Point
251st Company was quietly pushing out a branch gallery
from one of its mines. It was close timbered with R.E.
casing, except for the last four feet. Suddenly a small
hole appeared in the top left hand corner of the face,
through which a strong current of air began to blow into
our gallery. At first it was not quite certain whether
our gallery had struck into the broken ground of previous
craters, or into a German gallery, so the hole was plugged
with an empty sandbag and an armed listener posted.

After a period of listening and investigation, carried
out without lights as a precaution against being discovered,
during which sounds of talking and distant walking could
be heard, it was clearly established that we had holed into
a German gallery. It was decided to charge the end of our

gallery, packing the charge and tamping in such a way as to permit a person to crawl over it, and then to enlarge the hole and enter and examine the enemy gallery.

Loading had commenced, but at dusk, which was the conventional hour for firing mines, the men were withdrawn as a precaution. Nothing happened, so loading was resumed. At about 10 p.m., when Second-Lieutenant Hansen was completing the tamping, he was startled by a strong light flashing on him through a hole in the R.E. casing some distance back from the face. Immediately putting out his own light, he passed word back for detonators to be sent ; when they arrived, Lieutenant Hansen crawled back in the darkness to the charge and inserted them. This done, but before tamping could be resumed, a German once more appeared at the hole and shone a light through, making a lot of noise on top of the casing. In going back he broke through the thin layer of earth separating the two galleries ; his foot came through and actually landed in the middle of Lieutenant Hansen's back as he lay there half covered in dirt ! This commotion alarmed our men, and the gallery was soon cleared. Lieutenant Hansen managed to crawl out, warning was given to the infantry and the mine fired.

It would appear that the gallery into which we holed was one damaged by a previous mine at some point nearer the German lines. The sounds previously reported, no doubt, were the work of clearing the damaged gallery, this work being completed just as we were loading our mine. Our gallery must have skimmed just below his at a time when he was denied access to his gallery, and so we passed undetected.

IX

These are no more than typical samples of the work and experiences of the Tunnellers in the first half of 1916. The operations were fully local, and had no more than tactical possibilities. But now the scene switches south, where the long-awaited attack on the Somme front was about to break.

X

It is necessary at this point to chronicle the further development of the Tunnelling Companies. As the overseas contingents increased, they tended to become more and more self-contained, and to include special units. Mining is extensively conducted throughout the British Empire, and gives employment to large numbers of men. Here then was a source of material which could be drawn upon at once, and, with little training, be ready for immediate employment at the front ; naturally, when several of the Dominions offered to provide Tunnelling Companies, the War Office gladly accepted.

Canada was first in the field. In December, 1915, Captain A. W. Davis had organized the 3rd Canadian Tunnelling Company from mining sections in the 1st and 2nd Canadian Divisions. In March, 1916, the 1st Canadian Tunnelling Company, which was mobilized by Major Rogers in Eastern Canada, and the 2nd Canadian Tunnelling Company, recruited in British Columbia and Alberta by Major R. W. Coulthard, were in the line near Ypres with the 171st and 250th Tunnelling Companies respectively, for instruction. Shortly afterwards the 1st took over from 182nd Company at Armentières, and the 2nd from 172nd Company at the Bluff.

The New Zealand Tunnelling Company, which had been at Falmouth completing training under Major J. E. Duigan, also arrived about this time, and relieved a company of French Territorial Engineers at " The Labyrinth," but soon after was relieved by 185th Tunnelling Company, and proceeded to the Chantclere sector on the outskirts of Arras.

Early in the year Lieutenant-Colonel Fewtrell had been at great pains to select the personnel and equipment of the Australian Mining Corps of 1,000 men " prepared to serve at the Dardanelles or elsewhere." Here, evidently, was a man of foresight and ideas—alas, unused. Arriving in France in May, his men proceeded to Hazebrouck, in the form of a battalion with H.Q. staff. In this

formation is was no simple matter to fit them into the existing
scheme of organization, and it was decided to divide the
battalion into three companies, Nos. 1 and 2 going to
Second Army and No. 3 to First Army, all coming under
the administration of the Controllers of Mines. The
H.Q. staff, no longer being necessary, was broken up and
absorbed in various capacities. Of the specialists, Major
W. E. David was retained and attached to the staff of the
Engineer-in-Chief for special duty, and Captain Pollock
went to Second Army Mine School, and Captain Morse to
the Australian Electrical and Mechanical Mining and
Boring Company, generally designated as the A.E. &
M.M. & B. Co., and better known as the Alphabetical
Company.

The 1st Australian Tunnelling Company relieved 175th
Company, and the 2nd took over from 172nd Company,
while the 3rd relieved 255th Company at Laventie—
Fauquissart. Three more companies which arrived later
from Australia were used as reinforcements to raise the
existing companies to the higher establishment.

All these overseas companies were very welcome and
proved a great asset, their wide and varied experiences
infusing new ideas and methods. Further, they arrived
at a time when it was becoming increasingly difficult to
get good miners from England. In fact, none could now
be spared from the coal mines, where they were urgently
required to maintain the output of coal.

In April, 258th Tunnelling Company formed at Rouen
under Captain A. W. Pope, and in May proceeded to First
Army and billeted at Noeux-les-Mines. Two sections commenced at Hill 70 under the care of 173rd Company ; the
other two took over at Chalk Pits Sector.

At Hill 70 the trenches were in a very bad state, and
the miners had to be withdrawn at night owing to the
complete absence of any trench garrison. Soon after
taking over, the enemy exploded a camouflet opposite
Mine 23, doing some damage to our galleries and killing
five men by gas and two at the face, filling the mines with
gas, which took several days to clear. A few days later
two charges were fired simultaneously, in Mines 21 and 3,

with good effect. A raiding party found the enemy's trenches filled with debris; one mine listener was captured.

257th Tunnelling Company left No. 4 General Base Depot at Rouen in June for Béthune, Captain Hannay being in charge. Attached to the 3rd Australian Tunnelling Company for a few days' instruction, they eventually took over the line Winchester to Sign Post Lane. Soon after their arrival at the front No. 3 section, under Second-Lieutenant J. B. Templeton, took part in repelling an attack near the Ducks Bill, assisting the 5th Gloucesters, at the request of their Company Commander, who required reinforcements. In July, 256th Tunnelling Company was formed and Captain W. T. Wilson was placed in command. Entering the line on Vimy Ridge front, No. 3 Section took over from 184th Tunnelling Company part of their line, the other sections taking over " H," " I," and " G " sectors from the New Zealand Tunnelling Company. Four officers from 181st Tunnelling Company were temporarily attached to give the new company a good send off, but the sector was reported to be very quiet, few sounds of enemy mining being heard.

This was the last Tunnelling Company to be formed; there were now twenty-five British, three Australian, three Canadian and one New Zealand, a total of thirty-two in all, actively employed in mining at various places along the front, and covering a length of line about equal to half the total length of the British front. A census, taken in June, 1916, disclosed the fact that between 18,000 and 24,000 men were continuously employed on underground work, showing to what extent mining had developed. In fact, an uninterrupted lateral in front of our line extended from the La Bassée canal to Hulluch, *along which it was possible to walk underground for a distance of nearly four miles.*

Both sides had now perfected their defensive systems; pushing on with the next phase, offensive mining, the firing of mines became incessant. In June, 1916, when mining reached its zenith, along the First Army front from Laventie to Vimy Ridge (north end), seventy-nine British and

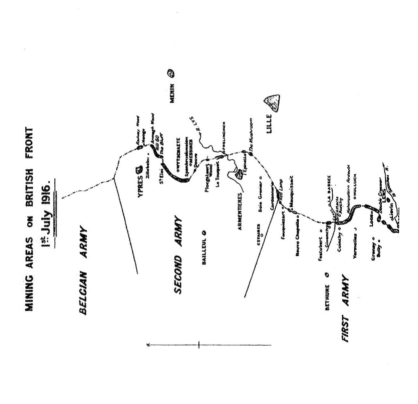

MINING AREAS on BRITISH FRONT
1st July 1916.

seventy-three German mines were fired ; while on the whole
front, out of a total of two hundred and twenty-seven mines,
one hundred and one were fired by the British and one
hundred and twenty-six by the Germans—or one mine
every three hours !

CHAPTER V

I

TO date, it will have been remarked, the Tunnelling Companies had been used exclusively in the desultory fighting of trench warfare. In the several offensive actions undertaken by the British Army—battles which, although insignificant in comparison with those of the latter half of the War, dwarfed anything in our previous military history—the Tunnellers had been ignored. Not that they felt any slight : tunnellers, though complete masters of their technical craft, counted themselves as novices in military matters. They professed no knowledge of strategy, and placed their services unrestrainedly in the hands of the men above, whose job was to think out plans. The much improved organization of the Tunnelling Companies, however, coupled with their direct representation on the staff of G.H.Q., meant that in future they were to be used in the serious operations which were contemplated.

To date, too, the efforts of the Allied armies had been just as desultory as the exploits of the Tunnellers. It was not until the dawn of 1916 that a really serious effort was made to co-ordinate the action of the Allied forces. At Joffre's headquarters on 5th December, 1915, the principle of a simultaneous general offensive was adopted. The main effort in the West was to be a Franco-British advance astride the Somme—the French flinging forty divisions into the fight, the British twenty-five.

Optimism has generally been a feature of military command throughout history, and there is always a tendency to make plans which, however good they may be, ignore the possibility that the enemy commander may not fall in with them. In this scheme the basis of the perfectly feasible scheme was smashed by Falkenhayn's vicious and sustained attack on Verdun. Nothing like this had been envisaged in the original calculations—on the contrary, some preliminary attacks on the German lines had been discussed. But as division after division was flung into the man-made wilderness of death about Verdun, so the French measure of participation in the grand attack gradually dwindled. Whereas in the first plans the British were to play the part of junior partner to the French, now the roles were completely reversed. Instead of the forty French divisions originally anticipated, only five marched to the attack on the morning of 1st July, 1916.

The battle-fields of the Somme differed vastly from the muddy plains of Flanders. Here were ranges of chalk hills and ridges, the one most immediately important being that which formed the watershed between the Somme valley and the basins of the Scarpe and the Scheldt. This undulating ridge, which effectively commanded the lower country to the west, had been seized by the Germans in the miscalled " Race to the Sea " in October, 1914, and held firmly ever since. On due warning of the projected attack—and in view of the superior observation commanded by the enemy, it was difficult to conceal the multitudinous preparations essential—the low hills, of great natural strength, were in thorough German fashion converted into veritable fortresses. To carry them was obviously the stiffest of tasks, but the confidence of the high command, and—born of optimism rather than experience—the enthusiasm of the new volunteer army made light of the innumerable difficulties.

The front of the Fourth Army, which was to carry out the main assault, was about fourteen miles long, roughly in the shape of a capital letter L. From Serre to Fricourt our line faced approximately to the east while from Fricourt to Maricourt it faced approximately north. Along the whole of this front the enemy held the higher ground ; in the northern sector, in particular, our lines on the edge of the low-lying valley of the Ancre were completely overlooked.

H

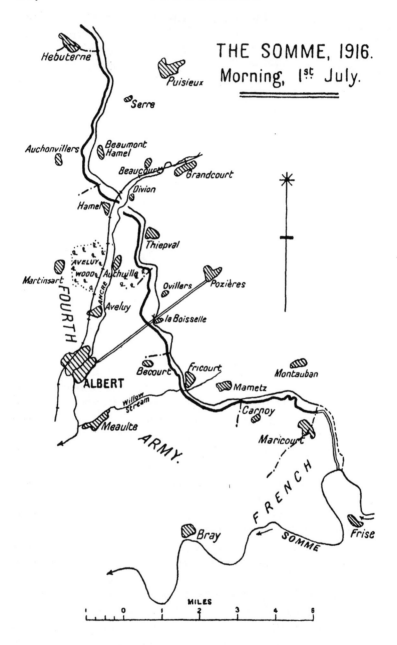

THE SOMME, 1916.
Morning, 1st July.

The Tunnelling officers involved in the operations, while appreciating the difficulties of their allotted tasks, were by no means dismayed. Their casual offensive efforts during 1915 had taught many invaluable lessons. The moral and material effect of well placed mines as an adjunct to infantry attack had been already demonstrated. Nevertheless, it had also been proved conclusively that the right to retain any ground won depended on the capacity to defend it. At St. Eloi, for example, the initial advantages had been neutralized by our inability to construct and maintain communication trenches to the newly-won position, which we had to evacuate. Keen brains analysed the tactical difficulties, and eventually evolved the ingenious plan of constructing the necessary communications across No Man's Land *before* the attack commenced.

The type decided upon was that known as the " Russian sap "—a covered communication trench or tunnel with the roof only a foot or so below the surface of the earth. A considerable number of these could be pushed out to points near the German trenches without undue risk of detection ; they would be broken out to the surface just prior to the time of the attack, and rapidly connected to the captured trenches. The tactical value of these saps can be estimated when it is realized that on the Somme front the opposing trenches were not a mere hundred yards apart as so often in Flanders, but that No Man's Land was in some places half a mile wide.

In addition to their use *after* the first assault, the saps were planned to assist the attack itself. Branches were to be dug near the terminals of the saps, and complete emplacements built for trench mortars and machine guns. These also would not be opened to surface until the moment of the attack, when the infantry would thus find immediate support at close range. The positions of the emplacements in the saps were chosen so that they would escape the enemy barrage.

Yet another valuable tactical idea was thought out by Tunnelling officers—the over-charged mine. The common mine blew up the enemy trenches and formed a crater with lips about six to eight feet high. The overcharged mines

were to carry charges far more powerful that those necessary merely to break the surface.   The additional charge
would force into the air a great volume of earth ; as this
fell, it would form a pronounced lip to the crater—eight to
ten feet high—an invaluable temporary breastwork to
shelter the attacking troops, who would be immune from
the serious menace of enfilading machine-gun fire along
No Man's Land from miniature salients in the German
trenches.

II

Five Tunnelling Companies were at the disposal of the
Fourth Army Commander for the preparation and development of the attack, in addition to the maintenance of the
existing defensive mining system.   They were distributed
as follows : Commencing on the left flank, i.e., the northern
end of the line, the 252nd Tunnelling Company's front
extended from Hebuterne to south of Beaumont Hamel.
Next came 179th Company, with a much longer front
extending down to south of La Boisselle, with 178th Company on a short front to Fricourt.   174th Company occupied a similar front opposite Mametz, while again to its
right 183rd Company was on the Carnoy-Maricourt
sector, adjoining the French Army.

On the VIII Corps front, 252nd Tunnelling Company
was constructing the nine Russian saps opposite Serre,
where a subsidiary feint was planned.   By April it was
working at full speed with no fewer that 1,900 attached
infantry, bringing the total strength of the company to
well over 2,000, equivalent to two battalions.

As the saps neared the German lines, work was stopped
by night to prevent detection ; the wide No Man's Land
was constantly reconnoitred by the enemy, and in spite of
the vigilance of our own patrols he succeeded in locating
John sap and fired a small charge in one of the emplacements, killing seven men.   A week later, a second charge
was placed in the same sap, doing little damage, but unfortunately two men were killed by gas and eight others
rescued with difficulty, all badly gassed.   The saps were

constantly blown in by shell fire, but this had been anticipated, and all were repaired and ready on the appointed
time, some very rapid progress being made—averaging
over one foot per hour.

North of Beaumont Hamel we held a strong point known
as the Redan—the most northerly point where actual
mining, as distinct from the saps, was in progress. Here
two mines, 57 feet and 62 feet deep, were in active contact
underground with the enemy, and a series of mines had
been fired by both sides. There was also a shallow defensive system here. Opposite Beaumont Hamel H.1 and H.2
mines had previously been started as part of a defensive
scheme. When the attack was planned, a mine to destroy
the Hawthorn Redoubt was an essential, so H.3 was

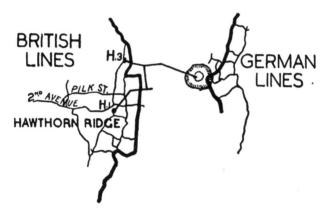

commenced. It was 75 feet deep, and was directed
against this German strong point some 1,050 feet away
on the Hawthorn Ridge. By the end of May the gallery
had been driven out over 900 feet, and was giving considerable trouble on account of the hardness of the chalk
and the large amount of flints in the face. From this
point it was essential that the work should proceed silently,
and, in order to facilitate this, the face was drenched with
water to soften it, and the chalk and flint prised out with a
bayonet, the lumps being caught by the hand to prevent

them falling on to the floor with a thud, and so disclosing our position. In due course the drive reached its objective, and a chamber constructed ; into this was loaded a charge of 40,600 lbs. of ammonal ; all was in readiness for " Zero."

South of H3 mine were two saps, First Avenue and Mary ; both had emplacements for Stokes guns, and were well out across No Man's Land. As the original plan was completed, additional saps were begun, but in most cases they did not get very far owing to the belated start. These Russian saps generally took their names from the communication trenches from which they started.

179th Tunnelling Company, which had been reinforced to over nine hundred strong, was on the front covered by the X and III Corps. On the 36th Divisional front, which straddled the Ancre River, ten shallow saps for Stokes gun emplacements were under construction south of the river to opposite Thiepval in the 32nd Divisional area. Peterhead was the most northerly of these, and was driven from the point where our line commenced south of the Ancre.

South of Thiepval, still on the 32nd Divisional front, two saps, Arthurlie and Sauchiehall, were being rushed out. Both had twelve feet of head cover and were intended for sixty-pounder trench-mortars.

Further south again, Inverary, a covered communication, was 234 feet out and within 30 yards of the enemy front line. Tyndrum, another covered communication, was started at the last minute and so it did not make much headway. Then came Sanda, a covered communication started by the 252nd Tunnelling Company. On account of the shallow depth it was smashed in several times by shell fire. This tunnel was over 100 yards long and was opened to surface and connected to the German line. It was used immediately for communications, and was invaluable to the infantry as it was the only means of communicating with the captured German trenches.

On the 8th Divisional front opposite Ovillers, two saps, Rivington in clay, and Waltney in chalk, were being driven. The former reached to within 30 feet of the

German line, and was eventually connected to it, the latter was driven out over 500 feet. From the end of Rivington sap the Germans could be heard walking in their trenches.

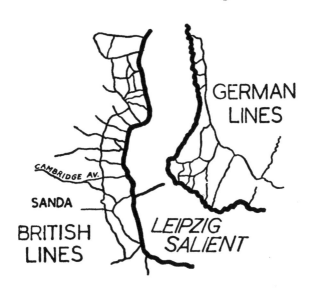

On the 34th Divisional front, astride the Albert-Bapaume Road, opposite La Boisselle, active mining had been carried on for some time, and No Man's Land was a mass of mine craters ; many of the shafts in this sector were over 100 feet deep, with galleries at four different levels. North of the road, a drive from S4·1 shaft 70 feet deep, had a twofold objective—the destruction of a prominent work extending out from the German line called " Y " sap, beneath which a 40,000 lbs. charge was placed, and secondly the formation of flanking protection. This drive did not go straight across No Man's Land. It was driven at an angle and then turned, thereby out-flanking the enemy mines ; thus, when we were near enough to blow, he was powerless to ward us off. Actually he was heard sinking down on us while we were cutting the charge chamber, but that did not stop us.

Further to the south, at Inch St., where a long incline shaft had been put down, two charges of 8,000 lbs each

were placed in No. 2 straight and No. 5 right to destroy
hostile galleries known to be near, while a little farther
south again a heading of 50 feet deep from Lochnagar
shaft was directed against the " Schwaben Höhe," a
formidable strong point in the German lines.   On nearing
its objective this gallery branched, and two charges of
36,000 lbs. and 24,000 lbs. each of ammonal were placed.
Lochnagar was perhaps the first deep incline, and had been
sunk to 95 feet by 185th Company as far back as December,
1915.   There was also a Russian sap in this area, Kerriemuir St., which was eventually connected to Lochnagar
Crater and the German front line.   For some time this was
the only means of crossing Sausage Valley, and were greatly
used by the troops, a whole battalion of the 19th Division,

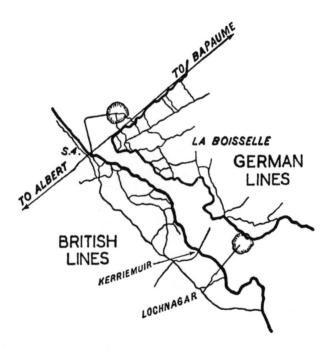

the 9th Cheshires, passing through it.   It was also used to
evacuate the wounded.   The last 150 feet of Kerriemuir
were excavated by bayonets, to ensure silent working.

178th Tunnelling Company was on the 21st Divisional front, a short one, the Tambour, opposite Fricourt, being the chief mining sector.   Here a number of deep shafts existed, varying from 69 feet to 115 feet in depth.   A compressor plant was in use, and pumping and hoisting were done by power.   The Tambour came in for a good deal of heavy shelling, sometimes for days together, and, in consequence, mine entrances were constantly closed. Below, the chalk was so hard that holes were drilled about 2½ feet into the face and charged with 4 ozs. of blastine. Usually four holes were fired as a "round," after which the shattered chalk could be worked easily and silently with a push pick.   The Germans appear to have adopted a similar method of working, as their rounds could be heard, but the exact position of them was difficult to locate.

Three Russian saps (Dinnet St., Balmoral St. and Purfleet) were being driven out in this sector for a novel purpose—at their terminals emplacements were to be constructed to accommodate flame-throwers !   Of these saps Dinnet St. only was subsequently used, as the German line opposite the other two was not captured.

In addition three large mines, against the German Tambour, were being driven, numbered G3, G15, and G19, G3 being about 90 feet deep.

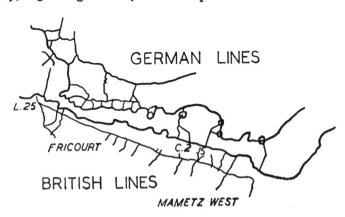

174th Tunnelling Company occupied about half of the 7th Divisional front, and was concentrated on the Bois

Français sector between Fricourt and Mametz West, where active mining was in progress. The enemy was close all round and at considerable depth, so that camouflets of 7,000 lbs. were frequently fired.

For the offensive, L25 sap was directed towards the famous " Aeroplane " trench, so called from its shape, a surface sap projecting from the German line. This gallery was connected to the Quarry by a drive of 750 feet long ; two machine-gun emplacements were constructed, but were not actually used in the attack, as the machine-gun officer could not be found and his sergeant had received no order !

Four mines were also to be placed under the enemy lines. Here again much accommodation was provided for the infantry by enlarging the mine galleries at such points where they could easily be protected against gas or possible enemy blows. Before the attack no less than fifteen hundred troops were accommodated in the galleries ; subsequently they were extensively used by reserves.

Two strong points, Bulgar Point and Casino Point, were attacked by headings No. 12 and No. 11, and eventually charges of 2,000 and 5,000 lbs. respectively were placed. In addition, numerous saps were run out along this wide front, where 183rd Company was working, off which emplacements for flame-throwers and machine guns were constructed.

On the Mametz West sector the saps were frequently damaged by the heavy bombardments. 14.1 received a direct hit on its entrance, which formed a crater with a diameter of 25 feet. A new entrance was cut into the crater. Eventually it was charged with 500 lbs. Two charges were also placed in 15 and its branch 15.1 ; these did considerable damage, destroying dugouts and machine-gun emplacements in the German lines. Eventually they were opened up to the craters and traffic was soon passing through them. A raiding party of one officer and fourteen men went over with the infantry. They entered the German mines, cut all leads, and evicted forty-three Germans from dugouts—they were much too occupied to take prisoners !

At Mametz East, No. 13 sap was out to within 80 feet of the German line. At this point a hole was bored with a

Burnside borer and charged with 200 lbs. A crater was blown, but after our infantry had passed over, a German officer and some men came out of a dugout and occupied the crater for some time. They were eventually disposed of, and traffic was passing through by 9.00 o'clock.

In Sap 12 at Bulgar Point, the charge failed to explode. The infantry officer standing beside the Tunneller with the exploder was a good soldier. He immediately led his party to the attack. A trench mortar bomb—one of our own—had landed plumb in a man-hole and cut the leads. The head cover of this sap was pulled in by the Pioneers and it was used as an open trench.

On the Carnoy Sector No. 11 was directed against a strong point called Casino Point, under which 5,000 lbs. was placed. In addition, numerous small galleries were driven, and contained Stokes gun emplacement and flame projectors. Several push-pipe charges were exploded, forming craters up to 180 feet long about 8 feet deep and 15 feet wide. Later these were converted into good communication trenches.

Some of the saps were mined to within 50 yards of the enemy in hard chalk. To soften the chalk and reduce the noise of working, augur holes were bored into the face and filled with vinegar. One sap was within 30 feet of its objective. An earth augur hole was put in and at 27 feet it struck into an officer's dugout. Loud talking could be heard for some time. When it ceased, the far end of the hole was plugged. Nothing occurred to indicate that anything suspicious had been observed by the enemy until next day, when picking was heard ; this, however, soon ceased, and the tunnellers completed their task undisturbed. The charge fired here destroyed the enemy's trench and two dugouts.

All the Companies had completed their entire programme of work, including dugouts for H.Q. formations, on time in face of continual interruption, and all was in readiness for " the day." By the end of June most of the miners had been withdrawn, and only repair gangs were in the line to keep the saps and mine entrances open. Delayed at first by unfavourable weather, zero was finally fixed at

7.30 a.m. 1st July, 1916. This postponement was most unfortunate for us. It gave the Germans a breathing space wherein they were able to relieve their tired troops, who had suffered a long bombardment, and to replace them by fresh troops.

III

The hours proceeding zero were of intense excitement. There could be no pretence that the enemy was not awaiting the attack—he had had the ample warning of a seven-day bombardment—but the saps might prove to be a tactical surprise. Under cover of darkness, many of the numerous saps and emplacements were opened to surface ; in others push-pipe mines were prepared.

The first mine to be blown, H3 under Hawthorn Redoubt, constructed with much labour by the 252nd Company north of the Ancre—was a colossal tactical blunder. Despite the reasoned objections of the Inspector of Mines, this was fired ten minutes before zero. In itself it was completely successful. The crater formed was 130 feet across, and 40 feet deep, while its greatest diameter was 335 feet. The Redoubt was utterly destroyed and (according to a German account) three sections of the garrison perished with it, while all the neighbouring dug-outs were shattered or blocked, entombing their inmates. But, unfortunately, the too-previous blowing of this mine gave the Germans ample warning of the immediate approach of the expected attack. Our infantry occupied the crater without great difficulty, and protected by its lip, established machine and Stokes gun posts. But, due to the unhappy warning, the Germans had ample time to man their other positions ; it was reported that they even stood upon the parapet of their trench to fire at the attackers, whence they repelled the advance so firmly that later in the day the crater itself had to be abandoned.

The responsibility of senior commanders in war is indeed heavy. In this case a casual decision on one detail of the operations—a mere matter of ten minutes—turned a potential success into failure and cost hundreds of lives.

At 7.28 a.m. " Y " sap, further south near the Albert-Bapaume Road, was completely destroyed, the mine explosion leaving a yawning cavern 165 feet in diameter. The total measurement across the lips was 335 feet. As desired, this mine threw up a high lip, cutting off fire from the north of La Boisselle, and affording protection under which the infantry could re-form before making the final attack. According to a German account, however, very few casualties were sustained by the actual blowing of the mine, as the area had been evacuated.

Lochnagar was fired at the same time ; the two charges formed a large circular crater 450 feet across the lips, and caused considerable damage, 350 feet of front line being obliterated, and the Schwaben Höhe destroyed. A German officer and thirty-five men taken from a dugout just beyond the damaged zone stated that nine dugouts equally full had been closed by the mine. These two charges were 30 feet apart in branches of a " Y." This was done to avoid making a chamber, which would have had to be very large to contain such a large charge. The mine cleared all the debris out of the crater, leaving it perfectly level, a very unusual occurrence.

At the same time two mines at the Tambour were fired. The third, at G.15, failed to explode. The detonators had been intact, and the leads had responded to tests. On being subsequently untamped it was found to be flooded and the charge saturated with water. The primers were found to have been blackened by the explosion of the detonators, but were themselves too damp to explode.

The mine which destroyed Casino Point saw a scene of drama. Apparently watches had not been synchronized, and the Tunnelling officer waiting to fire the mine was horrified to see our infantry scrambling over the parapet some minutes too soon. He was indeed on the horns of the proverbial dilemma—to fire or not to fire—that was the question. He fired. The mine—of 5,000 lbs.—was very successful, and much damage was inflicted on the German dugouts, trenches and machine-gun posts. Unfortunately, our own infantry, because of the premature start, suffered some casualties from falling debris.

During the day, 178th Company dug two trenches
across No Man's Land.   At 7.20 a.m. the flame projectors
in saps 3, 4 and 5 opened fire, and at 7.27 a.m. Casino
Point was destroyed, and eight saps were opened up and
by 7.50 troops were passing through them.   Of the

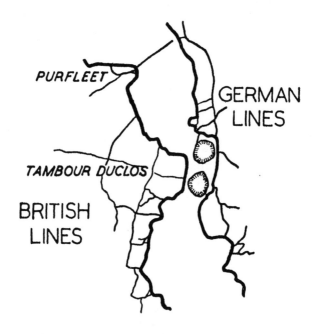

seventeen galleries made for emplacements, later to be made
into communication trenches, six only were used owing to
the failure of the attack.   On the twenty saps for communications only, sixteen were acually joined to the German
trenches, and in some instances were in use by the troops
within a few minutes of zero.
     Unfortunately many of these saps—so perilously con-
structed—failed to fulfil their real purpose here and at
other points along the front through lack of staff organization.   The work had necessarily been done in great secrecy
—so cautiously, in fact, that our own infantry knew nothing
of the existence of the saps !   On the VIII Corps front
very few of the attacking troops seemed to have heard a

word about their existence ; only in a few cases in this
sector were they immediately used by prearranged plan.
Others were " discovered " by the infantry almost by
accident ; some were actually unused throughout the whole
of this desperate day, and had it not been so tragic the sight
might have been classed as absurd—of runners and
reinforcements making the perilous passage of a No Man's
Land swept with steel, while a hundred yards away a
Tunnelling officer would be yelling invitations to " come
and use his sap," his voice unheard in the din of battle.

The saps that were used, however, amply fulfilled their
purpose. Runners, reinforcements, ammunition carriers,
found them a godsend ; cables and signal wires were run
through them, and later in the day they were immensely
useful in shielding the evacuation of the wounded. One
battalion commander declared that without the aid of two
saps on his front he would have been unable to hold on,
since any movement above ground drew a fierce fire.

In the northern sectors the Tunnelling Officers had a
heart-breaking experience. There the trenches averaged
almost a quarter of a mile apart, but an adequate number
of Russian saps had been pushed to within 50 to 30 yards of
the German lines. A 5.30 a.m. the Tunnellers began to open
them to the surface ; the work proceeded rapidly, and within
an hour the saps were open and the light trench-mortars in
position in their emplacements. At 7.20 a.m., ten minutes
before zero, these mortars opened fire ; such was the rate
of fire that in eight minutes each gun had exhausted its
allowance of 150 rounds, and in some cases it was estimated
that this mortar attack did more damage than the whole
of the previous week's artillery bombardment ! The
proximity of these Stokes guns to the German lines may
be judged by the fact that one officer was killed by a grenade
hurled by hand from a German trench.

At 7.30 our infantry left their trenches ; they marched
with the coolness of veterans, slowly, in long lines and in
four waves a hundred yards apart. This was their great
day—these were the men of the New Armies—the volunteers of 1914 and 1915, now confident of their military
powers, blooded in a dozen minor affrays. They had been

led to expect little more than a casual initial resistance—it
had been anticipated that our unprecedented bombardment
would have completely destroyed the first line of defences.
Unhappily this was far from the realisation. Secure in
deep dugouts, the Germans waited until the barrage
lifted ; then, with perfect discipline, they manned their
battered but very adequate trenches, ready to pour a deadly
rifle and machine-gun fire into the awaited attack.

With keen excitement the Tunnelling Officers in the
advanced sap-heads looked back to our trenches. They
saw the brave and determined civilian soldiers scramble
over the parapet and advance in lines that would have
delighted the heart of any general of a hundred years ago.
Then a hail of bullets whistled over their heads ; a minute
later the infantry were still in line, but were now stretched
upon the ground. Wave after wave was caught in that
merciless, withering machine-gun and rifle fire ; No Man's
Land was strewn with khaki figures, mown down in swathes,
like ripe corn before a sythe. Over part of the northern
sector not one single infantryman succeeded in reaching
even the sap-heads, much less the German lines. Yet the
saps were there. The great width of No Man's Land gave
the Germans ample time to man their trenches when the
barrage lifted. A few dozen men loosed from each sap-
head at the same moment would have seized the trenches
before they were occupied—mere dozens have succeeded
where thousands failed.

Imagine the thoughts of Tunnelling Officers as they saw
all their hopes perish in a few brief moments. And
imagine the hard things said when it was realized that
someone had blundered. The use of Russian saps
was a tactical device overlooked even by the Germans,
masters of the art of trench warfare. We had constructed
them, with skill and in peril, and their sole use was to provide
a grandstand for men who had to witness the agonizing
spectacle of thousands of their comrades being shot down
in striving to reach the spot where they stood—men killed
and wounded in an attempt to cross 300 yards of fire-swept
ground, when they could have passed underground in comparative safety. The men who penetrated nearest to the

German line were the tunnellers and those who accompanied them ; at their point of vantage they waited for those waves of " occupying infantry " which never had a chance of breaking. *This is actually one of the most significant incidents of the whole of the War.*

Farther to the south the prospect was more pleasing. Mametz and Montauban were captured, and Fricourt almost surrounded. The mining programme had proceeded almost without hitch ; all the mines caused damage and confusion in the enemy lines. Officers of the Tunnelling Companies advanced into the captured area at the earliest possible moment. Tunnellers were always ready to learn, and were not too proud to learn from their enemy. Consequently, a thorough examination was made of the German mine systems—some of which, incidentally, were connected to our own workings. Much useful information was obtained—one stroke of luck came our way when the diary of a German mining officer fell into our hands. A study of this revealed the comparative harmlessness of some of our previous mines—due to the German plan of evacuating an area suspected as being due to be blown up, and also the irregular manner in which enemy mining was carried on, in order to reduce the risk of being blown.

Generally the German workmanship was very good—if anything, a little more elaborate than essential. Even in hard chalk a good deal of unnecessary timbering was put in the galleries. From the German practice of marking the progress of each shift on the timber it was confirmed that our rate of progress was considerably faster than theirs. On the other hand, the Germans took much greater care in concealing the spoil ; they were minding their dumps while we mined their trenches.

In one mine we found an instrument by which the Germans picked up our telephone messages ; copies of numerous intercepted messages were lying about.

It has been noted that as mines on one level became exhausted by continual blowing, descent would be made to a deeper level. On some of the Somme mining sectors mines existed at 40 feet, 80 feet, 100 feet and 150 feet levels. But even then the Germans went deeper. While

I

our men were examining the German system on the Mametz
front they came across a deep system.   On examination it
was found to contain a gallery no less than 200 feet deep.
This gallery had approached quite close to our line.   At
such a depth, in hard chalk, it would have taken an enormous
charge to form a crater, almost equal to the total weight of
explosives used at Messines.   What would have been
the moral effect of such a mine is dreadful to contemplate.

IV

    For a few weeks the Tunnelling Companies played but
little part in the series of isolated efforts which go to make
up the Battle of the Somme.   On the right flank it was
considered that we were almost on the verge of open
warfare, and Tunnellers found themselves employed on constructing communications and roads.   They did not
grumble ; their mines belonged to siege operations.   If
open warfare were really at hand, then roads would be more
useful.
    But it was soon realized that the dream was premature :
the two squadrons of cavalry which patrolled the flank of
the 7th Division in the attack of July 14th were the last
mounted troops to be seen on a battlefield for more than a
year.   Our advances were of the nature of the " nibbles "
beloved by Joffre, and some of the strong points in the
German defences held up our best efforts for many weeks.
Best known of these was High Wood, dominating point
of the Bazentin Ridge.   From it the Germans commanded
observation miles behind the British lines.   It was actually
captured on July 14th but lost the next day.   Time after
time attacks were flung against it : whole armies of artillery
bombarded it continually for weeks on end ; yet still it
held.
    This was a war of three dimensions : when you cannot
get through a position or round it, then you must try to
get either over or under it.   Frontal attack having consistently and bloodily failed, it was decided to mine the

MINE CRATER AT LA BOISSELLE

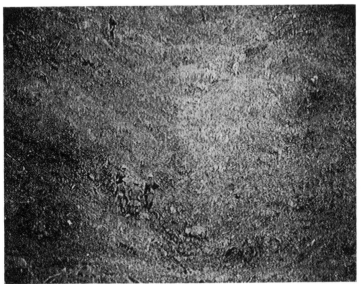

INTERIOR OF MINE CRATER IN HIGH WOOD

position. For this purpose 178th Tunnelling Company
was brought into the line.

The conditions for a successful mining venture were
anything but ideal. Such trenches as existed were continually bombarded, and communication was possible at
night only. This greatly hampered the removal and
disposal of soil from the mine and also the supply of stores
and material. To complicate matters further, the exact
location of the strong point was not known.

A shaft was sunk to 25 feet, and a gallery pushed out
with the intention of driving at least 400 feet, but for want
of sufficient time and delays owing to lack of material,
the gallery was charged at 320 feet, a point some distance
in rear of the German front line. The mine, 3,000 lbs.
of ammonal, was successfully exploded thirty seconds before
" zero " on the 3rd September, 1916, and the Black Watch
occupied the crater, with little resistance, and established
a machine-gun in it. Strong enemy counter-attacks by
bombing parties and cross-fire from machine-guns compelled a retirement to the original line, leaving the enemy
in possession of the mine crater, which he soon held in
force. Our infantry tactics in crater warfare were throughout the War decidedly inferior to the Germans, and the
number of occasions on which we were forced to relinquish
an initial advantage was very disconcerting.

A second time the miners were called in. The original
gallery was reopened, and a second charge of 3,000 lbs.
placed and fired on the 9th September in conjunction with
an infantry attack. It cut into the first crater and inflicted
heavy loss on the enemy, who was completely surprised
by this second explosion. The 1st Northants occupied the
craters, the enemy offering little or no opposition.

In addition to the mines, eight " push-tubes " were forced
out in this vicinity, but were not a success, only four being
completed and fired ; the conditions were distinctly
unfavourable for such work, the ground being matted
with tree roots.

On this occasion, however, the crater was firmly held,
and its commanding position contributed materially to the
eventual capture of High Wood.

Thereafter the Battle of the Somme continued its weary way, its only excitement being the introduction of the Tanks on September 15th. The Tunnelling Companies found their main occupation in the construction of trenches and dug-outs : as the autumn rains fell, conditions became deplorable—almost impossible, and forced a lull in the bitter struggle. Yet suddenly the damp fire of battle blazed again for a brief while, bringing to us our most spectacular success of the year. This time the scene was transferred to the northern edge of the Somme battle-field.

v

The July attack north of Thiepval had not been successful, and months of hard work by 252nd Company, during which time it had completed over 10,000 feet of galleries, had proved futile. In the weeks which followed, the enemy could not have failed to locate the exact position of many of our Russian saps, and therefore was in a position to destroy them at will. For this reason, order to reopen them in preparation for another attack were received with some misgivings and a certain lack of enthusiasm. Nevertheless, work was at once resumed at the Redan mine, where the defensive system was soon put in order.

At Hawthorn Ridge mine, the old H3 gallery was opened up and recovered for a considerable distance ; and when it became too crushed to reopen, a new drive branched off to reblow the original crater which the Germans had seized and consolidated.

Then work began on John, Mark, Excema, Cat and Beet saps, but owing to the impassable state of the trenches, work was impossible on the other saps. Later, four saps from new trenches between the Redan and Hawthorn mine—North Street, Hunter Street, South Street and Beaumont—were started. Work was also commenced on a big scheme to tunnel under Beaumont Hamel at a depth of 180 feet from a shaft, well back, called White City. This project, called the Great Eastern Tunnel, was soon abandoned as it was estimated that six months would be required for its completion.

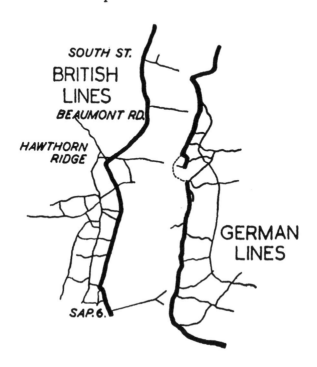

Meanwhile the enemy had not been inactive ; he fired a large camouflet in the vicinity of R.1 (1) and R.1(2), but work was not in progress there at the time and our galleries suffered slight damage only, though an officer and a sapper, no doubt actuated by the best motives, entered the mine to investigate without having taken the precaution of equipping themselves with " Proto " apparatus, and both were overcome and died from gas poisoning.

As was expected, the enemy soon began systematically to destroy our saps, in some cases by mines bored from the surface, in others by portable charges. In this he was quite successful, for in a short time Grey was blown three times, John five, Excema two, Bleneau three, Beet and Mark once each. These blows caused few casualties to the miners, but the infantry seeking shelter in the saps from the bombardments which followed the firing of the charges had numerous losses from gas. Much material damage was done, especially to Bleneau, which was practically destroyed. In retaliation, we fired a charge in Grey which cratered into the German trenches ; and in Cat, where the enemy could be heard working close to us at the time of the blow, 2,000 lbs. in three boreholes blew into his trenches, but the infantry raiding party attacking in conjunction with the mine failed to enter the German lines.

On 1st October, a new attempt was made to re-open John, Mark, Excema and Grey. The following day the Germans again fired a heavy charge between John and Mark, and of ten men who took shelter in the sap mouth, nine were gassed. Towards the end of the month, the saps were stepped up to within a few feet of the surface of the ground. H.3 mine was again charged with 30,000 lbs., and a smaller charge placed in Cat. No. 2. In the face of heavy bombardments, all the saps and mines were maintained intact. On one occasion eighteen men were entombed in First Avenue Tunnel, both entrances having been smashed in, but all were eventually rescued uninjured.

Immediately north of the Ancre River, where our front line had been advanced by digging new trenches, there were four more saps. 174th Company worked on these for about a month, extending them forward and making two connections back to Roberts Trench, while south of the river, where again new trenches had been made in advance of the old line, Peterhead and saps eight and three' of the original ten, were extended.

The attack took place on the 13th November, 1916, the mines being fired at " Zero "; H.3 was particularly successful and did considerable damage. The charge blew into the 1st July crater and covered the German trenches with debris.

So successful was the infantry attack that 252nd Company secured fifty-eight prisoners, including three officers, from a dugout. Six dugouts were closed. One of the officer prisoners stated that each dugout had held about the same number of men.

After the attack, 252nd Company was employed making new dugouts in Beaumont Hamel, clearing up and repairing German dugouts, salvage, road making, and fatigue work at rail head, and later on mined dugouts for infantry and signals.

The victory of Beaumont Hamel was the last phase in the series of attacks known as the Battle of the Somme. A *denouement* was to follow the main drama—when the Germans retreated to the " Hindenburg " Line four months later. The battle had been a deep disappointment ; its high hopes had vanished in its early days. Instead of the expected break-through, we had eaten into the German trenches so slowly that there was ample time to construct further lines. Yet the situation was not without its bright side. After all, we *had* driven the Germans from one of the strongest sectors of his front ; very much against his will, we had forced him back several miles. Unhappily, this fact had been accomplished at too great a cost in brave lives. A few more victories like this and we might easily be defeated.

The brightest gleam of all came from the conduct of civilian soldiers. They faced difficulties and dangers which would have staggered the veterans of the Crimea ; they suffered casualties which would have made the hair of the Waterloo Guards stand on end. At least Britain's men would not let her down ; men who could fight the battle of the Somme and still maintain their high *moral*— the future, at least, was not without hope.

The Tunnellers were as optimistic as the rest of the British Army. Their mines had battered the German trenches ; their cutely-planned Russian saps had scarcely been used. They would just have to try again.

VI

Although the Somme absorbed the main efforts of the Tunnelling Companies during 1916, the whole of the remainder of the front was continually active. There is a continuous record of mines exploded, craters seized and lost, of miniature pitched battles underground, of hard work and heroism. To describe all this in full would savour of repetition, for, except that our Tunnelling Companies were now more numerous and better equipped and organized, their work and adventures did not differ vastly from those of the previous year.

At Hill 70, in front of Loos, 258th Tunnelling Company was in contact with the enemy underground. A big blow from the upper levels had checked him temporarily, but later he was discovered to have worked beneath the crater. Another charge delayed him for a couple of days only, after which he was heard recovering his gallery and driving forward again. Obviously his mines were much deeper than ours, and had suffered little from our blows.

We had still another shot in our locker, fortunately. No. 3 shaft was down 80 feet, and the gallery was being pushed forward rapidly, but before it had proceeded very far it was turned to the right to form a chamber. While this work was in progress, the enemy was heard working very close, and sounds that indicated all too plainly that he was tamping were picked up by a geophone. Our miners were withdrawn at once and the trenches in the vicinity cleared. That evening the expected camouflet was fired, damaging our gallery back to the shaft. Repairs were soon effected and chambering resumed, but had made little headway when a pocket of gas was encountered; this, on being liberated, exploded immediately it came in contact with the naked lights. Gas continued to surge through the broken ground in such quantities that the air pumps could not keep the gallery clear. We were thus faced with a new difficulty—the problem of charging and tamping a gas-filled gallery.

No such difficulty interfered with the enemy, who continued to work forward, passing the end of our gallery. The situation now was very serious, as he was within striking distance of our trenches. The First Army Mine Rescue School lived up to its title and came to the rescue, and Lieutenant Smart, one of the instructors, was placed at the disposal of the Company. On the morning of the 16th September, 1916, the "Proto" apparatus arrived on the scene. Sapper Trueman, with a trained assistant and a fatigue man, was placed in charge to clean and recharge it, a duty which he carried out with great care and skill, so that no hitch occurred. The fourteen men specially trained to " Proto " work were divided into two shifts to work in relief. Lieutenant Smart led the first shift of six men, and after preliminary work began to place the charge. It was soon discovered that men wearing " Proto " apparatus could not handle readily 50 lb. boxes of powder, so it was made up into parcels of about 20 lbs. and placed in double sandbags. The shift remained below for two hours, and after a short rest Lieutenant Smart went below with the second shift.

The enemy was now working in his gallery very close to ours, a fact which greatly increased our difficulties ; extreme caution was necessary to ensure noiseless working, for the careless dropping of a bag of tamping, or bumping the gallery side with the cylinders of the " Proto " set, might result in disaster.

Though in constant danger from the gas-laden atmosphere, and in spite of wearing breathing apparatus, our men were comparatively safe from being blown so long as the enemy could be heard working in his drive. This he continued to do, no doubt confident that his mines had smashed us beyond repair.

By 4 a.m. on the 17th September, 5,000 lbs. had been put in and detonators placed. The next relief was in charge of Corporal McDougall, and during its two hours below it completed the careful packing of the greater part of the charge. It was thought that the charge would have sealed the gallery and that the air pumps would clear the gas, but after ten hours the gallery was still badly gassed. It was therefore decided to increase the charge by 1,000 lbs. Captain Henwood and Lieutenant Smart went down, and brought out seventeen boxes of ammonal from the 48 feet level ; this was placed in bags and added to the charge, and tamping commenced.

After about 35 feet had been put in the enemy ceased work in his gallery ; evidently he considered he had approached near enough to our line to be sure of smashing it with his blow.

During the next shift a slight accident happened.   The
man at the shaft bottom unhooking the bags had the
mouth-piece of his " Proto " set pulled out, the hook of
the winding rope catching in the breathing tube.   Somewhat alarmed, the man began to climb the ladder hurriedly ;
using the by-pass valve, he managed to reach the third
landing, where the air was better.   Here he was made to
rest and eventually reached the surface none the worse.

At last the tamping was completed right back to the
shaft, a certain amount being placed in the shaft bottom
to protect it from the force of the explosion.

At 6.45 p.m. on the 18th September, the mine
was fired.   Second-Lieutenant Ward, an eye-witness,
described the result as follows :   " In the case of the deep
charge a pillar of flame shot up, expanding as it rose.   It
burnt like a blow-lamp for quite ten seconds, and after a
further ten seconds, a loud hissing of escaping gas was
heard."

The good work done by the Mine Rescue School party
saved the front line from being blown.

VII

In spite of the increase in the number of Companies,
there never were enough Tunnellers.   Men toiled and
endured continuously, month after month, with no reliefs
available.   Difficulty and danger were dismissed by the
veterans as unworthy of comparison with sheer weariness.

As indicating the continuous nature of the work done by
Tunnellers, a most unusual entry is recorded by a Company
diarist for the 25th December, 1916 :   " No work.   First
time this has happened to this unit."

Again on the 31st :   " Corps Commander says no work
on New Year's day—that will give us two days' rest in a
week, after fourteen months working every day."

CHAPTER VI

I

THE story of the British Army in France during 1917 may be summed up in three words—Arras, Messines, Passchendaele. Yet the stories of the three battles differ vastly. In each case there was a ridge to be stormed as a first condition of success. At Vimy and at Messines the condition was fulfilled ; at Passchendaele it was not.

The principal physical feature of the Arras sector was Vimy Ridge, a stretch of downland some nine miles in length, extending from the River Scarpe at Arras to the Souchez River, dominating the Douai Plain, from which it rises abruptly. Its northern end is narrowed by the Zouave Valley, a bay of the Souchez valley. In the latter are the villages of Souchez and Carency, where in 1915 some of the fiercest fighting of the War took place, with changing fortune as the wave of battle surged to and fro— especially around the Sugar Factory, which was lost and won time and again, taking heavy toll of the resources of both sides. The losses of the French alone amounted to 150,000 men, and as late as 1917 there were still many unburied corpses lying about, grim relics of previous carnage. The outcome of the struggle left both sides clinging to opposite slopes of the Pimple, the northern extremity of Vimy Ridge, while towards the south the enemy occupied the higher ground.

Then for some time comparative quiet reigned, but the French made no effort to consolidate the line, being content to hold it by isolated posts, as their policy then was, relying on the rapid and accurate fire of the wonderful 75's for the real defence. Meanwhile, the Germans further strengthened their advantageous position by mining activity.

A further extension of the British front in 1916 brought to this sector the 176th Tunnelling Company from Givenchy ; 182nd Company, from Armentières, actually arrived several days before our infantry ; 172nd Company from The Bluff ; 185th and 184th Companies from the Somme, and the New Zealand Tunnelling Company. In addition, there were five French Companies in the Third Army area towards Arras. These were subsequently relieved by British Companies.

Now French and British trench policies differed greatly. The French adopted the principle of " live and let live " ; they did not believe in the frittering casualties of trench warfare, which, insignificant in themselves, eventually amounted to mammoth totals. Little attempt was made to disturb or harass the enemy, and generally he was good enough to respond in similar fashion. It need hardly be said that it was no lack of spirit which prompted this leave-well-alone policy ; the French man-power was limited, and the high command needed every man it could raise for its vast offensives. Consequently, trench casualties must be cut to the minimum.

The British plan was the exact opposite—a continuous and active hostility, disturbing to the enemy as to ourselves. For the first few days after we took over a sector the Germans got the surprise of their lives. Their peaceful undisturbed nights were gone for ever—there were actually cases where the French slept in one half of a village, the Germans in the other. These British, with their persistent patrols, raids, and bombardments, made life too exciting and rest impossible. Casualties, too, greatly increased.

There are, of course, arguments in favour of both policies. The British inflicted and received larger casualties, an essential part of a war of attrition ; the French conserved their depleted man-power, so that the staged attacks did not go short of effectives. The British theory was that such quiescence invariably led to a lack of combative spirit ; on the other hand, an unending sequence of trench affrays could easily dull the senses of the most

offensive fighter.   At the same time, however, it did
seriously affect the *moral* of the enemy.

When the British took over the Vimy sector they were
very surprised to find that the Germans held practically
the whole of the crest of the ridge.   In the battles of 1915
the French infantry had actually swarmed over the crest,
and the feat had naturally been blazoned to the world.
Very soon, however, they had been driven back to the
lower slopes, and this unpleasant fact had been disguised
even from their allies.

As on other parts of the front, a great change came over
the erstwhile quiet sector when the British took it over ;
peace gave place to interminable strife, and the Ridge
became one of the plague-spots of the front.   Underground the situation was even less favourable than our
miners suspected.   Nothing loath, they took up the
gauntlet, carrying the fight to the enemy's territory.
Cautious, yet cruelly persistent, they hung on to the enemy
like a pack of hounds at the flanks of a hunted stag, the
while he lashed out with camouflets, as the doomed animal
kicks at its pursuers, yet lacking the power to drive them
off.   " Football," " Broadbridge," " Irish," " Kennedy,"
" Love," " Momba," " Montreal," " Grange," " Crosbie "
and many more craters bit deeply into his flanks and did
much to wear down his strength and weaken his *moral*.
A map of this front looks like a strip of lunar landscape, so
pock-marked is it with craters from the Pimple to Arras.
Captured German documents bear eloquent testimony to
the moral effect on the harassed troops caused by our
aggressiveness.

The General commanding the 17th Reserve Division
found himself compelled to report thus : " The casualties
which we suffered by mine explosions and continual night
attacks aroused in me lively anxiety, which I communicated
. . . to the Chief of my Corps and his G.S.O.I.   Things
could not go on as they were.   If by attack . . . we
could throw back the British and so rob them of all their
mine shafts . . . we should have tranquillity."

The 163rd Regiment reported : " The continual mine
explosions in the end got on the nerves of the men.   One

stood in the front line defenceless and powerless against these fearful mine explosions."

Reserve Regiment No. 86 was equally despondent : " Our companies had suffered heavy losses through the British mines . . . we could not fight against the enemy any longer with his own weapons, for he was superior to us in men and material."

Hard pressed as he was below ground, the enemy sought relief by attacking on the surface and capturing our shafts. The circumstances were somewhat peculiar. A Divisional Commander on " the Ridge " fell sick ! a Deputy Chief of the Staff, General von Freytag-Loring-hoven, was given temporary command of this division to gain practical experience at playing the war game—this was one of the excellent rules of the German staff, that all officers from time to time should serve at the front. Through his influence at H.Q. he was able to secure almost un-limited ammunition and many guns—so many, in fact, that he was able to assemble no fewer than eighty batteries on the divisional front.*

On the afternoon of May 20th, 1916, an exceedingly heavy barrage was put down on the Berthonval sector, corresponding to the sector recently taken over by 182nd Tunnelling Company. By midnight all was quiet again. The Company Commander proceeded to the trenches to investigate. Nothing of the " line " could be found, and with considerable difficulty one mine entrance was identified. The only men encountered were those of the 2 a.m. relief, struggling forward in the darkness to take over in the mines ; they, failing to recognize any semblance of the line, were actually out in No Man's Land ! They were got back, and proceeded to repair the mine entrance. That was the last seen of them ; before they could get back the barrage again came down and they were trapped.

The London Division suffered heavily in the attack which followed, and the enemy made an advance of about 200 yards, gaining temporary relief. After the attack, a new and continuous line was constructed ; mining work

* See *Official History of the War.*

was redoubled, and a lateral connected with 176th Company's workings on the left. An incline, by good luck, holed at 60 feet deep into the end of 176th Company's old gallery, in which a large charge was placed. Actually, in spite of the lavish expenditure of men and ammunition in this local attack, the relief gained by the Germans was but fleeting ; within a few days we were under his line once again.

II

1916 had scarcely justified the high hopes with which it had opened. The results of the Somme were disappointing, and the casualties high. And, although the French had held Verdun, the sentimental policy of defending every yard of ground had bled the French Army almost to exhaustion. Nevertheless, at the end of the year the Allies still had a considerable numerical superiority in the west, and Joffre and Haig agreed to a continuance of the offensive policy. The Somme battle was to be continued, the British attacking to the north of the river, the French to the south.

The plans were no sooner made than cancelled. For some time the French Government had been uneasy about Joffre ; while his moral stability was invaluable, he was evidently no heaven-sent genius, and his neglect of the defences of Verdun had been disturbing. He was therefore " promoted to the rear," and Nivelle, a comparatively junior commander who had won fame by his unconventional methods at Verdun, became Commander-in-Chief. His plan was for a grand attack on a colossal scale on both flanks of the great salient about Noyon ; he was no disciple of the Joffre " nibbling " school, but planned to end the War by one vast victory. The British were to open the battle by an attack in front of Arras ; the enemy's attention and reserves thus attracted to this flank of the salient, the French could inflict a crushing blow along the Chemin des Dames front, from Soissons to Reims. They would break through the German line in forty-eight hours, and within a few days the salient would have disappeared. Such was the theory of the plan.

The Germans, however, were not content to leave the initiative in enemy hands.   In August, 1916, Falkenhayn had been replaced by Hindenburg—with Ludendorff, of course, as the *de facto* commander.   Ludendorff, like his predecessors, saw the difficulties of the German position ; unlike most generals on either side, however, he had no sentimental attachment to useless ground.   Accordingly he carried out a manœuvre of which an Allied commander would have been almost incapable—deliberately and unhurried he gave up several hundred square miles of ground, and calmly retreated to the well-prepared " Hindenburg Line " across the base of the Noyon salient.

The Hindenburg or, more properly, the Siegfried, Line was an almost impregnable stronghold extending from the Scarpe, via Bellicourt, St. Quentin, La Fère to the Aisne east of Soissons.   Its chief characteristics were defence in depth, both on the surface and underground, and a lavish use of reinforced concrete.   It consisted of two and sometimes three lines of deep, strongly-wired trenches, plentifully provided with deep dugouts, which gave complete shelter from the severest shelling.   Not only were the dugouts connected with the concrete shelters above ground, admitting of easy and rapid access to the fire step in case of emergency—they were also connected, at intervals, by underground passages to the support line.   They were further connected laterally by the Hindenburg Tunnel which ran the whole length of the line.   The Hindenburg Line possessed, in addition to its almost unassailable strength, the added advantage of shortening the line by cutting across the chord, thereby economizing in man power —a decided advantage at this stage of the war.

In passing, it is of interest to note that, except for a few listening posts here and there, no attempt had been made to protect the line by mining.   Incidentally, a little more acuteness on the part of our Intelligence might have forecast the preparation of a strong reserve line, for after June, 1916, there was a marked falling off in German mining activity—with the reasonable assumption that the pioneers were engaged elsewhere.

The strategy of the retreat was excellent but the manner

of its execution aroused many angry thoughts.   Two
years earlier this stretch of rolling downland had been one
of the most fertile corners of France.   The Germans left
it a desert.   In six hundred villages not one brick adhered
to another—the whole area was one huge ruin, an appalling
waste.   Maybe some justification could be pleaded on the
grounds of military necessity, since unharmed villages
provide shelter for troops, but this plea could scarcely be
extended to cover the destruction of young fruit trees,
which could not benefit an enemy for many years.   The
British were appalled as they saw the abomination of
desolation spread before them ; the fury of the French may
well be imagined—one division was actually recruited from
this very area.   The Germans hoisted a large notice * over
the ruins of Péronne : " Don't be angry ; just marvel ! "
But this was too much to ask, and the wilful desolation of
the province is one of the things held against Germany by
France to this day.

The retreat was skilfully conducted.   Only/occasional
patrols and machine-gun nests were left behind to delay
our advance : these were not difficult to dislodge.   The
greatest dangers of the advance were the devices of the
German engineers—methods of the anarchist and the
assassin.   Infernal machines and traps, cunningly designed
and craftily constructed, were secreted in cellars, dugouts,
under roads and railways, and other places where parties
of our troops were certain to congregate or pass.   The
existence of these devices was often unsuspected by our
men until they revealed themselves in no unmistakable
manner ; then, alas, it was too late.

The cellars of the Town Hall at Bapaume were left fur-
nished in a most elaborate manner, as though they had been
used as headquarters—for which they were admirably suited.
This " step into my parlour " invitation and the desire to
enjoy such magnificent comfort proved too alluring and
irresistible.   The invitation was accepted.   A party of
French local officials, including several deputies, anxious
to visit the territory so recently freed from the yoke of the

* *Nicht argern, nur wundern.* The board is now housed in the Imperial
War Museum.

K

invader, visited Bapaume shortly after its occupation by the British.   As no other accommodation was available the troops, eager to show their hospitality, provided the visitors with temporary quarters in the cellars.

Eight days after the occupation, at about midnight on the 25th March, 1917, the Town Hall was wrecked by an explosion.   The first delay-action mine of the war had added yet another form of frightfulness to the ever enlarging list.   Casualties were heavy.   Several non-combatants, including two deputies, were among the killed.

A few hours later the headquarters of an Anzac Brigade blew up.   The members of the staff were absent at the time and the losses were slight.   Soon other delayed action mines were reported.   Evidently the most urgent measures must be taken to combat this new and dangerous menace. In the South African War " anything hot or unwholesome " was passed on to the Mounted Infantry to be dealt with ; in the late War such things fell to the Tunneller's lot. Parties were organized immediately to scour the neighbour-hood ; places likely to contain mines were marked " out of bounds " until they could be examined thoroughly and declared safe.

At Beugnatre, Sapignies, Gomiecourt and Mory and other places north of Bapaume, mines went off before they could be located and removed.   At Ervillers the junction of the Bapaume-Mory road was suspected.   Work was pressed on throughout the whole of one day clearing the debris to locate the gallery containing the mine.   Over-taken by darkness before the work was completed, the men were withdrawn.   Shortly afterwards a mine exploded, gouging a huge gap in the roads.

All these were delay-action mines—that is to say, they were provided with a means of detonation concealed within the charge, and were not dependent upon the presence of the human element to set them off.   This lessened the likelihood of their detection, as leads or fuzes were not required.   They could be laid and concealed days, even weeks, beforehand.   Their uncanny hidden hand effect was demoralizing.   There is nothing quite so unnerving as unwelcome surprises.

But the secret of the firing device was soon discovered. Briefly, it depended upon the corrosion of a wire by acid. A striker, actuated by a spiral spring, was held at full cock by a wire. This wire passed through an acid solution which gradually ate through it and brought the striker into action, detonating the charge. There was also another type of device, the " booby trap." Innocent

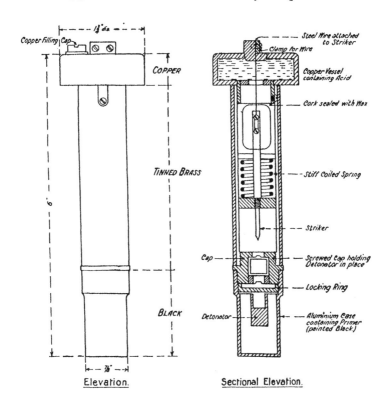

Elevation.   Sectional Elevation.

looking articles, likely to tempt the souvenir hunter, such as a book or a spiked helmet, apparently carelessly left upon a table, when moved would detonate a bomb or a small charge, and the incautious hunter was fortunate if he escaped with his life. A picture, hanging awry upon the dugout wall, when straightened would go off with a bang. A loose step in a dugout entrance, when stepped upon, would explode a shell hidden in a recess behind the timbers, or perhaps a mine which would destroy the whole entrance.

Examples could be multiplied a hundredfold ; the few quoted will suffice to show with what extreme caution the advancing troops moved, and how their progress was restricted and retarded until the ground had been examined thoroughly.

" Fools rush in where angels fear to tread." Many of the troops denounced as recklessly foolhardy the activities of the Tunnellers in their " booby-trap stunt," as it was called. None, however, considered them angels. Certainly no angels trod more warily than did those Tunnellers engaged in this particular work.

The use of these ruses was scarcely in keeping with our ideas of " playing the game." Men who had talked almost amiably about " old Jerry " now cursed him fiercely. Yet maybe he was no more than brutally logical. A British officer prisoner, interrogated by a German officer, remarked : " You Germans do not play the game." The German replied, " This is not a game. This is war." And, of course, as in love, in war all is fair.

But two can play at war with the gloves off. Some of our patrols adopted an expedient which was effective if not pretty. A German prisoner became a valuable possession instead of a nuisance : since duck-boards and dugouts blew up at the first footstep, let the German tread them first. If he knew of traps, assuredly he would then reveal them : if not—well, it was better for him to die than us.

Several hundred booby-traps and delay-action mines were located by the Tunnellers, often moving forward in advance of the infantry. The Inspector of Mines rendered very valuable assistance by collecting information, and circulating sketches and full descriptions of any new devices discovered, so that all companies were well posted with up-to-date information. The Tunnellers soon developed almost an instinct for locating and dealing with these ruses, so that, in spite of the extremely hazardous nature of the work, casualties were surprisingly few.

It may be of interest to record that during the period in which the delay-action mines were exploding near

Bapaume, the Germans were blowing craters on important roads well behind their front line in the Wytschaete-Messines-Ypres area, many of which they fortified. At the same time a lot of work was done on rear defences in the same area. Is it possible they contemplated retiring on this front also, in anticipation of our attack later in the year ?

III

The German retreat to the Hindenburg Line interfered seriously with the Allied plans. The Germans, in their retreat, systematically laid waste the country ; in particular, communications were utterly destroyed, wells fouled, accommodation ruined. Consequently it was necessary to modify the British share in the attack. The Vimy front, to the north of Arras, was unaffected, but further south the impossible wilderness impelled a drastic shortening of the front of the attack.

The capture of the Vimy Ridge was perhaps the knottiest problem confronting the British command. Here every advantage was held by the Germans, whose command of the high ground gave them observation well behind our lines. The scheme finally drawn up depended to no small extent on tunnelling activity. The mining programme included the destruction of strong points and the formation of craters to give flanking protection. Nor was this all : the British staff throughout the War was generally slow to learn its lessons, but it *did* learn. The causes of the catastrophe on the opening day of the Somme had not been entirely overlooked, and for the new battle underground communications and sheltered tunnels for attacking troops were to be vastly extended and to form an important feature.

The policy of a wholesale construction of infantry subways was also impelled by other causes. In the autumn of 1916, as has been stated, large numbers of German engineers and other troops were withdrawn from the front for work on the construction of the Hindenburg Line. An immediate and distinct falling off in mining activity was reported. This did not imply tranquillity in the line, however. As a compensatory factor, and perhaps to disguise the fact that the trenches were lightly held, trench mortar activity greatly increased—not only in the Somme area, but all along the British front.

Many more batteries were observed, especially of the heavy type, and, provided with an abundant supply of ammunition, a systematic bombardment was maintained on the trenches in which were our mine entrances. The communication trenches also received special attention, a practice quite in accord with the general principles laid down for mine warfare. The devastating effect of the trench mortars soon began to be felt. Mine and subway entrances were constantly smashed in, hampering work underground and interfering with the disposal of spoil on the surface.

The communication trenches were so damaged that sufficient supplies of mining material could not be got up, Consequently the rate of working was slowed down, and the weekly totals dropped considerably.

Along the First Army front, between the La Bassée Canal and the Souchez River, the ground was suitable for the construction of subways. Therefore, as a counter to the enemy's trench mortars, 251st, 170th, 253rd, 3rd Australian, 173rd and 255th Tunnelling Companies all commenced to construct subways. The other Companies who were working on Vimy Ridge were also engaged on subways. This work is described fully in the approaches to the battle.

The Cuinchy-Cambrin-Auchy front was well served by a group of about a dozen infantry tunnels, more or less regularly spaced along the front, the work of 251st Tunnelling Company. At Hohenzollern, 170th Company had several tunnels, of which the Saville was perhaps the best known. At Hulluch, The Quarries and Cité St. Elie, 253rd Company had North, South and Dudley tunnels, while at the Double Crassier, 173rd Company was engaged on similar work. Marble Arch, Bully Subway, Gum Boot and Rotten Row, were put in by 255th Company along the Calonne-Souchez front.

The work was greatly impeded in its early stages by the extremely wet weather, but afterwards very rapid progress was made, and in a short time no less than twenty miles of subways had been constructed. Ample dugout accommodation for headquarter and infantry formations was

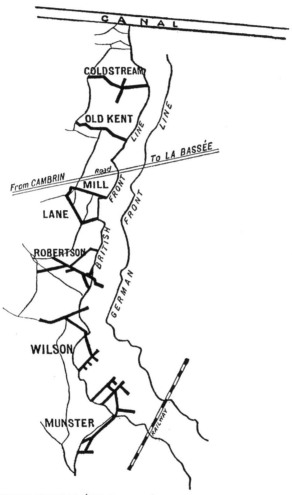

INFANTRY SUBWAYS (HEAVY LINES) ON THE CUINCHY-AUCHY FRONT.

included, and numerous exits connected to front and support lines. In cases where the subways were connected to mine systems, adequate gas doors were provided to prevent mine gases entering the subways.

In nearly all cases there was sufficient room for men in full kit to pass along in comfort, while at intervals passing places were provided. Many of the subways connected with machine-gun posts, and, for defence purposes, traverses were made, into which loophole plates were built. Generally the subways were lit by electric light—in order to minimize confusion, good lighting was essential. Most of the lighting and pumping plants were installed by the A. E. & M. M. & B. Company.

There can be little doubt that the subways were a decided success. In addition to providing shelter, they were used sometimes in connection with raids. They also gave a feeling of security and reduced casualties.

Perhaps the most elaborate of all the subways was Hythe Tunnel, constructed by the 3rd Australian Tunnelling Company. It connected the Hulluch-Cité St. Elie Road with a strong point on Hill 70 ; this, however, was not constructed until the early part of 1918.

Reinforced concrete Bascule doors were put in at the foot of the forward entrance inclines. Pivoted, the doors normally rested in a horizontal position, forming the floor of the gallery. On the withdrawal of a pin the door turned on its pivots into a vertical position. Stout timbers kept the door fastened, and a loophole commanded the incline. These Bascule doors were the modern counterpart of the ancient drawbridge and the portcullis.

IV

The benefit of the withdrawal of German miners was felt to greatest advantage along the Vimy Front—the scene of the potential attack. Here enemy mining activity subsided so considerably that we were able to withdraw many of our own miners for work on subways, of which more than a dozen were constructed.

A large number of companies were engaged on this work. From north to south, 176th Company was on the northern end of the Ridge, known as the Souchez Sector, where mining, on two levels at 60 feet and 110 feet deep, continued to be active. A charge of 6,000 lbs. at 135 feet deep had to be fired, as a vigorous offensive by the enemy had brought his gallery so near to ours that talking could be heard with the naked ear at ten feet back from the face. On two occasions when the enemy fired mines, no damage was done, but subsequent gas explosions did damage. Our main lateral for over 300 feet was damaged, and a fire started.

Three mines in preparation for the attack, one of which was to be under Kennedy crater, which the enemy had consolidated, and two subways, Gobron and Coburg, the latter being 873 feet long and having an average of 50 feet of cover, completed the programme in this area.

On the next sector, Berthonval, 182nd Company had four subways, Blue Bull, Vincent, Tottenham and Cavalier, all of which commenced in the Zouave Valley. Vincent eventually holed into " M " mining system, the main gallery of which was enlarged and driven to surface out in No Man's Land. At 1,270 feet Cavalier was connected to the front line.

Frequent raids harassed the enemy and kept him on the *qui vive*. After a heavy bombardment, during which gas was used, 182nd Company sent out four parties with the infantry, only one of which succeeded in reaching the German trenches. Second-Lieutenant A. E. Morris, R.E., the leader of this party, was wounded at the wire, but Lance-Corporal Medlicott gallantly carried on, entered the trenches, fired his mobile charge, and after making further investigations for mines, withdrew, bringing with him two other ranks who had been wounded.

Two days later an armistice, to remove the dead killed in the raid, was suggested by a German officer, who approached our lines carrying a yellow flag. This lasted two hours—a very infrequent event on the Western Front—the bodies being carried half-way across No Man's Land by the Germans and then handed to our men, who evacuated them through the subways.

As Vimy Ridge extends southwards it tends to flatten, so that the subways necessarily became longer. Grange and Goodman (the latter was no less than 1,880 yards long) had a series of heavy trench-mortar emplacements and the necessary casemates for ammunition. 172nd Company was on this sector and had, in addition to the above, several mines in preparation—one large one beneath "Broadmarsh" crater, which the enemy had fortified so that he could enfilade our line, and two smaller ones near the end of Grange.

Just prior to the attack, the enemy fired a series of about nine small mines, presumably for tactical reasons, which formed one long crater which became known as "Longfellow." The mine under Broadmarsh was then abandoned, as it was considered likely another crater would further restrict the passage across No Man's Land.*

On the Roclincourt-Neuville St. Vaast sector, 185th Company had numerous mine galleries, many of which were in the clay, while from the head of Zouave Gallery they had commenced, early in 1917, four subways—Zivy, Bentata, Douai and Barricade.

Two sections of 255th Company were employed in constructing two large underground reservoirs, capable of holding 50,000 gallons of water each, for the use of troops after the advance. These were well under cover, and pumping plants were installed to deliver the water into the tanks in the subways.

In " H " and " I " sectors near Arras, the New Zealand Company was working on a number of Russian saps, one of which holed out into the enemy's mine system. In another, one of our trench-mortars dropped a shell well short of the German lines on the shallow earth covering the gallery, which promptly collapsed ; a party of miners was cut off but was released after nine hours by a party driving a " rabbit-hole "† round the broken ground.

184th Company had relieved the New Zealand Company on " J " sector, and in addition were building heavy trench-mortar emplacements and the Fish Avenue Tunnel, while at Ronville 181st Company was engaged on dugout construction for Headquarters, signals, etc., saps in " H " sector and at the Caves.

---

* Many Battalion Commanders disliked mines on account of the difficulty of crossing a crater.
† Rabbit-hole : a small untimbered gallery ; literally a burrow.

All the subways had ample head cover, and were most elaborate—containing accommodation for Brigade and Battalion Headquarters, dugouts, assembly chambers, signal offices, bomb and ammunition stores, dressing stations complete with operating table, water tanks and water-bottle filling points, kitchens and latrines. Numerous exits gave access to support, front and assembly trenches, while others again came to the surface well out in No Man's Land. Signal cables were run through and into the mining system and were carried along the laterals ; thus uninterrupted communication could be maintained with units on either flank—a most important point.

Some remarkably rapid progress was made in driving the subways, which were 6 feet 6 inches high by 3 feet wide. Incessant trench-mortar straffing made the removal and disposal of the large amount of spoil produced a difficult and dangerous proceeding. Precautions to prevent flooding of the subways with gas necessitated the erection of gas doors and curtains, and kitchens and latrines had to be ventilated by boring earth augur holes to the surface.

Most subways were electrically lighted by plant erected and maintained by the ubiquitous Australian Electrical and Mechanical Mining and Boring Company. The lighting sets were petrol driven, and precautions were taken to store petrol in locked fireproof dugouts, adjoining the engine-room, and the exhaust was carried to the surface through a borehole.

Owing to the many chambers, exits, etc., elaborate plans and numerous direction boards and bright light signs were provided in order that the troops might easily find their way in these maze-like subterranean labyrinths. On the eve of the attack, special guides were posted at various points to control the traffic.

Even the rail head of the light railway was underground, and it was quite intriguing to see the miniature train, laden with stores and ammunition, disappear into the hill-side to be off-loaded and shunted in perfect safety after running the gauntlet across Zouave Valley.

IV

The provision of this vast series of underground tunnels was by no means the only contribution of the Tunnellers to the forthcoming attack. By their ingenious use of existing caves at Arras they made possible a tactical surprise.

Underground shelters and passages have been in use in France for hundreds of years, especially in Artois and Picardy, where they are called *muches* or hiding caves, in which the populace took refuge in times of riot or war. One tunnel, which ran from the neighbourhood of Armentières into the fortifications around Lille, was said to be large enough to permit a horse and cart being driven along it, and in this way supplies of food were brought to the garrison of Lille during the siege of 1793. Some again were so extensive that fodder and cattle were kept in them for long periods, water being supplied from wells sunk in the floor. The entrances were sometimes hidden in or near churches, schools or convents, in houses and even in wells. Similar underground chambers exist beneath the castles in the border country, and were much used in the days of the border forays, when Scotland and England were not such friendly neighbours as they are to-day.

The Germans are known to have used many tunnels and shelters to be found in the Somme area. The Kaiser himself, while on a visit to Tournai in December, 1916, stayed in caves close by the station.

The housing of a large army on active service in modern warfare is a difficult problem. All buildings, villages, towns and camps near the front where troops are congregated, are bombarded day and night, not only by artillery, but also from the air. Adequate protection against this must be provided if the efficiency of the troops is not to be impaired. To build this on the surface is too costly and laborious, so the only alternative is to " go to ground."

The French had made use of some small caves in the vicinity of Arras before we took over this area. Later, officers of the New Zealand Tunnelling Company, amusing themselves while off duty, discovered some openings which their curiosity led them to explore. A thorough investigation resulted in the discovery of more caves, and steps were at once taken to make these habitable. But these caverns were entirely distinct from the *muches*. They proved to be the underground quarries from which was taken the limestone used in rebuilding the city of Arras in the seventeenth century.*

It was found that two definite cave systems existed, one along the Arras-Bapaume road, the other along the Arras-Cambrai road. The New Zealanders and two section of 184th Company were concentrated on developing and preparing the caves, making entrances and exits, connecting them by tunnels, securing the roofs and generally cleaning up ; making the roofs safe was no easy matter on account of the height of the caves, but by trimming off the loose chalk and building huge sandbag pillars, most of them were made quite safe and the doubtful ones were railed off and not used. This work was done so well that even during a bombardment the injuries from falling chalk were few and slight. The excavated chalk from the tunnels was dumped into the caves and levelled off, making an even floor, reducing the height, and so making timbering less difficult.

In all some twenty-five caves of various sizes were found and linked up and transformed into underground barracks complete with every modern device, including gas doors, ventilating plant, " electric light, running water and the usual offices," as the house agent would say. In this way dry, warm and safe accommodation was provided for 11,000 troops during the coldest months of the whole campaign. In fact, the work was delayed as sufficient timber and material could not be delivered—through limitations on the vehicles permitted on the roads by frost precautions.

From the caves, tunnels were driven forward—St. Sauveur's Tunnel to connect with the five subways in

---

* Just as, outside the walls of Jerusalem, are Solomon's Quarries, from which material was taken to build the Temple.

" I " sector, which had numerous exits well out in No
Man's Land, and Ronville Tunnel connected to R.I.
From I·54 and I·56 push-pipe mines were eventually
blown and, soon after zero on the morning of battle, connection was made with the German front line on either
side of the Cambrai road.   Thus troops actually passed
from the security of the caves direct into the German
trenches !

ARRAS CAVES AND SUBWAYS.

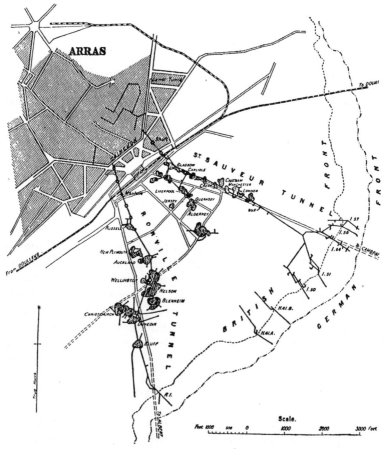

Another important feature added further to the utility
of the caves and was ingeniously adapted.   The moats

round the Citadel at Arras are fed from the Chrinchon stream, which is then carried beneath the city by a large well-built brick sewer, passing eventually into the river Scarpe. Two footpaths, one on each side of this conduit and well above water level, made it ideal for the passage of troops.

Tunnels were driven back from the caves, and the sewer became incorporated with the subway system. Tramway tracks along the tunnels facilitated the handling of supplies and ammunition. And so it was that troops descended underground at several places in the centre of Arras and emerged in or near the German front line, having travelled in perfect safety a distance of nearly two miles.

In all about seven miles of tunnels and subways were constructed in a little over four months, constituting the most important tunnelling work undertaken up to that time. That the value of the tunnels was enormous will be agreed by many thousands of grateful infantrymen, who probably owe their lives to them.

VI

The first day of the offensive—April 9th, 1917—was apparently the greatest success the British had achieved to date during the War. Many factors contributed to our initial success ; our artillery concentration was infinitely denser than anything we had yet achieved ; a new gas shell recently introduced was devastating in its effects. The delicate act of the timing of the creeping barrage had been mastered. Nor was the contribution of the Tunnelling Companies unimportant. On more than half the battle front battalions were able to take up their battle positions at the last minute from the safe seclusion of tunnels and caves ; thus the disheartening and often disconcerting pre-battle casualties which are so upsetting to the *moral* and equilibrium of the attack were avoided. At the cost of losses which were insignificant compared with the slaughter of the Somme, home and Canadian troops swept forward astride of Arras, and in the initial stages of

the battle captured no less than 13,000 prisoners and
200 guns.   Considering that all possibility of surprise had
been surrendered by the policy followed by the British
command, this achievement was almost remarkable.

For Tunnellers April 9th was a busy day.   Not only
had our tunnels to be maintained, Russian saps to be
broken to surface, and the culmination of months of work
supervised, but the rapid advance meant that the whole of
the enemy mining system south of Calonne fell into our
hands.   Numerous parties of tunnellers went over to
examine the enemy mine systems, remove or render harmless any mines found, collect equipment, and locate and
examine dugout accommodation for the infantry.   Many
mine plans, listening reports and other documents fell into
our hands.   176th Company found a copy of orders
issued by the 79th Reserve Infantry Brigade, dated 5th
April, 1917, giving details of another prospective attack
on a front of 3,200 yards " to remove the mining danger."
For once the Germans were too late !   Other parties were
detailed to search for and remove traps and ruses along the
roads and railway lines and other likely places in the newly-
captured area.

Officers from 172nd Company located two German
subways, Schwaben and Volker, secured numerous
prisoners sheltering therein, and cut the leads of demolition
charges placed near the entrances.   One officer of 182nd
Company, on reaching the enemy trenches, was greeted by
a large party of Germans with their hands up.   Escorting
them across to our lines, they suddenly came under machine-
gun fire from a part of the line which had not then been
taken.   Throwing themselves on the ground until the fire
ceased, they rose as one man and raced for our lines, hotly
pursued by the officer—yelling curses at them and brandish-
ing his revolver in approved wild west fashion.   Visibly
swollen with pride at his achievement, he almost burst
with indignation when, instead of commendation, he
received a mild rebuke for having " brought " the prisoners
to the wrong H.Q.!

VII

The latter stages of the battle, unfortunately, did not
fulfil the high promise of its first day—they seldom do.
The failure of the French offensive on the Chemin des
Dames front, however, led to a decision to pursue the
battle before Arras in order to distract the attention of the
enemy. Improvised attacks, nevertheless, were hardly
likely to make much headway against the strong and determined German defence. In such warfare the Tunnelling
Companies had little opportunity of distinguished service,
and contented themselves with the construction of dugouts, camps, and trenches, or adapting to military purposes
the numerous small caves in the battle area.

VIII

There are two memorials to the tunnellers to-day in the
green and pleasant land which was once the bloody battle-
field of Arras. Near the crest of the Vimy Ridge the
Canadian Government has purchased a considerable stretch
of ground in memory of the men who fought and died on
those scarred slopes. An imposing memorial has been
erected, but far more interesting are its environs, which have
been maintained in their war-time condition. Here is a
maze of trenches, barbed-wire, and the medlied rubbish
of a battlefield. As a necessity to permanence, sandbags and duck-boards have been reconstructed in concrete,
and the eyes of an ex-service man may well open wide as he
beholds their ordered array. But one exhibit is at least natural,
for one of the tunnels (Grange) burrowed in preparation for
the grand assault has been retained in its primitive yet
practical state. Here it is not difficult to recapture the
atmosphere of bygone days ; every effort is made to assist
—even to the litter of equipment and rum bottles (empty).
The walls are freely decorated with unique specimens of
trench " art," of which only the most piquant specimens
have been deleted by the Censor. There must be hundreds

L

of autographs, roughly scribbled by soldiers as they waited
for the word to advance to victory or death.   An inscription
near the mouth of the tunnel is well worded : " These
walls are sacred to the names of the soldiers who inscribed
them during their occupation in the war of 1914-1918.
Please omit yours ! "

The other memorial is even more intriguing.   Among
the mines blown by the tunnellers at the moment of attack
were two known as Lichfield and Zivy.   Both destroyed
important German strong points, but were the scene of
bitter fighting before the last desperate resistance was
overcome.   When the burial officer of the Graves Regis-
tration Unit arrived on the scene the atmosphere was still
unhealthy, disturbed by continuous fire.   Whether because
of this or whether he had the insight of an artist, we do not
know, but he decided to use the craters as cemeteries.   In
their depth were buried the men who fell in the miniature
battles about them ; wisely, their bones have never been
disturbed.   To-day a significant stone wall surrounds each
crater, and its scroll records the names of the men who lie
within its circumference.   The crater has been filled in,
and a green carpet of tended grass covers what once was a
sudden scene of angry desolation.   Over one hundred men
lie in these unconventional graves, and of all the beautiful
monuments raised by the Imperial War Graves Commission
none are more beautiful nor more imposing than these.

CHAPTER VII

I

IN addition to feverish operations on battle fronts, Tunnellers were continuously engaged in sectors which might be classed as comparatively quiet. To detail the whole of their work would require a huge volume, which might be too boring in its sameness. A glance at one or two of the sectors must serve as an indication of the rest.

From the very commencement of mining on the Western Front, Givenchy had been one of the high lights, and remained so until the end. Givenchy—the name will long linger in the memory of thousands of Guardsmen, Canadians, and men from the County regiments, who at one time or another took part in its defence—a small scattered village on rising ground sloping up from the La Bassée Canal, commanding a view towards the town of La Bassée in the east, and to the north over low-lying, marshy ground beyond Festubert. Like most other sectors, it had its periods of storm and calm. At one period the blast of war had subsided so completely that, at the notorious " Windy Corner," one could buy the London daily papers, a day or two old, from a mere lad, calling his wares in a thin, piping voice.

At the canal, the lines were about 500 yards apart, gradually converging as they swept north, until at Duck's Bill, a small salient in the German lines, they were very close together. From this point they were more or less parallel until, at Sunken Road, they splayed out again over the flat country, leaving Givenchy exposed and somewhat isolated.

Most of the mining took place at the northern end of the sector, though 176th Tunnelling Company had succeeded, after great difficulty in overcoming excessive water, in sinking a shaft near the Canal. During 1915, a number of shallow " rabbit-holes," just below grass roots, had been put in from surface saps " F," " D," " H," " K " and " J." Exposed to enemy raids (on several occasions the Tunnellers had to eject the enemy from sap heads before they could enter the mines !) and too shallow to be effectively blown, they were anything but an asset. However, they were kept open and used as listening posts while deeper systems were being developed.

Towards the end of the year the Sunken Road inclines were extended into the blue clay, while Red House, White House, Orchard, The Warren, Hope Street, Bond Street and Duck's Bill were all down twenty, and in some cases thirty feet. All these shafts gave trouble with water early in 1916, and power pumps had to be installed in some. Red House was a particularly wet mine. A winze had been sunk through the clay into the chalk, which contained artesian water, and although a special pumping fatigue of thirty men came on every eight hours, the water gradually rose until it was only a few feet from the shaft top. White House, Orchard, and Duck's Bill were also flooded. These floodings were regarded as an assurance that the German workings, slightly deeper than our own, would also be flooded, and therefore so long as they remained in this condition we were in no immediate danger of underground attack.

But the miners did not remain idle while the workings were flooded. The opportunity was taken to sink more elaborate shafts. At the Sunken Road two sections of 180th Company had been relieved by a like formation of 255th Company, who at once commenced Bunny Hutch shaft almost in the front line. The officer in charge here, " Birdy " Dixon, was probably the biggest officer in the Tunnellers, and the shaft was in keeping with his stature. The pent-house * was an elephant shelter sunk well below ground level and covered with tons of broken bricks from ruined houses ; upon these railway rails were placed in two layers at right angles, then a gap or bursting space

* The covering over the top of the shaft.

and more rails, the whole being covered by thousands of filled sandbags packed and rammed, thereby utilizing the spoil and solving the dumping problem to a certain extent. The shaft was 8 feet by 5 feet with two compartments —one for haulage or winding, the other for ladders, pumps and pipes. The shaft sets were 8 inches by 6 inch squared timber, the longer beams being 9 feet in length, and the problem of transporting such heavy and cumbersome material to the site and erecting it within a few dozen yards of an alert and vigilant foe was no light undertaking— it all had to be done at night. Manhandling the awkwardly shaped segments of elephant shelters over the wet and broken ground—they were too large to be taken along the communication trenches—through an almost incessant barrage of rifle grenades and trench-mortars was a severe test for the carrying parties. The work was naturally not popular, but was carried out with great courage and without cessation. Until the pent-house was completed all traces of work had to be concealed very carefully before dawn, as any carelessness in this matter invited disaster.

On its return from Gallipoli, 254th Company took over from 176th Company, and in the spring of 1916 succeeded in de-watering several of the flooded mines. Later several new shafts were sunk, including one at Shaftesbury Avenue.

Both from " E " sap, Shallows and Bond Street came reports of enemy mining at no great distance away. Both were charged. As the " E " sap workings were slightly in advance of, but not so deep as, Bond Street, it was decided to fire the shallow mine first, followed by the deeper almost immediately afterwards. This plan miscarried, as the concussion from the first mine broke the leads of the second. Twelve hours later they were repaired and the charge exploded successfully. This mine had the desired " fougasse " * effect as, by blowing through the side of the crater formed by the first, it threw up a high lip on our side of the elongated crater formed, but no lip

* Fougasse—a very ancient military mining term. It described a mine intended for purely *surface* effects—equivalent to those of an enormous trench mortar, using a hole in the ground as the mortar. Its effect is to scatter debris, earth, etc., over the attacked position.

on the German side. Tons of debris were hurled on to the German trenches, and enemy mine timbers appeared in the crater. But the Germans must have had a deeper gallery which had not been damaged, for two days later they retaliated with one of their most successful blows against us.

On 22nd June, 1916, for two hours a rain of shells, including heavies, fell upon our saps, front, reserve and support lines. At 2.50 a.m. the enemy exploded a large mine, completing the destruction of two saps, wire and front line trench over a considerable distance, and inflicting losses on the garrison. To add to the confusion, a strong enemy raiding party entered our lines, but was later ejected by the remnants of the 2nd Royal Welsh Fusiliers, who gallantly counter-attacked. The crater, the largest on the Givenchy front, was known as " Red Dragon," the sign of the Division to which the 2nd Royal Welsh Fusiliers belonged.

" Red Dragon " is also connected with one of the most poignant incidents in tunnelling warfare. Considerable damage was done below ground when the enemy mine was fired. The main drive from Shaftesbury Shaft had not proceeded very far, and five men were in it at the time of the blow. The shock broke some of the timbers near the shaft, causing a fall of roof and cutting off the men. Relays of workers set to work at top speed to release the trapped men. After twenty-four hours a small opening was made through the soft fallen ground and broken timber. Three men scrambled through it to safety.

It was then discovered that a smaller fall of roof had occurred near the face. Of the two men remaining in the gallery, one, a big man, was badly injured by the fall near the face ; the other was Sapper William Hackett. The opening which the rescue party had driven through the outby fall was too small to permit the injured man to be passed through, and as there was immediate danger of further falls, Hackett was ordered to come out. Well knowing his fate, he steadfastly refused to leave the injured man, saying : " I am a Tunneller. I must look after my mate." Scarcely had he finished speaking when both men were overwhelmed by a fall of clay which filled the gallery completely. All efforts to re-open it failed. For this calculated act of courageous self-sacrifice Sapper Hackett was awarded the Victoria Cross posthumously. "*Greater love hath no man than this, that a man lay down his life for his friend.*"

Shaftesbury Shaft received such a buffeting that finally it collapsed, and new shafts were started. These were equipped with electrical pumps and were therefore able to overcome the water trouble. Such rapid progress was made that we were able to make the new line, built behind "Red Dragon" crater, secure underground before the enemy could strike again and drive home his advantage, and very soon we had a gallery out beyond the far lip of the crater. As expected, an approaching enemy gallery was detected, and allowed to come quite close before a charge was fired. Next morning, on looking into "Red Dragon" crater, the officer on shift was astonished to see the head and shoulders of a German soldier protruding from the side of it ! He was extracted and made a prisoner. A second man scrambled over from the crater into our lines and gave himself up. On being questioned independently, each prisoner related a similar story. Just before our mine was fired, they said, a fatigue party, about forty strong, came to work for the mining company. These two men had been posted as look-outs in the crater, into which a German gallery had holed, while the remainder of the party were resting in the same gallery immediately above our charge. By some strange chance, these two men escaped unhurt, while the rest of the party must surely have perished.

For months after this blow the enemy showed extreme lack of enterprise. This enabled us to develop our defensive mines and push out our galleries as far as necessary.

In May, 1917, sounds of enemy mining were again picked up, but work was carried on so irregularly that, at first, it was thought to be surface work. The sounds approached nearer. At length the sound of falling earth was picked up by the geophone, and we were now unmistakably aware of its significance. Cautiously the enemy

advanced, little knowing that his every movement was as
well known to us as if we were actually watching him in
his own gallery, so proficient had listening become. Then
talking was audible, which meant that he was very close.
Finally a charge of 9,000 pounds of ammonal was put in
our own gallery and fired at 7 a.m. on the 10th August,
1917, forming a large elliptical crater, which we immediately
occupied.   It was given the name of Warlingham, and
proved to be the last mine of the War fired by the British,
251st Company having the distinction of thus striking the
final blow.

On this front three small mines, which did no damage,
were fired by the enemy in September and October,
after which no other mines were fired by either side—except,
of course, demolition and delay-action mines.   After the
decline in mining activity towards the end of 1916, as we
have already noted, the Tunnellers were concentrated on
the construction of subways.   The increasing use of heavy
trench-mortars by the enemy caused many losses among
the infantry, and destroyed communication trenches.   Subways were a very effective reply to this, and a large number
were constructed along the Givenchy, Hulluch and Vimy
Ridge front.   But it was on another sector that Tunnellers
helped to develop another tactical idea—the use of subways
and saps during a raid.

II

Raids were cordially detested by the infantry.   The
necessity of cutting the enemy wire by trench mortar and
artillery fire meant that ample notice was given to a vigilant
opponent, who almost invariably prepared a very warm
welcome.   Consequently, a raiding party knew in advance
that at least half its number would never return—usually
the proportion was even more staggering.   Yet raids were
very necessary in " quiet " periods—particularly for the
identification of the German divisions, and for the valuable
information a prisoner might give.

The dangerous part of the raid was the rush across
No Man's Land, well covered by enemy machine guns.

The wider No Man's Land, the greater the danger. But Tunneller officers, impressed by their experience on the Somme, repeatedly suggested that raids should be made from tunnels or Russian saps pushed into No Man's Land, thus greatly reducing the dangerous stretch of ground to be traversed. After one or two experiments in this direction, a raid on a large scale was organized, and the tactical arrangements were left almost entirely to the Tunnellers.

On the 10th June, 1917, the 2/4th East Lancs. carried out the idea on a front of about 100 yards a short distance south of the Béthune-La Bassée road ; a party from 251st Tunnelling Company, consisting of Second-Lieutenant Woods and five other ranks, took part. Three subways served this front. For the purposes of the raid, Mill Tunnel, on the left, had been continued forward beyond our front line into a group of craters, but was not broken out to the surface until the last moment. In this tunnel the left assaulting column assembled, secure, *and within 50 yards of its objective.*

Lane Tunnel, the central one of the three, housed the reserves, and was connected to the front line close to the dugout used by the officer commanding the raid. From here telephone cables were carried through the mine lateral into Robertson Tunnel on the right into Battalion Headquarters. An advanced dressing station was constructed in this tunnel so that the wounded could receive attention immediately. The troops attacking on the right assembled in Robertson Tunnel.

Three minutes before the appointed hour, a decoy mine was fired some little way to the left. A listening post had been advanced and a charge placed beneath the near lip of a group of craters. It was so placed in order to " fougasse " the enemy trenches, and was very successful. Taking advantage of the distraction caused by the mine, the infantry, nearly two hundred strong, left the tunnels and went forward into the German trenches almost as easily as when " finger " (the code for these operations) was rehearsed at Le Quesnoy. The miners followed immediately. After a brief search a mine shaft was found, partly obstructed by debris from the " fougasse." Posting four

infantrymen, attached for the purpose, on guard at the
entrance, Lieutenant Woods and his party proceeded below

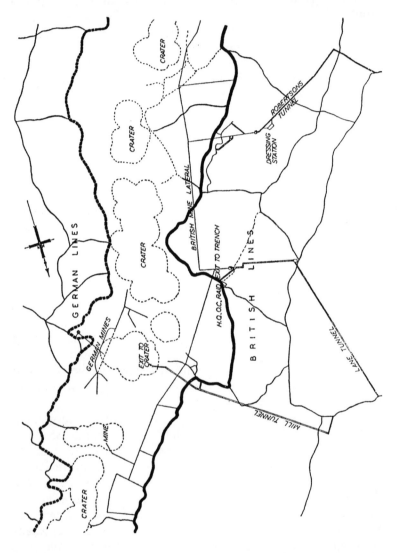

to make an examination. None of the enemy was
encountered below and a complete survey of the workings
was made. Placing portable charges in position, the party

withdrew, bringing with them some listening appliances found in a dugout and detectors found in ends of two listening posts. Hearing the reports of the mobile charges after they had emerged from the mines, the party withdrew, having spent an hour and a half in the German lines !

The infantry took numerous prisoners, including one officer, and sustained slight losses only. The raid, in fact, was one of the most successful of the whole of the War, and attracted such attention by its results and particularly by its slight cost that Sir Douglas Haig himself came to inspect and congratulate the raiding party.

III

An awkward situation arose at Hill 70, when the capture of some enemy trenches brought our new front line directly across the centre of the German mining system, leaving many yards of lateral and branch galleries behind our line, while he still retained possession of some of the entrances. Before being driven out of their line, however, the Germans had succeeded in destroying the mine entrances so thoroughly that an exhaustive search by the 3rd Australian Tunnelling Company failed to locate a single one in the newly captured line.

But their listening, carried out in the lower levels, gave them a very good idea of the German lateral and some of the galleries. From the face of No. 1 D.D. Main, which was being extended in front of our new line, intermittent working could be heard to the left, which was thought to be the enemy re-opening one of his mine entrances. Then for several nights in succession the sound of walking could be heard, coming from the same direction as the previous sounds.

The infantry were informed and a raid organized, in which three shafts were destroyed by a party of Australians who accompanied the raid. At one entrance leads were found and cut.

No. 1 D.D. main was rushed out to a point known, from listening reports, to be close to the enemy's galleries :

it was charged with 10,000 lbs. of ammonal, but not
fired.

While this work was in progress, the enemy was heard
again, working at night, in a vicinity where one of his
shafts had been destroyed in the raid, probably repairing
it. He succeeded in gaining access to his workings, and
on the 8th July, 1917, fired a mine which formed a crater
near our line.

Another of our galleries (parallel to 1 D.D. Main, but
in rear of our new front line), which we had been pushing
forward, holed into the enemy lateral at a point where our
front line crossed above it, and where our listeners had
located the German lateral. An investigating party entered
the German workings and found that the charge fired on
the 8th July, 1917, had not been tamped and several cases
of explosives were still about. The leads had been carried
through the whole length of the lateral and were found
to be those cut during the raid on the 28th June, 1917.
Indications were found of two other charges being prepared at points behind our line. The galleries were close
timbered throughout. When surveyed, it was found that
in all 774 feet of enemy mine galleries had fallen into our
possession, and that our listening had been accurate.

There is always a great pleasure in getting something
for nothing. Tunnellers were always delighted at the
capture of enemy galleries—the idea of all his labour
being used for his own destruction was naturally amusing.

IV

In August, 1916, during the tenure of the 3rd Canadian
Company on the Hill 60 front, an intermediate gallery
known as D. Break, was driven to the left off the deep
offensive incline. This gallery was at 50 feet deep and
intended to " back up " the shallow system. Bearing
round to the right, it ran parallel to the main incline for
some distance, then again curving right-handed under
trench 39 it became D.R. Just behind trench 39 a lateral
was broken out to the left, but had only advanced about

ten feet when suddenly a rush of water burst in the face, flooding our workings, the men in the gallery having a narrow escape. After several days' hard work on the pumps, the water was reduced sufficiently to allow an examination.

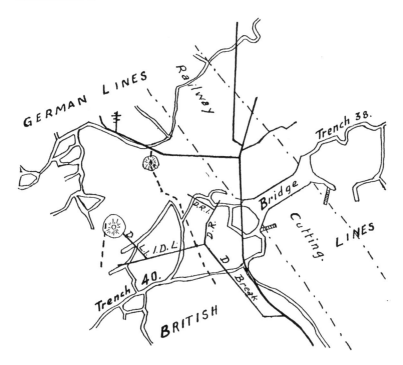

It was discovered that we had holed into a damaged German gallery, which had penetrated, unknown to us, to a point 100 feet behind our front line. The usual tools and sandbags and a portable electric lamp were found, also something more unusual—an oxygen cylinder, which was presumed to have been used to ventilate the gallery, no other method being discovered. By the end of August 230 feet of this German gallery had been recovered and it was used as a listening post, though a geophone could not be used in it on account of the dripping water. The regular and constant dripping of water sounded on the geophone like picking. By great good fortune the end of this gallery, and the shaft from which it had been driven, were wrecked some time previously by camouflets fired from our listening posts in the shallow workings. Thus the portion of the gallery which we had captured was denied to the Germans. Had we not been so fortunate and the enemy had been able to fire a charge in this gallery, the result would have been disastrous.

Meanwhile, by the end of September, tunnel D.R. was completed and back from the face of it D.R.I. was commenced. From this face Lieutenant Clarke, the listening officer, picked up with a geophone a series of tapping sounds which could not be identified, and at first were thought to be mining sounds. The taps occurred at regular intervals of several minutes and each series contained the same number of taps. Furthermore, towards the end of each series the rate of tapping increased. No other sound was audible. The direction from which the sounds emanated was easily determined by the use of two geophones and a compass, and the distance estimated to be about 70 feet off. The point indicated was plotted on the mine plans. Constant and careful listening over a period could reveal no more. For the moment we were completely baffled. At last, by clever deduction, it was surmised that the taps were accounted for by a windlass being allowed to run free, the bucket increasing in speed as it neared the shaft bottom, the tapping sounds being caused by a loose handle or the spindle of the barrel bumping in its frame. During the winding up, the pressure would prevent the taps, and so this operation could not be heard. Very soon the truth of the surmise was established to be correct. Proceeding along the captured gallery as far as possible in the direction of the point previously indicated on the plan, the enemy could be heard working in frantic haste to re-enter his lost gallery, little knowing that we had got there first. A suitable charge rendered this area immune from attack for some time.

Foiled in this attack, the enemy attempted a thrust in another direction, hoping to find a chink in our armour. I.D.L. had been continued beyond the captured gallery in an easterly direction as a lateral front of trench 40, and from it D.L.I. branched off in the direction of the German lines. On October 19th listeners at the face heard sounds indicating that a German gallery was approaching from the left, some distance ahead. A premature blow was not to our advantage, so work was stopped and an " ear " kept on the German gallery. Soon sounds were heard to the left growing fainter, at the same time becoming increasingly louder on the right of I.D.L. Thus spotted from two points, the exact course of the gallery was easily located and, as it would pass the end of I.D.L., the enemy was allowed to proceed.

With great restraint the Canadians withheld their hand though not their ear, and allowed the enemy to approach close to trench 40. Then at last came the " third day's frost " in the shape of a couple of well-placed charges in the shallow right on the line of, and above, the intruding gallery, not only " nipping the bud," but blasting the whole tree so that no more branches were thrust out to molest us in this vicinity.

Great accuracy was needed in calculating the amount of explosive required in these mines in order that the maximum damage be done the enemy without injury to our deeps.

Intermittent mine warfare continued on this front, but it was confined to the shallow galleries. This was greatly to our advantage, and we exploited every method of keeping the enemy continuously on the *qui vive* in the shallows, so as to distract his attention from our far more serious mining in the deeps.

v

A long, narrow, terraced spoil bank along the north side of the cutting through which the Ypres-Commines canal passes terminated in a mound some thirty feet above normal ground level. Called by us " The Bluff," and known to the Germans as *die grosse Bastion* (*englische*), it was handed over to us by the French early in 1915. As an observation post it was of great importance, overlooking, as it did a large sweep of enemy trenches, a fact which made its retention essential. The Germans saw to it that we were not permitted to retain our legacy unchallenged, and at once developed an attack underground, and soon the Bluff became as a noisome festering sore, continually breaking out.

Our front line trench No. 29 ran round the base of the Bluff, numbers 30, 31, etc., extending northwards to the left, in front of which the ground became marshy. The 28th Division took over this front from the French, and were at once ordered "to push forward saps and mines against the enemy." This they proceeded to do ; in March, 1915, 171st Tunnelling Company started two shafts in trench 32. The nature of the ground and the lack of proper material soon brought these attempts to an end, and a new start was made behind trench 32 and in trench 29. Soon afterwards the scattered sections of 171st Company were recalled to Ypres, and 172nd Company extended its front to the left, as far as the Ypres-Commines railway line. In April, 172nd Company was fully occupied at the Mound, St. Eloi, but found time to start a shallow defensive system north of the Bluff.

Early in May, Captain Johnston, V.C., left 172nd Company to take up appointment with the 15th Brigade, and Captain W. C. Hepburn took over the command. By the end of the month, five or six shafts were being put down in trenches 31 to 34. From these and other shafts a shallow mine system developed, and not long afterwards contact was made with the enemy mines.

Lieutenant Williamson, while on his rounds inspecting the workings in front of trenches 32 and 33, discovered that the Germans had broken in and installed a listening apparatus. This he quickly dismantled, at the same time sending out to the magazine for explosives. The news soon spread, and another officer joined him. Continuing their investigations, they entered the German gallery, but had not proceeded far before they were fired upon. Withdrawing round a bend, they placed in position the small charge which had arrived, lit the fuse, and hurried out of the gallery, which in a few moments was destroyed. This was on the 5th October, 1915.

So began a series of underground encounters, remarkable

for initiative and daring, carried out with the greatest hardihood over a period of two years, each successive incident outdoing the last, until, finally, the Germans were driven back and lost the whole of their mines.

As the ground was very soft, much use was made of the Burnside borer, and numerous small charges were put in and fired, especially from the craters (which were fast increasing on this sector), to destroy enemy galleries. It was the practice to keep two or three bore-holes, spread out fan-wise, in advance of the working face, as a precaution. In " B " sap the boring tool came into contact with something solid. After careful probing with the borer, it was concluded that it had come up against the timber of a German gallery. Working with the utmost caution, and using only a bayonet to dig away the clay, our gallery was advanced right up to their gallery timbers, unknown to the Germans. Removing some of the timbers, Second-Lieutenants Brisco and Hibbert entered and proceeded to investigate. They encountered a party of Germans and immediately opened fire upon them with pistols. Taken completely by surprise at being molested in their own gallery, the Germans fled, leaving behind one of their party. Returning to our gallery to fetch the portable charge left there, Second-Lieutenant Brisco placed it in the German gallery and touched it off.

About this time—November, 1915—the Germans, who had blown us rather badly on several occasions, again succeeded in firing a large mine, doing considerable damage. However, much to the relief of the new commanding officer, Lieutenant Syme, 175th Tunnelling Company took over some of the mines near the railway line, thus freeing 172nd Company to concentrate on the Bluff.

In " B.2 " mine connection was made with our old " C " gallery ; it was discovered that the Germans had got there first and established a listening post, but their listening was so badly conducted that they were unaware we had re-entered our lost gallery.

Second-Lieutenant Brisco placed 40 lbs. of ammonal within a few feet of this post, and also an improvised listening apparatus consisting of a funnel, made from an

M

army biscuit tin, inserted into a length of rubber piping. The piping was carried through the charge and the 10 feet of tamping back along our gallery, and for some time every movement and conversation of the Germans at this point could be heard distinctly by our listener.

Owing to the continuous wet weather throughout December, underground work was delayed, the appalling condition of the trenches making them almost impassable. The wet had another and most unexpected effect. One morning, towards the end of December, it caused a subsidence in the large crater in front of " E " shaft, disclosing the open end of a German gallery ! Scrambling over the top into the crater, the intrepid Brisco entered and explored the gallery for a considerable distance. Hearing the Germans approaching, he withdrew to the entrance, whence he commenced to fire at the enemy, compelling them to retire. Barricading the entrance with sandbags, he then returned to our lines. At 6.15 p.m. the same day the enemy fired a mine, destroying and closing the end of the gallery, but doing no damage to our line or galleries. Undoubtedly the unlucky subsidence had ruined weeks of his work.

Early in 1916, New Year trench was dug on the canal side of the Bluff, and connected round the Bluff to trench 29 by the Loop. This was quite an innovation, as until this time the canal itself had been considered sufficient protection. Shafts were at once started in these new trenches, and also a small tunnel through the Bluff for communication purposes.

In the meantime, the Germans were stealthily and assiduously pushing on with a big scheme which culminated on the night of January 21st, 1916, when the face of the Bluff was ripped open by a series of heavy mines. Considerable damage was done to the trenches and the tunnel in the Bluff, but, for some unknown reason, no infantry attack followed, and we proceeded at once to consolidate the crater and reconstruct the trenches, unmolested by the enemy, and the situation remained much the same as before the blowing of " B " crater, as this was called.

Encouraged by this success, albeit unexploited, the

Germans redoubled their activity underground. Listeners reported the approach of an enemy gallery towards B.2 mine in trench 32. A charge was put in at once, together with the usual listening tube. Fifteen feet of solid tamping was placed against the charge, then an air space of five feet, followed by more sandbags, at which sat the listener, his ear glued to the listening tube through which the enemy's movements could be heard. On 11th February the listener reported that the Germans were removing the timbers of our gallery. Second-Lieutenant Brisco immediately went down and cautiously approached the tamping. Soon he was joined by Second-Lieutenant Laroque, who brought in a mobile charge of thirty pounds of gun-cotton. As noiselessly as possible they removed the tamping till but a single row of bags remained. Here they sat patiently awaiting developments. Four hours later the Germans had made an entry into the air space, and one of their miners cut the leads of our charge, and also the listening tube. The undaunted Brisco, deeming the moment ripe for action, pulled away the few remaining sandbags and fired upon the astonished intruder, wounding him in the jaw. The mobile charge was placed inside the junction and fired, forming a crater extending towards the German lines and throwing up a considerable quantity of mine timber. Only slight damage was done to our gallery.

The ground in front of the Bluff was difficult to mine, firstly because of much surface water, secondly on account of its churned up state through constant blowing, artillery and trench mortar bombardments. This and the incessant rains caused subsidences in the craters. After one of these settlements the end of another German gallery was seen in the side of the January crater. From our trenches a bearing was taken on to a light seen in the gallery, thus giving us the line of the gallery. A listening tube was placed in position, and the gallery barricaded and a listener posted in the crater. Soon the Germans returned and could be heard tampering with the tube. After dark a party went out into No Man's Land to bore down to the gallery. A rabbit hole was also started from the side of the crater,

in case the boring party were not successful in locating the
gallery. This proved a wise precaution. The Germans
were very vigilant, and by the light of flàres the boring party
was spotted and fired upon, the ubiquitous Brisco and a
sapper being wounded. Retiring behind the lip of the
crater, boring commenced again and soon reached the
gallery timbers. A charge of gun-cotton was fired, forming
a small crater and smashing a length of the gallery.

These measures, nevertheless, were not sufficient to
stop the enemy. On the afternoon of the 14th February,
1916, after an intense bombardment which obliterated the
front line, the enemy fired a mine under the old " B "
crater in front of the Bluff, burying a platoon sheltering
in the old gallery known as the Tunnel. Two minutes
later two more violent explosions occurred just north of
the first. Following the mines, the German infantry
attacked from the Bluff to the Ravine. By morning the
enemy was in possession of all the mine shafts in the sector
—ten in number. All the miners in them were either
killed or captured.

On 2nd March, 1916, however, we regained the Bluff.
By a clever *ruse de guerre* the Germans were lulled into a
false security. For days prior to the attack designed to
recapture the Bluff, the artillery put down on the front
line an intense bombardment lasting only a few minutes,
followed by a lull, and then another bombardment.

The methodical Germans got into the habit of remaining
under cover during the lull. On the day of the attack
the gunners lengthened the range during the lull, so that
the returning barrage fell on the support and reserve lines.
Our infantry swarmed over. Completely surprised, the
Germans were caught in the dugouts ; many even had
not time to don their equipment before they found themselves prisoners.

Four parties from 172nd Company went over with the
infantry to examine mine shafts and make sure that no
device for blowing up the trenches had been left. No. 3
party, led by Lieutenant Lyster, encountered strong
machine-gun and rifle fire from the entrance to enemy
workings in " B " crater. Overcoming this by bombing,

he and a sapper went below, and made a rapid survey of the workings. During an encounter with a party of Germans, Lyster received a wound which compelled him to withdraw his party. Before doing so, however, he was able to fire a portable charge which wrecked the gallery. The other parties located shafts, but they were so badly damaged that access was impossible. In the newly captured German line a shaft was found in the fire trench only 15 feet deep and long since abandoned.

The loss of the Bluff caused a rupture of the cordial relations existing between two regiments of German Grenadiers. The 124th Grenadier Regiment had captured the Bluff from us in the attack on 14th February, and when it retired to lick its wounds it was relieved by the 123rd Grenadier Regiment. It could find no excuse for the loss of the Bluff, purchased as so high a price. " The 124th," says the divisional history, " have never been able to forgive the Grenadiers ; there ensued a certain tension between the two regiments not overcome during the whole length of the War, in spite of many later fine successes in common."*

For over a twelvemonth the Germans had kept us " pegged down " round the end of the Bluff, where a nest of small craters, connected by numerous rabbit holes, had been blown and re-blown. Breaks into each other's workings were almost a daily occurrence. We were cramped, hampered for want of elbow room. Yet action was essential, but we were in no shape to deliver a real blow. Had the enemy not blown " B " crater several times without reply from ourselves ? To avenge this insult a scheme was evolved whereby two deep shafts were to be sunk well down into the blue clay, deeper than anything so far attempted by us in this sector, and connected by a lateral. The line then would be secure at least against underground attack.

In April, 1916, 172nd Company, which had borne the heat and burden of the day on this part of the front since its formation, and which had brought off the first big mining venture of the War, was relieved by the 2nd Canadian Tunnelling Company. Before leaving, it had

* See *Official History of the War.*

commenced an infantry subway through the Bluff in order
to provide better and more secure access to the trenches.
Off this a caisson shaft was started. The first attempt
proved abortive, as the caisson struck tree stumps below
the original ground level.

In May yet another change took place. This brought
the 1st Canadian Tunnelling Company on to the scene. A
second attempt to sink the caisson met with success, so
much so that in a few weeks the shaft was down 90 feet
in blue clay. Soon the main drive was making rapid progress, the Canadians, meanwhile, having acquired the art
of " clay-kicking."

For some time we had been in possession of very valuable
information giving the depth and the general direction of
the two enemy galleries from which " B " crater had been
blown. One was a tunnel from the canal bank, the other
a drive from a small shaft in the front line. They were
connected just in front of the German lines, and also again
where they converged near the crater, while two small
exits gave access to the crater itself. Later Canadian
Corps Intelligence reported " much new earth visible.
This may indicate tunnelling." The report gave us no
indication of the nature of the earth. Obviously it was not
blue clay, as it was dumped over the parapet near the canal,
not far from the small shaft. It was known that the
galleries were only 15 feet deep, so that the spoil
would probably not differ greatly from trench earth ;
thus its exposure over the parapet would not arouse
suspicion.

It was now more than five months since the last big
mine was fired at the Bluff. Surely this inaction was ominous ? Instinct and the " much new earth " led Major
North, of the Canadians, to the conclusion that something
was about to happen. He therefore took the precaution
to appraise the Corps Commander of the situation.
Accordingly artillery support was arranged for in the event
of an hostile mine going up. At the same time the
garrisons in the craters and the front line were reduced to
the minimum. Scarcely had these arrangements been
completed when the anticipated mine, or rather mines,

were fired. A huge bean-shaped crater, later to be designated " A," was gouged out of the Bluff behind " B " crater. No infantry attack developed, no doubt due to

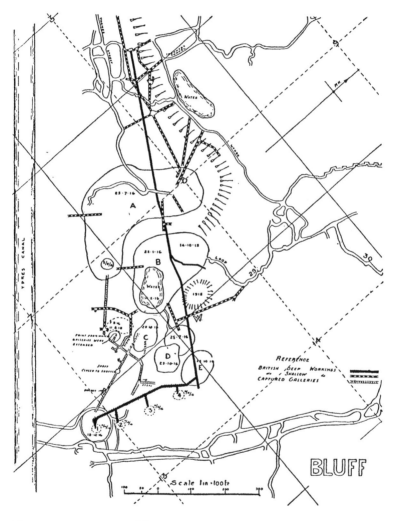

the promptness with which our pre-arranged artillery barrage came down. Major North established a great reputation as a prophet as a result of his very accurate forecast of this blow.

Below ground, the face of the deep Bluff drive was within the effective radius of the mines, and of the three men working there, one was killed and the others injured. The gallery timbers were damaged for a considerable distance, and as the ground was very heavy they were replaced by steel " I " beams. From a prisoner it was learned that about 15 tons of explosives were used in blowing " A " crater.

For months the Germans had tried to deprive us of the Bluff by blasting it out of existence, and they were succeeding gradually. Nevertheless the German official Bulletin's claim that they had " blown up the great British bastion beside the canal, together with its garrison," was slightly exaggerated. Our actual losses were slight, and the damage suffered was out of all proportion to the size of the huge crater. An impartial review of the situation forces one to the conclusion that this was a good outflanking movement successfully carried out. The repeated blowing of " B " crater, seemingly from the same galleries, was, no doubt, but a ruse to distract our attention while the more important work of getting round our flank was being developed unmolested. On the canal side of the Bluff we had little or no protection underground, relying mainly on the state of the ground to parry any thrust in that direction.

We now were in a very unenviable position indeed. Should the Germans renew the attack from the " A " crater gallery, we were in no position to counter them. The deep gallery was not far enough advanced to be of any use, unless the attacking gallery endeavoured to outflank " A " crater and approach on the canal side of the craters. In that case the correct policy was doubtful—whether to blow from it and so disclose our position, or to continue undetected with the prospect of effecting a *coup de main*.

One thing was certain—at all costs the enemy must be denied access to his gallery. The quickest and most direct way to it, from our point of view, was from the surface. Thus it was decided to adopt the bold and dangerous plan *of digging down into it*. Without delay a small party commenced to bore into the far lip of " A " crater at a point where the Germans had been heard working. They were detected. A small charge by the enemy killed three of them. Nothing daunted, others literally stepped into the breach.

In order to locate the gallery at a point nearer the German lines, Captain Spencer and a party stealthily made their way out into No Man's Land by night. Dropping into shell hole after shell hole, they listened, with a geophone, over a wide area. At last the expected sounds rewarded their enterprise. The following night a small charge was fired in the bottom of a shell hole immediately above the gallery at a point 150 feet from " A " crater. This gave some small measure of protection for further work in this exposed position. Two bore holes were then put down and fired. Night after night this went on, the charges increasing in size as the crater grew deeper : this was an unusual operation—mining in No Man's Land ! After two charges had been fired on the morning of 11th August, 1916, mine timber was exposed at the very point where the listeners had located the gallery. This was indeed encouraging—for us !

The following night the gallery was entered from " A " crater and followed to the point where it had been blown in by our charges on the surface. This success gave us a breathing space. Two days later the enemy fired a small charge on his side of the block. By so doing he played into our hands, for it meant that he had lost 200 feet of gallery since he blew us a week previously, and caught our men in " A " crater ; even more important, it meant that, for the moment, we had staved off an attack. The captured gallery proved to be most useful, providing a basis from which we were able to develop our shallow defensive system in front of " B " crater. Connections were made, linking up the craters, giving protection to troops going to and from posts in them. Also a drainage tunnel was started from " A " to the canal.

During this time the Bluff gallery had made steady progress, and early in September, 1916, was under the middle of " B " crater. At this point a branch was turned off to the left to form a lateral and connect up with one coming from the deep shaft at the Ravine. About this

time also several severe earth tremors were felt at the
Bluff ; no damage was done, but time was lost as, according
to standing orders, the miners withdrew.   These tremors
were caused by German camouflets, blown against our suspected galleries.

Then, on the 22nd October, 1916, three mines were
fired by the enemy, forming three craters in front of " B "
crater.   Reading from the canal side, these were lettered
" C," " D " and " E."   No serious damage was caused by
these blows, but Corporal Hodge and three miners working
in the shallows between Trench 29 and " B " crater were
buried.   A rescue party working from " B " crater was
driven off by bombs.   Three of the men succeeded in
digging themselves out—the fourth was killed—but on
reaching the surface they had the misfortune to come under
fire from the enemy, and they returned to the sap.   That
night our infantry took possession of " C " crater.   Three
weary and bedraggled miners managed to struggle back to
safety, and reported to their officer just as he was about to
post them as " missing, believed killed in action."

In the second week of November, two small charges
were fired in the German crater 50 yards in front of " A "
crater, throwing up a considerable quantity of old mine
timber.   Lieutenants Murray and MacPherson listened in
the crater and heard sounds of enemy mining.   About a
week later we encountered a German gallery beneath " C "
crater, and an interchange of small camouflets followed in
which we got the better of the deal—not before time.

Decidedly our star was in the ascendancy.   The Bluff
gallery had succeeded in passing beneath the craters
undetected.   Near the German lines it had been turned
to the right and ran along towards the canal, almost
parallel to them.   From this again four branches, about
100 feet apart, headed straight for the line.

At 6.35 p.m., on December 11th, a total charge of over
10,000 lbs. was exploded successfully in these four branches.

Each night for a week prior to firing these four camouflets,
an officer's patrol had been out in No Man's Land.   One
of these patrols located an enemy gallery at a point about
75 yards from our lines.   About ten minutes before the

I.W.M. Photo

Rescue of Trapped Miner by Sapper wearing Proto Set

blow, two officers and eight men went out to this spot. As soon as the charges exploded they commenced to dig down into the gallery. At midnight they found it, tamped with sandbags. At ten o'clock next morning all the bags had been removed and men, wearing "Proto" breathing apparatus, entered it. It was so full of gas that only a short reconnaissance could be made. The following morning (13th December, 1916), the gallery was again entered and surveyed. A quantity of mining material was found, which included a new type of listening apparatus, complete. The bodies of two Pioneers of the 324th Saxon Pioneer Mining Company were also found. By this *ruse-de-guerre* no less than 700 feet of undestroyed enemy galleries were now in our possession, connected to our shallow system, and consolidated into a defensive. At last the Bluff was safe—from underground attack, at least. This was one of the most successful underground flank attacks of the War, to say nothing of its ingenuity and audacity.

The capture of practically the whole of the German mines was not without its lighter side. On first entering the workings, it was seen that at a rough estimate at least 500 feet had fallen into our hands. This information, in code, was phoned back to our lines. The code was not extensive enough to convey all the information the party had to report, so a little ingenuity had to be used. "Cunningly dissembling," like Ulysses, the sender ended his message "Johnnie Walker." At first this was rather confusing, as it was known that no person with that name had accompanied the party. Could it be a hoax? . . . Then the trade slogan of a large and important firm came to mind. It was as plain as daylight now. They had already captured 500 feet of gallery and were "still going strong."

On the 18th December, the enemy sprung a mine directly over our No. 1 camouflet (of 11th December, 1916) which formed a crater just in front of his line. This he consolidated. In all probability the charge was placed in the remains of the canal tunnel. It proved to be the last mine of any consequence in this sector.

In the third week of the New Year, the 2nd Australian

Tunnelling Company relieved the 1st Canadian Tunnelling Company, and by way of a greeting the enemy flattered us by imitating our methods.   It was not good policy to allow us to occupy so much gallery so near to his line, so he began to destroy the confiscated gallery by firing charges on the surface.   As there was no point in keeping these shallow galleries open, since we now had our own deep levels, and the Germans knew their exact position and could destroy them at will, the timbers were withdrawn and the gallery allowed to cave in.   In the meantime a defensive gallery had been driven round the front of " C," " D " and " E " craters and the 30 feet level developed, while in the deeps listening and pumping was carried on, and the damaged ends from which the four camouflets were fired were also recovered.   At long last the Bluff was adequately protected underground.

While this work was in progress nothing was heard of the enemy.   For a time at least he seemed to have had enough.   In fact it was learned, from a prisoner, that the mining company had been withdrawn and was having an easy time in billets.   But he had not abandoned mining entirely, and soon again he was heard working towards us, coming in between two of our listening posts.   Both were charged speedily, but as now we were in the stronger position firing was delayed.   When at least we did decide to fire there was a negative result—the leads had been cut.

As the tamping was being removed to repair the leads, the Germans could be heard untamping from their side. It developed into a " cat and mouse " sort of business, each keeping a " listening ear " on the other.   At the exact minute, while separated by only a few rows of sandbags, each side ceased untamping.   It was a hectic moment. Should we blow now, or defer in the hope of engaging in hand to hand combat with the intruder and driving him back still further ?   The Germans settled the query by blowing.   As a result, one officer and four sappers were gassed.   But we had yet another card to play.   A bore-hole was put in from another post, and the enemy gallery smashed in by a small charge.   Yet the Germans were in no mood to throw in their hand without a struggle.   Several

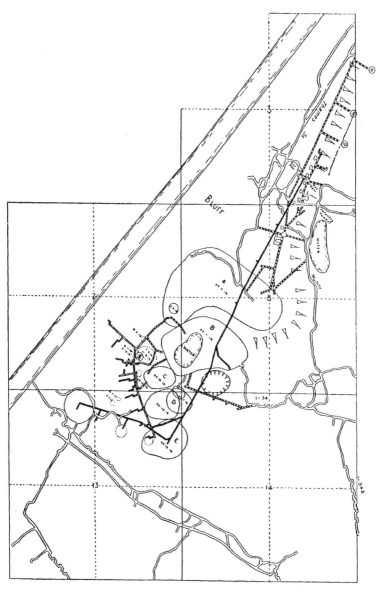

THE BLUFF—PROTECTING GALLERIES.
DEEP LEVELS IN THICK LINES, INTERMEDIATE LEVELS SHADED,
SHALLOWS DOTTED.

attempts were made to break into our workings from the craters. Then, as often happened before when the German miners were hard pressed, the heavy trench mortars came to the rescue and pounded in most of our mine entrances, as well as many of the shallow connections between craters.

To make the situation more unpleasant, the shallow defensive system became flooded. Water poured in from " D " and " E " craters, doubtless as a result of the trench mortar bombardment. This, however, did not prove so serious as it might have done, since the water was got away to the canal through the drainage tunnel, though it was some days before the mines could be entered because of the mud and slime left behind.

Next the Germans " were discovered working noisily towards No. 3 post." But these attacks were almost futile compared with the smashing blows of January, February and July of the previous year. From a winning position, a crafty and determined foe, giving no quarter and seeking none, had, after delivering what might easily have been a knockout blow, been cheated out of the full fruits of his success. Defeated at his own game, outflanked so successfully and decisively as to render his efforts innocuous, deprived of the initiative by troops as determined as himself, he relinquished the final honours, acknowledged defeat, and mining ceased. The successful attack on the Messines—Wytschaete Ridge on the 7th June, 1917, finally closed the mining chapter in this sector.

Riven, distorted, lacerated by the fell hand of war, wearing its wounds as eloquent, though silent, testimony of the grim struggle waged above and below ground for its possession, it yet stands a memento to foe and friend alike —The Bluff.

CHAPTER VIII

FOSSE 8

TUNNELLERS were constantly called in to the aid of our Intelligence officers because of the facilities they were sometimes able to offer for listening in to conversations between Germans. At first sight, however, there is nothing to connect tunnelling with the activities of spies. Now it is well known that the chief difficulty of a spy in war time is not the gathering of information, but its transmission to his headquarters. Various methods were used by both sides in getting information about each other's movements, and varied were the channels along which the agents passed. As far back as 1915, it was suspected that the Germans maintained communication with their agents behind our lines through the workings of the coal mines of the Béthune concession (a series of mines near Noeux-les-Mines). This view was further strengthened by the fact that a certain house in Les Brebis, the occupant of which was said to be in sympathy with the Germans, escaped shelling, while almost all the others were more or less badly damaged by shell fire. This was, of course, sheer fiction, since artillery fire is not sufficiently accurate to spare one house in a street. Nevertheless, this house was much sought as a billet !

The Béthune-Lens coal mining area was, as is usual, a somewhat confused jumble of shafts, galleries, and levels. Many of the mines belonged to one company, and often the galleries were served by several different shafts. Naturally, when in 1914 the actual course of the front line trenches was being debated by hand-to-hand combat, no attention was paid to civilian mining rights ! Thus, in front of Annequin, the line ran over a gallery which connected shafts behind our lines with others in German hands—for Fosse 8 (i.e. the shaft of that number in the

Béthune concession system)—just behind the German trenches, was directly connected with Fosses 3, 4, 9 and 12, all within our lines ; a glance at the plan on page 193 will make the position immediately clear.

There now seems no doubt that these shafts were constantly used by the agents of both sides, as soon as the trench line settled down, as a means of going and coming. The first alarm, however, did not concern spies, but the French mine officials were afraid that the Germans would destroy the shaft tubbing, or pierce the water-bearing strata in an endeavour to tunnel our trenches from the upper mine levels, and in either case would flood the coal mines.

In July, 1915, Second-Lieutnant Dixon and a party from 170th Tunnelling Company made an inspection, and after much difficulty succeeded in reaching the bottom of Fosse 8—inside the German lines—and found the shaft blocked with debris. He reported that he did not consider it practicable to utilize the coal mines for offensive or defensive mining by either side. Here the matter rested for some time, G.H.Q. keeping an eye on the situation meanwhile.

It was not till 1916 that the matter of communicating through the coal mines again cropped up as a result of certain trifling incidents ; in order to check this danger, the French mine officials agreed to build concrete barricades in all roads* connected to Fosse 8. These stoppings were actually commenced but were only built up about four feet high, leaving sufficient room above for the passage of men and ventilation. Actually, a certificate was rendered to us by the French intimating that the stoppings had been built up and " were in order." It seems fairly obvious that at this period the French were using the pits as an underground passage for their agents, even at the risk of the Germans using them similarly.

During this time, however, the pumps at the foot of Fosse 8 were worked continuously, keeping the mines free of water, and listeners were stationed at the 240 metre

---

* In coal mining headings or roads are the main communications, such as would be stopped by barricades. The military mining term, gallery, is seldom, if ever, used in connection with coal mines.

level, but no coal was won. Had complete stoppings been
built across the roads leading to Fosse 8, access to the pumps

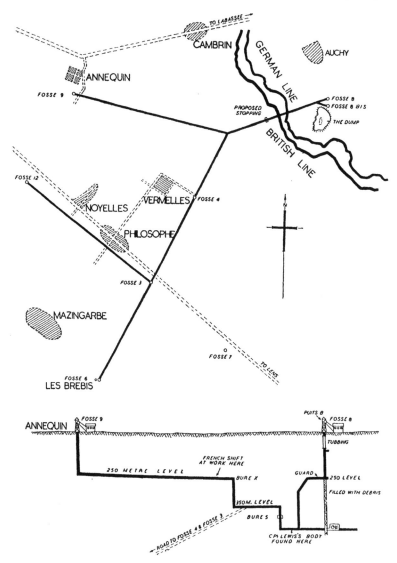

would have been cut off and the mines perforce would
flood.

N

Soon after Fosse 8 fell into German hands, railway wagons and other heavy material had been hurled down the shaft, ripping away the cage guides, ladders, pipes, etc. Carcasses of horses and mules, mingled with the corpses of the slain, formed a confused mass which filled the shaft to the 240 metre level. By means of a small hoist, however, it was possible for the Germans to descend to this level.

In August, 1917, Fosse 8 again began to be used as a dump for wire rope, dud shells and other similar material, but no chalk or other spoil from tunnelled galleries was noticed. The French observers also reported that the Germans carried out some work near the shaft top the " nature of which cannot be ascertained," but it partially closed the shaft.

The French mine authorities were now greatly alarmed and, convinced that the Germans were about to break the tubbing, as indeed they were in a position to do so at any moment, since the action from below on our part would be powerless to prevent them. In consequence of this activity on the part of the Germans and agitation on the part of the French, Major Manning, O.C. 170th Tunnelling Company, made an examination of the underground situation. A few days later the Company received orders to detail a permanent guard of twelve miners to furnish a post of three armed men, one to be a listener, and be on duty continually at the bottom of Puits* 8 and 8 bis, in order to prevent espionage and to report any unusual proceedings on the part of the enemy. The guard was posted forthwith. Telephonic communication between the post and Brigade H.Q. was established, and Brigade was responsible for immediate action in the event of anything unusual being reported to them.

By this time the French mine officials were thoroughly alarmed, and felt certain that the destruction of the tubbing was imminent. Furthermore, they were convinced that the Germans would flood the mine with gas. Consequently a stopping was built in Bure† 5 with all possible haste. In

---

* The terms *Fosse* and *Puit*, for shaft, are both commonly used in France.
† Bure—a minor shaft.

the course of this work, the telephone wires, leading to our post, were broken.

On the night of 25/26th September, 1917, two signallers were sent down the mine to repair the broken wires. After chatting for a few minutes with the French workmen building the stopping, they descended by the winze in Bure 5.

Soon afterwards the French workmen received a message that the Germans were bombarding Fosse 9, and they withdrew at once. About the same time the Germans discharged a large quantity of chloro-picrine, a highly lachrymatory gas down Fosse 8. The signallers had not gone far before they detected the gas, which had been released at the top of the downcast shaft and was rapidly carried along the mine roads by the ventilation current.

Donning their respirators, they endeavoured to make their way to Fosse 9, but the gas was in such concentration that it penetrated their masks, and only one succeeded in reaching the bottom of Fosse 9, where he was found suffering from gas poisoning.

At this time the men underground consisted of one N.C.O. and six other ranks of the 170th Tunnelling Company on guard at the 240 metre level, Fosse 8 and 8 bis, together with two French listeners, two French pumpmen at the 350 metre level Fosse 8, and the one signaller who had failed to return.

About 10 a.m. on the 26th, 170th Tunnelling Company received warning from the French mine authorities of the discharge of gas down Fosse 8. Immediately rescue parties were organized. Lieutenant Wood and eleven other ranks, equipped with apparatus, went down Fosse 9 at Annequin and succeeded in reaching a point about 1,000 metres from the shaft, when they were compelled to retire, as the gas penetrated their masks and affected their eyes.

Reinforced by Lieutenant Robertson and nine other ranks, they made several more attempts to get through, but could not proceed beyond the point first reached. Then Captain Thirlwell and his party relieved Lieutenant Wood's men, who by now were all affected by the gas.

The second party succeeded in reaching Bure X, which they descended, only to be forced to return owing to the failure of their respirators to withstand the high concentration of gas.

Between 1 and 2 a.m. on the following day the enemy began to shell Fosse 9 and Fosse 4 with mustard gas. The whole of Thirlwell's party were badly gassed, and he and another man died from the effects.

After consulting with the French, it was decided to abandon further rescue attempts from Fosse 9, but to work from Fosse 4 at Vermelles. Fosse 4 was a downcast shaft, and for some distance a party would have the advantage of better air.

Captain Brown and party went down Fosse 3 and found the air good as far as the junction of the roads from 3 and 9. It was noticed that the gas had followed the main ventilating way, so that hopes were high of finding the men in some recess of the main road.

In order to prevent gas penetrating between the skin and the mask, this party had taken the precaution of securing their masks with adhesive tape, and thus avoided to a great extent the trouble to the eyes experienced by previous parties. This attempt succeeded in reaching Bure 5 before being compelled to return. Here again the trouble was that the respirators could not stand up to such a heavy concentration of gas.

Although there was little real hope of rescue, a final attempt was organized. Lieutenant-Colonel Dale-Logan, R.A.M.C., managed to secure some improvised respirators, made by using the face pieces from the latest German respirators and fitting them to our breathing tubes ; as one drum was not large enough he had two joined together. These were thoroughly tested in a gas chamber and found to be quite efficient.

There was an air compressor plant at Fosse 3, and the pipes led along past Bure 5. It was decided to tap this supply and lead on air at 70 lbs. pressure into a station or chamber built of brattice cloth in which respirators could be changed, so that the party would be well prepared for the final dash.

Lieutenant Gibbons and party left at 10 p.m. on the 28th, and succeeded in getting all material to the point A. Captain Roberts followed with a party and completed the depot at A. Lieutenant Wheler completed depot B on the following day. At 6 p.m. on 30th Captain Brown and twenty-five other ranks left to make the final assault. They descended Bure 5 and found the body of Private Shanks. This indicated that the men had tried to escape, and therefore could not possibly have survived so long in such an atmosphere. Further risk at rescue was not justified and so that attempt was abandoned.

The gas eventually cleared sufficiently to permit of the mine being entered for short periods without respirators. The French were notified, and it was decided to take immediate advantage of the situation to block Bure 5. Accordingly at 9 p.m. on the 1st October, Captains Brown and Roberts and a party, with two French winch men and a party of French miners, descended to complete the first clay seal in Bure 5, after which our men were no longer necessary. Captain Brown made his way along the road towards Fosse 8 for about 500 yards from Bure 5, and found the body of Corporal Lewis. Captain Roberts tapped the compressed air pipe line, taking a branch down the winze to the point where the work was to be carried on, and assisted the French in making the seal. Two men from the 170th Tunnelling Company acted as sentries, and were ready to deal with any of the enemy who might venture in to explore. The road eventually being sealed by a five feet thickness of brickwork, Fosse 8 was completely cut off from the mines in our area ; the French miners considered it impossible for the enemy to approach the stopping and destroy it from their side, owing to lack of ventilation.

The French Minister of Munitions, in person, expressed his generous appreciation to the commanding officer of the 170th Tunnelling Company for the services it had rendered.

The situation at Fosse 8 and Fosse 9 was probably unique throughout the War. We have told, briefly and plainly, the story of one dramatic episode—an unusual episode, for very seldom were circumstances propitious for the deliberate use of gas underground, where Nature usually provides quite as much gas as a miner wants to encounter. The more intriguing stories of these mines must, alas, remain still untold. That the French used the galleries for the purpose of passing agents behind the German lines is now certain, and that the Germans used them for the same purpose is at least highly probable. Even the writers of spy fiction never visualized more thrilling possibilities than this strange situation suggests.

CHAPTER IX

I

THE failure of Nivelle's plans and the consequent mutinies in the French army meant that the burden of offensive action against the Germans now lay exclusively on the British shoulders. This question is more fully discussed in the following chapter. Sir Douglas Haig planned an ambitious series of operations with the avowed intention of driving the enemy from the Belgian coast. Though this would never have exercised any great influence on the submarine campaign (though it would have robbed the German Channel-raiding destroyers of a convenient operating base), it would certainly have been a resounding success, easily the greatest of the War. The value of an operation cannot be measured solely by its practical results. The Zeebrugge raid of St. George's Day, 1918, had comparatively little effect on German submarine activities, but it was more than justified by the exhilarating influence on a drooping Allied *moral.*

The Flanders scheme envisaged, first, the seizure of the Messines Ridge, which commanded the southern flank of the Ypres salient : then a grand attack in front of Ypres. Once the defensive system of the Germans had been broken, our Fourth Army was to push forward in the coastal area, while a division was actually to be disembarked near Ostend. The enemy once on the move, it was argued, he would find it difficult to halt. This might have proved correct—had we ever got him on the move.

In preparation for this tremendous offensive, therefore, we took over (in June, 1917) the coastal sector from the Belgians and French. It was by no means an easy area. The front was narrow and cramped ; on one hand lay the sea, on the other a man-made ocean—the inundated area in which part of the German advance was engulfed in the early days of the War.   The support line was just east of the Yser, across which all stores and materials had to be carried on three temporary wooden bridges.   They were also used by the troops as a means of entrance and egress.

In June, 1917, three Tunnelling Companies were sent into this sector—the 2nd Australian, 256th and 257th ; later on 184th Company followed.   The Australians at once began offensive mining towards the Grand Dune, and the construction of subways from front to support lines, tunnelled dugouts for Battalion Headquarters, and so on.   257th Company was employed on subways in Nieuport, and 256th Company in the provision of shelters in the dunes and in well sinking.   All this work was in sand, the conditions being entirely different to those on any other part of the front.

Everything was proceeding perfectly smoothly—*except that our plans had become the common property of those least intended to know them.*

On the 10th July the Germans began an extremely heavy bombardment of the sector, using guns up to 42 c.m. calibre and paying special attention to the bridges.   By midday these were all destroyed, and the few troops remaining alive to the east of the Yser were isolated.   Still the bombardment persisted.   In the evening, after the bombardment had lasted all day, the enemy attacked.   A party of tunnellers and some few infantry had taken shelter in the subway ; their ordeal was by no means concluded, for the Germans began to drop bombs down the ventilating shafts, and actually played a flame projector down the entrance.

Sapper James O'Connell of the Australians was particularly unfortunate—he suffered wounds from both, but he managed to secure some bombs as he came out of the subway, and made his way to the canal, keeping the enemy at bay with bombs.   Here he received a bullet wound in the head and fell into the canal.   He managed to drag himself out and took shelter in a dugout, where his wounds were dressed by Second-Lieutenant E. P. Hargraves.

The situation was now critical ; to remain meant capture, yet an attempt to escape meant almost certain death. But O'Connell decided to take his chance. Thrice wounded as he was, he walked down to the shattered stump of a bridge and, plunging in, swam across to the other side. No sooner had he scrambled out on to the farther bank than a cry for help came from the river. Heedless of his own plight, O'Connell again entered the water and with great difficulty assisted the non-swimmer to the bank, where he himself was pulled out exhausted and taken to a dressing station. For his bravery he was awarded the D.C.M.—which he surely deserved !

A precarious foothold was retained east of the Yser, communication being maintained by floating bridges made of cork mats fastened together ; the agility of an acrobat was required to negotiate them.

II

Thus, even had our assault on the Passchendaele Ridge been successful, it would have been extremely difficult to have launched an offensive on the coastal sector. The action, compared to others of the year, was trifling, but its importance was such that it might have been vital. Nor did it tend to increase the concord between the Allies, and for a time the French and Belgians looked at us askance. They had held the Nieuport bridgehead for nearly three years, and we had lost it—save for a perilous enclave— in three weeks !

The battle, too, gave forcible illustration to many often overlooked military truths. We learned—or ought to have learned—the folly of advertising a prospective offensive. The Germans again pointed out the incalculable advantage of surprise. It was revealed, too, that an army with a mind solely set on the offensive tends to neglect its defences. The French had learned this lesson from many bitter experiences. The British, having been continuously on the offensive for over two years, had forgotten it. And the Germans, themselves teachers of the lesson, were to forget it themselves—on 8th August, 1918—" the black day of the German Army."

III

As a result of this very unexpected rebuff, work was now concentrated on the provision of shelters and the construction of subways at Nieuport and Nieuport Bains. The whole area was subjected to very heavy shelling, in which gas shells were freely used ; our losses were heavy, one Tunnelling Company suffering over one hundred casualties in a week.   With the completion of the subways, and the disappearance of movement on the surface, the shelling subsided.   256th Company succeeded in sinking " elephant " * shelters in the sand dunes, thus providing shell-proof accommodation for considerable bodies of troops by a quick and inexpensive method as compared with the ordinary " cut and cover."   The difficulties of all underground work were tremendous.   The sand was dry, fine, wind-blown, and would pour in through the slightest gap between the timbers.   In the event of a bombardment near a spot where work was in progress, work had to cease and the face be boarded up, otherwise the concussion of the bursting shells would bring in the face.

On one occasion the sand poured in with such force that the man in the face was knocked down, and in a few minutes was buried in fine sand ; it took an hour and a half to stop up the hole and free him.

184th Company made underground shelters at Kent, Surrey, Brisbane and Norfolk Camps, and as far back as La Panne dugouts were provided.   The Australians put down a number of bore-holes on both sides of the Yser to determine the suitability of the ground for driving a subway beneath the river.   Suitable blue clay was found at about 80 feet deep, but the subway was not commenced. Work in the dunes was very unpleasant as the sand got into everything.   Food was gritty, and all suffered more or

---

* Semicircular shelters roofed by stout corrugated iron sheeting.

less from sand colic. The horses died of it, and a post-mortem examination of one animal disclosed no less than 56 lbs. of sand in its stomach !

When this sector was eventually handed back to the French, they were surprised to see we had done so much work, especially their artillery, who were delighted to find shell-proof shelters for their use. Much of our labour in this sector was, however, wasted, for the coastal offensive never materialized ; instead, its force was spent in the swamps of Passchendaele.

CHAPTER X

I

MESSINES is to the Tunneller what Waterloo was to Wellington. Never in the history of warfare has the miner played such a great and vital part in a battle.

In the early days of 1916 Sir Douglas Haig had begun the planning of the great British offensive on the Somme front. He realized that no easy task confronted him ; he had to assault a highly fortified ridge, held tenaciously by courageous, well-equipped troops. Consequently, although his hopes of the battle were high, he prepared for failure. Should the initial blow on the Somme fail, the British effort would be transferred to Flanders, and General Plumer, commanding the Second Army on the Ypres front, was instructed to make his plans for offensive action. Unfortunately, military results are seldom so clear cut as the plans envisaged. The Somme assault was a partial failure, partial success. It is only natural that a commander should see his successes in higher light than his failures ; consequently Haig persevere ' vith the Somme campaign, and the Belgian offensive v ostponed.

Plumer, however, had carried out hi. instructions and had made his preliminary plans. Even when he knew that his army was not to attack, the preparations continued. In particular, he fastened on to one essential—he realized that before any advance could be made on the Ypres front, the bastion defending the southern flank must be stormed. This was an almost insignificant eminence known as the Messines-Wytschaete Ridge. Although its height was puny in figures, it was of immense importance in the Flanders plain. Quite apart from its value as a flanking bastion to an advance, its possession by the Germans was highly inconvenient even in quiet times, for its gentle eminence commanded our front line system and communications, and even gave the Germans a unique side view of the defences of the Salient. This naturally, they were not slow to exploit.

Through the summer and winter of 1916 unceasing labour brought our plans towards reality. Plumer aimed that the first shock of the assault should be delivered by mines—unprecedented alike in numbers and size of charge. The staff work was as good as the technical ability of the Tunnellers. If genius is an infinite capacity for taking pains, then Plumer was a genius. He himself never pretended to the claim, but he had the confidence of the sound soldier who has learned from his own and other people's mistakes. He rightly considered the capture of the ridge as a siege operation, and tackled it as such. Probably no battle of the War received such continuous and detailed thought as this ; nothing which could be humanly foreseen was overlooked.

Months before the blow was delivered, all preparations were complete. As we shall see, a large number of tunnels had been driven out under strong points in the German lines, with many excitements in their driving. Then followed a period even more tense ; the mines were laid, but if the enemy discovered them the effect would be ruined. Tunnellers never knew more anxious moments during the whole of the War.

After the British thrust at Arras, intended to distract the German attention, the French had launched an ambitious offensive on the Chemin des Dames. Nivelle, the new Commander-in-Chief, had raised the highest hopes ; he had openly proclaimed his intention of finishing the War by one gigantic brusque attack. A battle seldom goes as it is intended ; Nivelle's was lost before the first shot was fired. It has often been described as a fiasco, but this is scarcely fair. Nivelle did capture ground and prisoners, and his casualties were not more excessive than those of similar operations. But the results, compared with the high hopes and rash promises, brought dismissal to Nivelle and mutiny to the French army.

The French had borne the brunt of the fighting on the Allied side, and had worthily upheld their tradition of being among Europe's finest soldiers. Time after time they had advanced against the enemy in futile attacks—bodies against bullets. Not even the most appalling casualties in the slaughter-house of Verdun had appalled them. Yet after Nivelle's failure there were mutinies in more than thirty divisions. The result was mental rather than physical. It was no strike of cowardice—there was no talk of throwing up the sponge. Soldiers were still willing to die—usefully; they were no longer willing to be slaughteredt they demanded a higher standard of leadership.

Since there never was any question of handing over the War to the Germans—the men manned their trenches as firmly as ever, and only declined obedience when ordered to the attack—the immediate crisis passed rapidly. Nevertheless, it was obvious that many months must pass before the French army recovered its *moral*. Cleverly nursed by the new Commander-in-Chief, Pétain, it was very soon convalescent—yet it was in no state to withstand another Verdun. Thus it became the duty of the British to hold the attention of the Germans for the remainder of the year.

For this purpose Haig turned to his postponed Flanders offensive—the dislodgment of the Germans from the Belgian coast. Quite apart from the fact that it was a project near to his heart, it offered the best immediate results in that its initial preparations were already complete, for the capture of the Messines Ridge was an essential preliminary to the main operation. Consequently, when Haig (on 7th May, 1917) asked Plumer when he could strike his blow at Messines, Plumer could answer without hesitation, " A month to-day "—and keep to his word. Yet, as Captain Liddell Hart says, " The calm confidence of this business-like statement betrays no sign of the anxiety suffered, nor does it do justice to the will power demanded of Plumer in carrying through his purpose." *

* " A History of the World War."

In the pages which follow are detailed at necessary length the contributions of the Tunnellers to the most complete tactical operation of the War. As we have seen, the Messines sector—particularly about Hill 60—the Bluff and St. Eloi—had been continually active in mining warfare. From the middle of 1916, however, the energy of the Tunnellers was bent to more than the usual desultory operations—no less than a mining attack on the Ridge itself—the same scheme, vastly enlarged and in much greater detail, as Norton Griffiths had envisaged the previous year.

II

The details of the Messines mines are treated as from north to south of the sector. While it is difficult to avoid a little apparent repetition, since one mine is very like

another, each individual story has something of interest
—sometimes of death and danger, sometimes of technical
difficulty.

From the Ypres-Commines canal south to La Douve
River, a tributary of the Lys River, the enemy had enjoyed
the decided advantage of occupying the higher ground
ever since the line settled down, which of course meant
that, in winter, all the water from his trenches drained into
ours.   The numerous woods and other natural features in,
or just behind, his line had been fortified, and in addition
many strong points, such as " Rag Point," " Bone Point "
and " Hop Point," to mention but a few, had been constructed.   Later, the position had been strengthened still
further by the construction of reinforced concrete " pill-
boxes," which were dotted about the whole hill-side.
Furthermore, his artillery was well hidden and amply
protected behind the ridge, which afforded excellent
observation over our lines.   Therefore the whole situation
presented a formidable bastion calculated to resist the
strongest attacks—above ground.

The actual line itself was in the form of a large arc,
from which jutted small salients at such well defined places
as St. Eloi, Bois Quarante, Hollandscheschuur, Petit Bois,
Maedelstede Farm, Peckham, Spanbroekmolen, Kruisstraat, Ontario Farm and La Petite Douve Farm.   These
tempting targets were too tantalizing to the Tunnellers
—more especially as the mistaken policy had been adopted
of exploding mines more or less indiscriminately, to give
the impression that we had more miners at work than
actually we had ;   later, as has been said, this was superseded by a policy of concentrating on a given area.

The story of the Messines mines is a protracted one—
not so much on account of the time taken in driving the
galleries and placing the charges, but because of the
inordinate lapse of time between completing and firing them.
It begins as far back as May, 1915, in the comparative
early days of mining, when the far-seeing Norton Griffiths
visualized the ultimate capture of the whole Ridge.   He
conceived the idea of concentrating 172nd and 174th
Companies—the only ones then on the whole front from

Hill 60 to Fauquissart—on the St. Eloi-Wulverghem sector, " and by a good mining offensive straighten out an advance our line from St. Eloi to Messines." As the ground was suitable for such a project—clay was known to exist at a suitable depth—the proposition was to attack with at least six deep mines, 50 feet to 60 feet deep, with minimum charges of 20,000 lbs, and so break the line in as many places.

Obviously the scheme possessed possibilities, but was presented in such a nebulous form as to stand self-condemned for lack of detail. But Colonel Harvey, at G.H.Q., saw that it could be made practicable, and together with Major Norton Griffiths thrashed out the details ; thus, when the revised scheme was forwarded to Major-General G. H. Fowke, Engineer-in-Chief, he at once submitted it to the General Staff.

When the scheme was first mooted special precautions were taken to maintain secrecy, as far as possible, and the mines were always referred to as " deep wells in connection with water supply," a ruse which succeeded remarkably well.

Both 171st and 172nd Companies had been mining in the vicinity of Hill 60 since their formation ; here fighting had been carried on incessantly at an average depth of 15 feet. Two or three camouflets a day, mostly small charges it is true, were fired by both sides ; while gas above and below ground, holing into each others galleries, and sometimes into charged mines, to say nothing of raids and bombardments, the miners' lot was not a happy one, though exciting enough for the most hardy and venturesome. Nevertheless, a state of virtual stalemate existed here on the V Corps front, and the only alternative, short of giving up mining entirely, was to go deeper. By order of General Allenby, then in command of the corps, a deep offensive was directed against the Caterpillar and Hill 60.

III

The formation of new Tunnelling Companies, and the departure of 174th Company for the Somme front, provided

o

the opportunity for a reshuffle of companies, and in July, 1915, 175th Company "right closed" and took over Hill 60 front from 171st Company, the latter going to Ploegsteert. Soon after taking over the new front, 175th Company started a new adit at rail level from the north side of the railway cutting at a point about 220 yards behind our front line. Continuing on the level for some distance, the drive then descended on the incline, thereby greatly increasing the difficulty of penetrating the waterlogged sand. This, and continuous fighting in the shallows, hindered progress, but after overcoming almost insuperable difficulties, the blue clay was at last reached, and the incline continued until it was 90 feet below normal surface level. Known as the Berlin Tunnel, this mine became quite famous, or infamous ; it was specially detested by innumerable infantry working parties because of the seemingly never ending amount of soil and water they had to remove from it.

Early in 1916 progress was again delayed. In consequence of " information received " from a German miner, who previously had worked at Hill 60 and was captured at the Bluff, who said that a hostile gallery was being driven to attack the right abutment of the bridge across the railway cutting, work was stopped on the main drive and a branch off it to the right was rushed out to ward off the attack. In due course a heavy camouflet was fired which had the desired effect. So great was the explosion that 200 feet of the Berlin Tunnel was serious damaged. This charge was fired right below a German deep shaft and wrecked his entire system. No crater was formed. The force of the explosion travelled along the German galleries and blew out a shaft in the shallow level. Some months afterwards a prisoner was taken on the Somme front, who stated that he had been working at Hill 60 when the blow was made. He said that the ground was so bad that the Germans never succeeded in sinking a new shaft. It is true that the ground on the German side of the railway cutting was almost a bog, and in the attack of 7th June, 1917, there were cases of men being actually engulfed in the morass.

However, when the 3rd Canadian Tunnelling Company relieved the 175th on this front and cleared up the damage, 800 feet of gallery was still intact. Their first work was to break out 60 N. to the left to attack Hill 60. Another branch to the right to replace the one destroyed by the mine of 12th April was also started. 60 N. proceeded without further interruption for some time, until it ran into bad ground just short of its objective, but near enough to do damage with a large charge. Rather than risk pushing the gallery further in bad ground, a charge chamber was started, but the ground was so bad that this caved in, yellow clay appearing in the rush of water and slurry, indicating that the drive was almost out of the blue clay bed. The face was baulked up and securely sealed against any further inrush, and a series of small chambers put in on each side of the drive ; on completing these, 53,500 lbs. of ammonal and other explosive was placed in position, detonators inserted, and leads tested and registered.

Owing to the scattered nature of the charge, extra precautions were taken to ensure speedy and complete detonation. The ammonal was placed in petrol tins, and 7,800 lbs. of guncotton in slabs was packed into the spaces, and tamping began.

Then a set-back occurred—C.N. drive ran into bad ground and the face caved in. Plugging the end of the galley, C.N.1 was started on the right, stepping down some 15 feet to get into firmer ground. Then turning left, it continued without further interruption till it reached the German second line of trenches, well below the Caterpillar hill. By mid-August, 1916, chambering commenced and, when finished, charging began. But no sooner was this well under way, when another and more serious peril overtook it. The whole of the Berlin Tunnel became flooded, and the charge cut off by water from the captured German gallery in the intermediate level, fully recorded in a previous chapter. To make matters worse, gas from a camouflet filled the mine.

The installation of an electric power plant gave promise of a speedy end to the gas and water trouble, as manual labour on fans and pumps would be superseded. But the promise was not fulfilled—at least not at once. Frequent breakdowns occurred, and the hand pumps had to be used again. Ultimately the mine was de-watered and the remainder of the charge put in and tamped. The flooding had not damaged the charge, as the whole 70,000 lbs. of ammonal was in water-tight tins—a very wise precaution.

Special carrying parties were needed to handle so large a quantity of explosive, and it was a great relief when it was all safely loaded without mishap. In order to ensure detonation, precautions were taken with the wiring. Three independent sets of leads were inserted in each charge, permitting of nine circuits—no fewer than sixty detonators being distributed through the charges.

The 3rd Canadian Tunnelling Company accomplished excellent work on this difficult front. Under the able guidance of Major Davis, C.E., they had acquitted themselves well in abnormal circumstances in placing two large and deep mines far into the enemy's territory, while at the same time warding off his continuous attack in the shallow levels, and constructing a deep dugout system.

In the first week of November, the 1st Australian Tunnelling Company relieved the Canadians on the Hill 60 front.

The two mines had been intended for immediate firing, but the change of policy meant that they would not be fired for some time to come. It was then decided to sink a vertical steel-lined shaft to replace the long incline, as the latter was more likely to be put out of action than a vertical one.

Started by the Canadians just before leaving, the Berlin Shaft, as it was termed, 6 feet in diameter, was sunk to 94 feet deep by the Australians, and from the bottom a gallery was driven to the foot of the incline. Along this all the water was drained back to a large sump and pumped up the shaft by power. The new shaft effected a great saving in labour and also greatly improved the ventilation, which had continuously been bad. From this shaft also a deep level defensive system was put in, and an offensive gallery pushed out towards a strong point called the Snout, but lack of time prevented its completion.

As " B " left proceeded, sounds of enemy mining became so plain that there was little doubt that he was sinking a

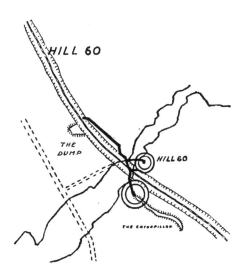

shaft almost on top of our gallery. Working as quietly as possible, a charge was placed and fired. Shortly after the blow, two large columns of smoke were seen issuing from the enemy lines close to the railway cutting, indicating that the charge had blown into his shaft, and must have caused extensive damage. It also damaged the leads in " A " mine, for a galvanometer test gave a negative result. This was indeed serious, as at the moment " A " mine was useless as it could not then be fired.

By some misunderstanding, the rate of progress in the galleries dropped to about one-third of the normal (about 8 feet a day), and this allowed the enemy to get in a couple of good blows which did considerable damage and inflicted losses on the Australians. One heavy mine formed a crater between Anzac shaft and the cutting, and almost over " A " mine gallery, doing some damage and breaking the leads. Several miners were cut off in the shallow workings but were rescued a couple of days later.   One of the released men reported that, soon after the blow, he heard a windlass working.   This sound had been reported previously and seemed to indicate shaft sinking.   Captain Pollock and Lieutenant Clarke, two experts from the Second Army Mine School, were called in and conducted a series of listening tests, the results of which confirmed the Company listening results, but as the shaft was estimated to be too far away to reach our mines before the day of battle, the Germans were allowed to work on, though their progress was carefully checked by the listeners.   It was a very near thing, as he was close enough to destroy the mine in " A " had he been aware of its existence.*   Had the attack been postponed a few days—and up to this stage of the War our attacks generally had been postponed—it is very probable that our work in this sector would have been ruined.

At the same time as these large mines were being driven, fighting was almost continuous in the upper levels.   This policy we encouraged, as it kept the enemy occupied and prevented him from going deeper.

IV

Smarting under the sting of the blows at St. Eloi in March, 1916, the enemy retaliated by delivering a counter-attack which won back all the lost ground and the craters, which he consolidated.   Not content with this, he continued to shell and trench-mortar our lines opposite with such good effect that 172nd Company found it impossible to carry out work there, so it concentrated on the Bluff. Soon, however, it was relieved by the 1st Canadian Tunnelling Company.   The shelling went on for months—in fact it was not until August, 1916, that the Canadians were able to commence a deep shaft, Queen Victoria, well back near Bus House.   Rapid progress was made in sinking, and

* This delayed action on our part was made possible by our knowledge of the German rate of progress.   This was first discovered on 18th June, 1915, by 174th Company when they broke into a German gallery at Houplines and found that each shift recorded its progress on the timbers, a practice the Germans persisted in to the end.

in less than three weeks the shaft was down over 100 feet deep.   At 30 feet a station was put in and from it a drive started, and also a chamber to house a power plant, which was installed early in October.

The main drive proceeded steadily though cautiously, as knocking sounds aroused suspicion.   These sounds continued, but much to our relief they were found to be caused by the enemy working in the craters, probably on dugouts, not mining.

The clay was hard and progress was slow.   Further delay was caused by continuous caving in of the ground ; later work was stopped to connect the main gallery with the old workings, driven by 172nd Company, which were reclaimed and developed and soon made contact with the enemy.

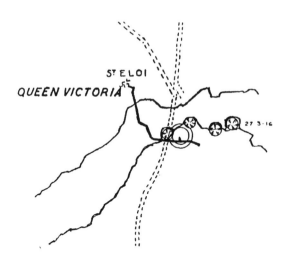

The main gallery, which had been flooded during the stoppage, was de-watered, cleaned out, and again continued. By a devious route it succeeded in outflanking the enemy and soon reached its objective behind Nos. 2 and 3 craters. By the end of May, 1917, an enormous charge of almost fifty tons of ammonal had been placed and tamped.   This constituted the largest single charge of the War, and without doubt the largest in the history of military mining.

The drive continued beyond the charge towards craters 4 and 5, but lack of time prevented them being reached.

At the same time the Canadians had carried out a great deal of work at the Ravine and the Bluff, but it is specially to their credit that the Queen Victoria drive reached its objective, as the enemy had excellent observation over our lines from our old crater lips.

v

In November, 1915, the 250th Tunnelling Company relieved the 177th, and became custodians of a front of nearly 3,000 yards, extending from Bois Carre south to opposite Kruisstraat Cabaret, with Wytschaete village opposite the centre. The various "beeks" or small streams made the ground so wet that even the trenches could not be dug more than 2 feet deep, the parapet being built up with sandbags. Yet shallow defensive mine systems had been constructed along this front in the surface clay-sands, but as the head cover was only 17 feet, the galleries frequently caved under bombardment.

The shafts, without exception, were situated in the front line for the simple reason that there was no second line ; sinking was no easy task—in fact more than one shaft had to be " tethered " * to tree trunks to prevent " deserting " altogether.

Realizing the inadequacy of these mines, Major Cropper suggested to the Canadian Corps, who occupied this front at the time, the desirability of deepening the existing shafts to the clay bed. A few days later, orders were received to begin a deep offensive scheme, and at once 250th Company proceeded to deepen the shaft in M.2 trench to attack the Hollandscheschuur salient.

Sinking to 58 feet, a drive was broken out and soon

---

* " Tethered." A large shaft cannot be sunk without a *collar set*, i.e. a frame of big timber on which successive sets are hung. In soft, wet ground it is difficult to keep the collar set in its proper position, square and level. Small shafts using R.E. casing were kept in position by lashing the first set to stakes with wire or rope as laid down in the R.E. Manual of Military Mining.

passed beneath the enemy front line only 130 yards away, and by March had reached a point 100 yards behind it. In order to preserve the secret of deep mines in the event

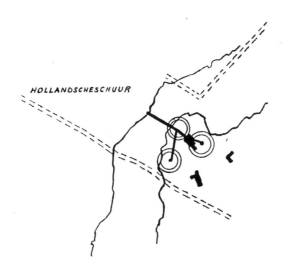

HOLLANDSCHESCHUUR

of an enemy raiding party entering our line, the shaft penthouse was made to resemble a dugout with two inclined entrances, protected by a machine-gun. A second shaft was also commenced in case the original should be destroyed.

Heavy shelling of our trenches near the shaft head delayed progress for a time, and as it showed no signs of abating, all work on the mine had to be stopped, and it flooded. There seems little doubt that the enemy located this shaft head. Certainly he registered several direct hits upon it.

In May, however, work was resumed, the shaft pumped out and cleaned. At 800 feet work was begun on a charge chamber, somewhat shorter than originally planned. The enemy, however, became suspicious, and began to fire heavy mines in his own lines, fortifying the craters. The first of these, fired on 21st May, 1915, was to the right of the main drive and was named by the Germans " Cöln." The second and smaller was to the left, fired on 11th June,

1916, just as our main drive had been completed.   It was called " Cassel."

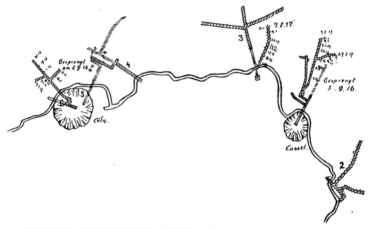

CAPTURED GERMAN PLANS OF THIS OPERATION, SHOWING METHOD
OF DRIVING GALLERIES FROM CRATERS.

A month later, No. 1 mine, having reached its objective, was loaded with a charge of 34,200 lbs.   Under the Nag's Nose, branches on each side of the main drive were driven, and two smaller charges were placed—one under the Nag's Nose, the other behind Cöln crater, with a total charge of over 50,000 lbs.   The very bad surface conditions and the proximity of the German lines made the placing of these mines no easy matter.

VI

Petit Bois, or S.P. 13, was perhaps the most remarkable of all the Messines mines.   Sheltered by the ruins of Vandamme Farm, some 500 yards behind our lines, the shaft was started, late in 1915, by 250th Tunnelling Company, and soon was down to 58 feet.   A gallery began at 55 feet.   Then it was decided to go deeper still, and by the end of January the shaft had reached a depth of 97 feet and 25 feet of gallery driven, its objective being a salient in the German lines. The original breakaway at 55 feet was then converted into a pump chamber.

A month later a second shaft had been sunk to 88 feet, and arrangements made here to accommodate mechanical plant. An air compressor, and electric light plant, were installed on the surface, while down below a chamber was got ready for a mechanical excavator.

A miniature " great shield," such as was used to cut the tunnels for the London tubes, was, with difficulty, man-handled to No. 2 shaft. The next problem was to lower it down the shaft ; as it weighed over half a ton, this was no easy matter. However, it was accomplished without mishap, and in due course the shield was erected, tested, and ready to start cutting a tunnel 6 feet in diameter. Needless to say, miners watched the experiments with a mechanical tunneller with great interest and great things were expected of the machine.

March 4th was the eventful day ; at 11 p.m. the cutter began operations, and actually cut 16 feet 8 inches at the rate of 2 feet per hour. Hope ran high, for at that rate we soon should reach Berlin ! But all was not well, and the promise was unfulfilled. ¡The machine developed an unexpected tendency to " dive." Adjustments failed to arrest this ; even by exerting a pressure of 2,500 lbs. per square inch on the two bottom hydraulic rams, the only effect was to burst the pipes. When cutting ceased, the clay swelled and pinched the tool, so that it had to be dug out ; this frequently happened. After much delay and many alterations and adjustments, the machine again started under favourable conditions and cut 18 inches in twenty minutes. But that proved a last despairing effort. The expert in charge left in high dudgeon, to return no more—and, as no profane hand dare touch the sacred machine, it remains to this day, covered in shame and 80 odd feet of Flanders soil, so that no mortal eye may gaze upon its abysmal failure. So ended a venture on which great hopes were set. Indeed, rumour had it that even the battery positions far in rear of the enemy line would be mined and blown up on the day of the great attack ! Nor did the Tunnellers raise one voice in protest ; in fact, they rather encouraged the circulation of these wild rumours.

Meanwhile the main gallery from No. 1 shaft made good progress, advancing at the rate of 100 feet to 150 feet per week ; but this also brought its problems. The most reliable form of manual ventilation proved to be the ordinary blacksmith's bellows, connected to 6 inch store piping, the joints being sealed with a solution of pitch. But even this method became ineffectual after about 1,200 feet. At the face the air was fairly good, but the return air began to " hang " about the middle of the drive. As this means of ventilating became inadequate, the power driven compressor was installed and proved quite successful.

S.P. 13 gallery had started 5 feet by 3 feet, but when " clay-kicking " started it was reduced to 3 feet 10 inches by 3 feet 4 inches. This, however, proved too small and the size was increased to 4 feet 4 inches by 2 feet 8 inches. The pressure from roof and sides became so great that the ordinary timbers were splintered to matchwood. This pressure was caused by the blue clay expanding after exposure to the air. Larger timber also proved too light. At last the difficulty was overcome by spacing the sets at 2 feet centres, and " easing " the clay between to relieve the strain.

The enemy now began to shell heavily localities likely to conceal shafts. This seems to indicate that he had knowledge of our deep mines. The shelling continued over a period, the compressor house being hit, and although no vital damage was done, work on the mines was held up.

On resuming, the main drive at 1,500 feet passed under the German lines, and 100 feet farther on a " Y " was started. This had not proceeded far before another delay was caused by a breakdown of the electric light plant. Progress was also slowed down on account of the length of the drive, and because of the extra amount of spoil coming down from the two faces. Then, swift as a tropical storm and without warning, disaster befell.

At 6.30 on the morning of 10th June, 1916, the enemy fired two heavy mines at the shoulders of the salient just outside his own lines. Blue clay was exposed in both the craters, indicating that the galleries from which they were blown were at a considerable depth.   As was his practice, these craters were incorporated into his trench system, sniping and bombing posts and machine-gun positions being constructed in the forward lips.

The northernmost of these blows was almost directly above our S.P.13 gallery, and was fraught with disastrous results to us.   The main gallery between 1,250 feet and 1,500 feet was competely smashed in, and twelve unfortunate men working at or near the face were trapped, imprisoned in the confined space in the undamaged end of the gallery.   Their predicament was desperate.   Every breath they breathed poisoned the fetid, though precious, air so vital to their very existence. . . . Was there no hope of release ?   Must they all suffer the tortures of a lingering death in the utter darkness 100 feet below ground ?   There was just a chance, feeble enough, and the knowledge that their comrades would spare no efforts to effect their release no doubt gave them hope.   Rescue and repair gangs were rushed to work with all possible speed, the miners gallantly working in frantic haste in an endeavour to release their entombed mates.   It is traditional with miners that they never spare themselves or despair of rescuing their comrades.   Night and day they strove with relentless determination amounting almost to frenzy.   For six and a half days they toiled with breathless energy, their half-naked bodies begrimed with clay and bathed with the sweat of exhaustion and anxiety, straining every muscle lest they should be too late.   At last, it seemed an age, the broken ground was passed and a connection made to the undamaged gallery.   By this time, however, it was quite hopeless to expect to find the men alive.   An eager search proved their worst fears to be only too well founded.   Body after body was found—eleven in all.   It was presumed that the twelfth was buried under the fallen gallery.   The workers were therefore withdrawn to allow the foul air to clear from the gallery.

Later they returned to the gallery, and to their utter amazement they discerned in the dim, uncertain light, something moving.   This, they thought, surely must be supernatural. Under the circumstances they well may be pardoned for showing some diffidence. But their apprehension was momentarily only ; scarcely believing their eyes, they saw the sole survivor crawl back from a living grave.

This man, Sapper Bedson, told how the entombed men had, collected at the broken end of the gallery, where a little air was coming through the air pipe which they disconnected. They then began by turns to dig their way out. This effort they soon abandoned and spaced themselves along the gallery. Gradually, however, they were overcome by the foul air, and in three days all but one were dead. Bedson, however, was an experienced miner. He avoided the broken end, where heavy air accumulated, and lay by the face, which was a little higher. He comforted himself by the reflection that a party of coal miners were entombed for thirteen days and then rescued alive.

He kept his head marvellously. His only food consisted of two Army biscuits and a bottle of water. He dare not eat the biscuits nor drink the water. From time to time he rinsed out his mouth with water and returned it to the bottle. To keep himself warm he improvised a suit from sandbags. Every night he slept on a crude bed made by placing sandbags on a bogie truck, winding up his watch before retiring ! And when after six and a half days he was rescued—hauled through a small hole in the broken ground—his first words were : " For God's sake give me a drink ! It's been a damned long shift ! " He was taken to the shaft on a mine stretcher placed on a bogie wagon in charge of the M.O. At the shaft he was rested for two hours. During this time his mind was quite clear and he could answer quite sensibly.

Even then Bedson's perils were not all over. As he was being carried down the communication trench he and his bearer party had the narrowest of escapes from shell-fire !

Bedson had already suffered his share of war's scars. Wounded on this very front in 1914, after recovery he was sent to Gallipoli, where he was wounded again. Now, returning to Flanders—this time as a Tunneller—he had to undergo an ordeal grave enough to try the stoutest heart.

Yet, when he had recovered from his appalling experience, his first act was to volunteer to return to his old unit ! It was rightly considered, however, that he had "done his bit," and he was given a job at the Base Depot.

A great amount of repair and reclaiming had to be carried out before work at the face could be resumed. This done, the right branch of the Y was advanced to 1,874 feet and a charge of 41,150 lbs. placed—not without interruption, for the enemy still continued to probe for our suspected mines. At 1,800 feet the left branch received a charge of 32,850 lbs., and was tamped back to the Y branch.

During the last few days of August tapping was heard at intervals in the crater above S.P.13, and three charges were fired by the Germans in this area—on successive days —no doubt from mines driven from the crater of the mines fired on 10th June. These charges were heavy enough to break the leads to our mines outside the tamping, and the main gallery was badly shaken, necessitating repairs and retimbering. It was an anxious time, but fortunately was not prolonged. For some unexplained reason the enemy suddenly discontinued his mining activity and we suffered no more interference in this sector.

VII

Probably the most ambitious plan of the whole deep offensive scheme was undertaken by 250th Tunnelling Company.

Late in 1916 two "tubbed" shafts about 200 feet apart were sunk, just off Park Avenue, in the rear of a small but pronounced salient in our lines due west of Wytschaete, and connected up at about 50 feet deep. Just off this connecting drive, two interior shafts were put down a further 80 feet and forward drives commenced, the one from No. 1 shaft turning to meet No. 2. These lower levels were connected by a cross-cut gallery, and then ran out parallel for a considerable distance ; No. 2 then turned to the right in the direction of Maedelstede Farm, at the

shoulder of a re-entrant in the German line, while No. 1
proceeded on to its objective in Wytschaete Wood, some
2,600 feet away and well behind the German line.

Early in 1917 the enemy fired several heavy camouflets
in this area ; as a precaution, the men were withdrawn
from the face for about three hours each day. To cope
with the spoil from these two drives, a covered tramway
was built running back to Turnerstown. At night the
spoil was trammed back to dead ground, built into block
and very carefully camouflaged in order not to disclose
our work or draw fire to it. But this and the withdrawal
of the men caused delay, and after No. 1 drive had been
driven to 1,320 feet, it became obvious that it could not
reach its objective in time ; consequently work was concentrated on the Maedelstede drive, and at 1,610 feet this
was chambered, charged,* tamped, tested and reported
ready for firing on the 6th June, 1917—one day prior to
zero !

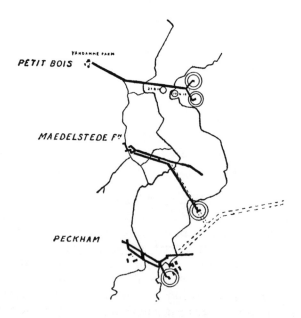

* The charge placed here was only 1,500 lbs. smaller than the record charge
in Queen Victoria Mine.

VIII

Another of the deep offensive mines, Peckham, was started behind trench G.2 by 250th Tunnelling Company. Owing to illness in the Company, brought on by the severe weather conditions, No. 2 section could only muster forty men for work in the trenches when, on the 18th December, 1915, a start was made on this shaft. Like the other mines, it derived its name from its objective in the German lines, Peckham Farm in this case.

Early in January, 1916, the shaft was completed at 65 feet, and the main drive started ; from the very first it gave trouble on account of heavy ground, box settings being necessary.

As an additional precaution, an auxiliary shaft (No. 2) was put down to 70 feet, and in hard blue clay a gallery was broken out to connect with No. 1 drive ; a compressor dugout was also constructed.

In the main drive progress was slow owing to the nature of the ground. Here the clay seemed to swell more rapidly, and in expanding crushed the ordinary mine timbers to splinters : larger sets were essential, and with some difficulty were placed in position.

In March No. 3 section of the 1st Canadian Tunnelling Company took over in the main gallery for instruction, two sections of 250th Company going to the Bluff, after its recapture by us, for urgent work. This, of course, was a temporary arrangement only, and No. 2 section was soon back again in its old haunt. By now the drive had advanced 500 feet from the shaft ; the ground throughout being extremely heavy, it required retimbering with heavier sets, squared timber 7 inches by 7 inches being used. When these repairs were finished, the drive was in good condition and half a section of 2nd Canadian Tunnelling Company came in for instruction.

By the end of the month the face had advanced beyond our front line ; to ensure silent working " clay-kicking " was then employed. Progress once more became slow, this time on account of enemy bombardments, which

P

increased in frequency and intensity, interrupting work, while on 29th April the Tunnellers lined the parapet and assisted the infantry in repelling a raid. Trench-mortaring also increased. With the exception of a mine, there is nothing so destructive or more effective against mining and shaft heads as a large trench-mortar bomb. The work of months may be destroyed in a moment by one lucky shot. Indeed, heavy trench-mortaring is part of the policy laid down by the Germans as a counter to mining. In this way three shafts were lost.

Then tramming became almost impossible owing to the unevenness of the floor—caused by the clay swelling—and work at the face was held up while the old track was ripped up and a new one put down. In preparation for charging, the cross-cut between the shafts was cleaned out and floored and used as a temporary magazine. At 1,145 feet " A " branch of the gallery was beneath its objective— Peckham Farm—and a month later the chamber had been made and charged with 76,000 lbs.

In the meantime " B " branch had advanced to 370 feet from the " Y " formed with " A " branch, and ran into bad ground ; the face caved, causing an inrush of water and sandy clay, the men at the face making good their escape with difficulty. As there was no possibility of reclaiming this gallery, a dam was built across it at 120 feet from the face ; it was abandoned, and a new drive broken out to the right. This, too, after passing the end of " B " drive, ran into bad ground at 1,341 feet and, as it was impossible to make a chamber, was abandoned. Yet another attempt was made with " C " gallery, also to the right of " B," at an angle of 45 degrees and directed against a new target. Starting in good blue clay, this drive made good progress towards its new objective, the support line, the spoil from the face being used to tamp " A " mine, thereby saving the long tramming back to the shaft. Then, like the other drives, " C " gallery ran into soft wet ground, and a few yards at the face were lost before the end could be dammed off. Nevertheless, a series of small chambers were made, into which a charge of 20,000 lbs. was loaded. As it was so wet, the precaution was taken of placing the primers in bottles, the necks being sealed with tar and pitch, and the leads placed in armoured hose-pipe.

All this time water had been causing a great deal of trouble and could not be kept down by hand pumps ; consequently an electric pumping set was installed. This was not a success and breakdowns were frequent. A new pump had to be installed ; in the meantime, the hand pumps not being up to their task, the whole mine flooded, the water rising in the shaft above the top of the gallery. The new pump soon de-watered the mine, which then was found to be half full of sand and slime. But worse was to come —the main gallery had collapsed completely, cutting off both charges. Repair was out of the question. Nothing remained but to drive a new gallery and pick up the leads of No. 1 mine first. A new gallery was broken out from the shaft about 10 feet above the old and to the side of it. In place of pit props, steel joists were used in this drive, which was driven for almost 1,000 feet before it was considered safe to break into the old drive, at the out-by end of the tamping. Accurate surveys and plans had been made of the original gallery, and it was located exactly where it was expected to be found ; a connection made and new joists joined, in March, 1917, some two months after beginning the new drive.

Fortunately for 250th Company, there was little or no interference from the enemy below ground near these mines, but this advantage was more than offset by the heavy trench-mortaring above, while treacherous ground and excessive water created enough difficulties below.

IX

Spanbroekmolen was another of the mines started by 250th Company in December, 1915. The stunted remains of a small wood offered some concealment, and after several unsuccessful attempts to penetrate below 15 feet, No. 3 section got a shaft down to about 60 feet and had driven the gallery 90 feet when, in the third week of January, 1916, it handed over this mine to the 3rd Canadian Tunnelling

Company.   Delayed by shortage of men, this newly-formed company did not get going till the end of January.

After three months of steady work the face had been advanced to 790 feet without incident.   Then another change occurred, 175th and 3rd Canadian Companies exchanging sectors.   But 175th Company made a very brief stay at Spanbroekmolen, and within a fortnight they handed over to 171st Company.   So far the chief feature of the mining programme in this sector had been the frequent and delaying changes of units !   However, at 1,717 feet * the drive reached its objective, and towards the end of June, 1916, the charge was completed and all in readiness.

The postponement of the Second Army attack led to the selection of additional objectives still further behind the German lines—one being Rag Point, a stronghold no less than 1,200 yards from the shaft.   Through a somewhat ambitious project this, it did not deter the Tunnellers. Just behind our front line, at a point 665 feet from the shaft, a station was made, and an incline started to go to a depth of 120 feet below the surface.   This branch gallery had been driven 1,140 feet by mid-February, 1917, when the Germans sprung a camouflet in the vicinity, doing little material damage, but destroying the sense of security induced by the hitherto unmolested progress.   A week later, just as the face of the drive reached Narrow Trench, the German front line, another and closer blow damaged 500 feet of the incline and also some of the main gallery. These blows were unmistakable evidence that the enemy had deep shafts in this vicinity, and, rather than disclose our presence by firing counter-mines, the idea of reaching the further objectives was abandoned.   Owing to the shape of the line, almost the entire length of this drive was under No Man's Land.

On the 3rd March, 1917, another enemy camouflet shook the main gallery so badly that the leads were broken. On investigation, it was found that the drive was so completely damaged that it was considered advisable to redrive

---

* Figure coincidence specialists might like to remark that 1,717 feet were completed by 171 Company in 7 months.

it rather than attempt repairs. No time was lost in starting the new gallery, and the work was rushed ahead with all possible speed to recover the lost charge. At 1,172 feet a cross-cut holed into the original drive and the leads were picked up, but on being tested were found to be broken at a point further inbye—i.e., a point farther away from the shaft.

By the end of April the new gallery had been driven to 1,429 feet, and began to approach the ground shaken by the blows, when gas was encountered. As the drive proceeded and approached nearer to the scene of the blows, gas was met in increasing quantities ; several miners were overcome, three being asphyxiated. A gas-tight stopping was then built across the drive, and a new drive broken out to the right to skirt the gas-drenched broken ground. Another test indicated that the break in the leads was still farther in, and, driving on, the chamber was at length reached. To save time, the old circuits were not repaired but a priming charge of 1,000 lbs. of dynamite was placed in contact with the original charge, into which was inserted a new set of leads, and 400 feet of tamping completed the job a few hours before zero ; the mine was once again ready, after having been cut off for three months !

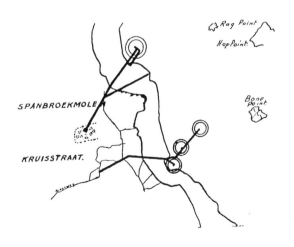

X

Kruisstraat was yet another mine commenced by 250th Tunnelling Company late in December, 1915. The shaft was located in the battered remains of a small spinny just off Kingsway, a communication trench leading to D.5, our front line opposite Kruisstraat Cabaret. Early in the New Year the recently formed 182nd Tunnelling Company took over this work when the shaft was only a few feet down. Three weeks later, when the shaft had reached 35 feet deep, the 3rd Canadian Tunnelling Company relieved, and made such good progress that, by the end of January, the shaft was down 66 feet including the sump, and about 50 feet of the main gallery driven.

Work continued without incident until April, when the 3rd Canadian and 175th Companies then exchanged sectors. At the end of April yet another change-over took place, 171st Tunnelling Company coming in when the drive had reached the 1,051 feet mark, showing that in spite of the frequent changes good progress had been maintained. No further reliefs were ordered, and work proceeded normally until June, 1916. Our staff then received warning of an enemy gas attack and immediately ordered the " gas alert," which naturally retarded progress in the mines, as it was in force for several days before the gas was released.

At 1,605 feet No. 1 charge of 30,000 lbs. of ammonal was placed. A short drive of 166 feet to the right of the gallery was run out, at the head of which a chamber was made and a second charge, also of 30,000 lbs., was placed beneath the German front line. This completed the original scheme.

Then a new objective was decided upon, and preparations were made to restart the main drive. Almost immediately the clay became exceptionally hard, and progress was slow. Then a stream of water poured in through a fissure in the floor, necessitating the making of a sump, into which the water was collected and from which it had to be bailed constantly. At length, after two months' work (on 25th

August, 1916) the new drive had reached its objective, no less than 720 yards (nearly half a mile) from the shaft, a chamber made, and 30,000 lbs. of ammonal placed under the German *third* line ! This was the longest gallery of the whole series of mines. Then followed a long period of water bailing, repair and maintenance until February, 1917, when an enemy camouflet caused some damage and flooded one of the charges. A new chamber was cut and loaded with a further charge of 19,500 lbs, making the fourth charge of this series. All four mines were ready by the 9th May, 1917.

XI

From Hill 60 to Kruisstraat the geological formation is very much the same, except that from the Bluff to Petit Bois the Kemmel sands are missing. But south of Kruisstraat an entire change occurs ; all the sand and clay beds disappear, and the blue clay is overlayed by grey limon or plateau sands only, in places very wet, and about 100 feet in thickness. These conditions made shaft sinking extremely difficult, and 171st Tunnelling Company had to abandon two shafts, one of which had been " tubbed " on account of the ground " caving " in the shaft bottom.

" Third time lucky " runs the saying, and they tried again in Hanbury Support north, behind Boyle's Farm. This time their efforts met with success, for, without further let or hindrance, on the 28th February, 1917, four weeks after starting work on the pent house, a " tubbed " shaft was down to 95 feet deep, including the sump. A week later a shaft station had been put in and chambers excavated for air and water pumps, and the main drive started. A feature of this shaft was its " telescope " design, the tubbing decreasing in diameter as the shaft descended.

When the drive had proceeded about 100 yards a chamber was made and from it an interior shaft was sunk 30 feet deep, and a new drive started in blue clay, having 120 feet of head cover. At 540 feet the face ran into very bad ground, water and quicksand surging into the gallery to such an extent that a strong dam had to be made, resulting in the loss of 100 feet of gallery. This company had had a similar experience of this nature in trench 127 and promptly dealt with the situation. A new gallery was branched off to the left and inclined to go below the soft ground, which, in all probability, was an ancient river bed.

This loss of gallery and damage to the pent house by shell fire delayed progress to such an extent that it seemed impossible for the mine to reach its objective and be completed on time. However, by the end of May the drive was beneath some ruined buildings, known as Ontario Farm, just behind the German front line. A week later the drive had been chambered and charged with 60,000 lbs., leads connected up and tested, tamping put in and all ready on the 6th June, 1917, a day before zero—a very near thing.

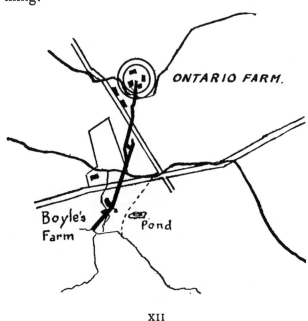

XII

In March, 1916, the 3rd Canadian Tunnelling Company started No. 4 or Q.1 shaft in trench 135, north of the River Douve, a small stream running from west to east across No Man's Land. This was a " tubbed " shaft,

5 feet 6 inches in diameter, and some difficulty was experienced in getting down to the blue clay. Then 171st Company took over and continued sinking to 80 feet, and in the second week of May broke away and drove the main gallery 104 feet towards Petite Douve Farm. After that progress became slower on account of water trouble, sumps being put in along the drive. At 865 feet the drive had reached its objective and a charge placed.

About the same time a branch was broken out to the left, and within a week had advanced 134 feet—a fatal point, as it turned out. By the 23rd August, 1916, the chamber charge in the branch gallery was completed, and charging was about to commence. The following day an unsuspected enemy gallery was heard—so close that it seemed to be on the point of breaking into our gallery. By this time the charge had been completed in the main drive, but being unwilling to fire it and thus disclose our real position, a small charge was placed in the branch gallery at the point nearest to where the German gallery had been located. When this charge was placed, definite orders were issued that it was not to be fired unless an entry was made into our gallery. So small was the partition of clay separating us from the enemy that he could be heard plainly talking and laughing.

Owing to the condition of the ground, it was thought that a small charge would completely disrupt the waterlogged sand above the clay and so cause flooding of the German workings, leaving our main charge intact—though also flooded.

The Germans did actually break into our gallery, but our charge was fired on August 24th, 1916.

Observers in our trenches saw a large cloud of grey smoke rise in the enemy lines in the vicinity of Petit Douve Farm. This indicates that the force of the blow exerted itself along enemy gallery.

Nine hours after the blow our mine was entered and slight damage only was found. The water then had not greatly increased and there was no gas. The leads to the main charge were intact and at that time it could have been fired.

The placing of the charge of 1,000 lbs. in the branch needs explanation. It was not placed at the face or end of the drive, as is usual, but at the point reached by the branch drive at the end of the first week's work, mentioned previously. Before the charge could be placed, twelve feet of solid tamping was put in on the inby side, then 500 lbs. of ammonal followed by 5 feet of solid tamping. Then came a second charge of 500 lbs. and 8 feet of solid tamping. To strengthen further the tamping, heavy timbers were strutted across the gallery. The charge was contained in watertight tins to protect it from the water. The mine closed all but 75 feet of the branch.

At the time it was thought that our camouflet had effectively stopped the Germans. But their system must have been more extensive than we imagined it to be, for four days later the enemy blew a large camouflet which shattered about 400 feet of our main gallery, killing four men engaged in effecting repairs necessary after our blow.

The exact position of the enemy camouflet could not be located at first as it did not form a crater. Later, from an aeroplane photograph, it was located about one-third of the way across No Man's Land from the enemy's side, and to the north of our main gallery.

The camouflet wrecked our gallery so completely that it could not be recovered, and we had to abandon the charge. It also destroyed some of our shallow defensive lateral. This was the only charge which was lost through enemy action.

Some weeks later we captured a prisoner belonging to the 45th Bavarian Division, XXXIII Reserve Corps. In a statement he said that a deep shaft existed at Weihauchtshof (or, as we knew it, Petite Douve Farm). Work in this sector, he said, had eased off since our camouflet was fired.

Major Paul Heinrici, in his book, *Der Ehrenbuch der deutschen Pioniere* (the Book of Honour of the German Field Engineers) states that at Weihauchtshof (i.e. " Christmas Court ") in August, 1916, " A shaft 20 metres, inclined to 30 metres and a new gallery driven." But the miners were not strong enough and shaft heads were often blown

in after great efforts had been made to cover them.   He
also complains that help and material were very scarce.
He further states that in June, 1916, a conference decided
to give up mining in the hope that we also would desist.

When we blew the German H.Q. wanted to know what
their miners were up to.   The usual reply was that we (the
British) had had twelve months' start of them.   The
Pioneers were disappointed at the " lack of appreciation
of the situation displayed by G.H.Q."

In order to deny the enemy access to our lost gallery
all pumping ceased and the gallery was allowed to flood.
Surface water from the trench was also drained into the
shaft.   The water from our mines was percolating through
the loose ground, formed by the blows, into his workings,
and his companies were fully employed in pumping alone.
The Tunnellers appreciated the joke—the Germans pumping the water from *our* mines !   Consequently, each time
the water level was lowered in our shaft, a fresh volume of
water, specially stored for the purpose, was released into
it.   Thus the Germans were kept constantly busy, and it
was certain that, even if the continuous flow of water did
not induce him to abandon his mines, at least it would
occupy labour which might be employed on more profitable
work.

XIII

Trench 127 was due south of Messines and north of
Ploegsteert Wood.   Here at the end of December, 1915,
171st Tunnelling Company started a deep offensive shaft
in the front line.   After passing through greyish loam and
quicksand (limon), stiff blue clay was reached at less than
40 feet deep.   On the 1st February, 1916, the shaft was
completed at 75 feet deep and the drive started, and went
so well that at the end of February it was 451 feet out.
Normal conditions continued and the good progress was
maintained ;   the face had advanced almost to 700 feet
from the shaft when, without the slightest warning, a run
of quicksand burst into the drive from the top left hand
corner with such suddenness and force that in less than

five minutes 35 feet of gallery was filled, the men working at the face being almost overwhelmed. Lieutenant Frayling, who was on duty at the time, immediately built a temporary dam of sandbags about 100 feet back from the face. A permanent dam of concrete stiffened with expanded metal was then erected, behind which a 30 feet wall of sandbags was built up, and a second concrete dam put in.

The run was most unexpected and occurred at a point at least 70 feet below the surface. Major David, the geological expert from General Headquarters, was of opinion that the drive had holed into an ancient river channel, possibly the bed of the Douve River in preglacial times, filled with surface sand.

A new drive was broken out and inclined down so as to dive beneath the bad ground, and by the end of March the new drive had at least 90 feet of cover and was out 761 feet from the shaft. Here a branch gallery turned off to the left and ran out 250 feet, where it was chambered and charged with 36,000 lbs. of ammonal on the 29th April, 1916. The main drive was continued without incident to 1,357 feet, and charged with 50,000 lbs. of ammonal by mid-May, 1916.

XIV

171st Tunnelling Company began sinking M.2 shaft for the mine at Trench 122 at the end of February, 1916, and with little difficulty got through the surface loam and reached blue clay at about 30 feet deep.

Four weeks later the shaft was down to 78 feet, and preparations were in hand to commence the drive. It was driven beneath a road for a distance of 450 feet, and then turned left towards its objective, a network of trenches on the north side of the road. It reached its objective without incident, and by the 14th May, 1916, a charge of 20,000 lbs. of ammonal had been placed and tamped ready for firing.

At 350 feet from the shaft, a branch to the right was directed against Factory Farm, through the ruins of which

ran the German front line. At 600 feet from the main
gallery the face of the branch was beneath its objective ;
the drive was chambered and charged with 40,000 lbs.
of ammonal on the 11th June, 1916.

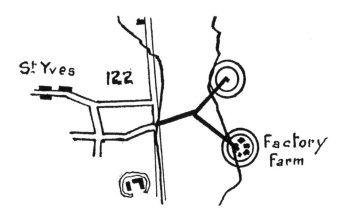

The chief feature of these mines was the remarkably
good rate of progress maintained. In one week the average
footage per shift was 27·8 feet, while a fortnight later this
was eclipsed by an average of 31·4 feet per shift. This
would be first class work under ordinary peace-time conditions ; in its actual circumstances it was outstanding.

xv

The Birdcage at Ploegsteert Wood—the Germans called
it Ducksbill—was the scene of some of the early mining,
and here the 174th Company had blown the German
line on two occasions in June, 1915. Soon after it was
relieved by 171st Company, and towards the end of the
year, preparations were made to sink two shafts as part
of the deep offensive scheme.

At the north-east corner of the wood trench 121 formed
a right angle, and it was immediately behind the elbow
that M.1 shaft was put down, and early in January, 1916,
was completed at 84 feet deep in stiff blue clay. A month

later, when the drive was out 100 yards, sounds were heard
indicating that the enemy was working in a gallery above.
Work was suspended and a period of very careful listening
followed.   After the danger passed, work was resumed,
great care being taken to work as silently as possible.
Then normal working was resumed, but the precaution
was taken to branch out to the right, with a gallery to
protect the shaft from being outflanked.   This gallery
inclined up to 60 feet below the surface to act as an intermediate level, and as soon as it had gone a few yards from
the main drive a chamber was cut.   The branch soon
reached its objective, Le Pelerin.

A few days after commencing M.1, the second shaft,
numbered M.3, was started nearby, also in trench 121,
but 171st Company had so much work on hand that this
shaft could not be worked continuously for lack of men.
These two shafts were connected by a drive, and later a
third shaft, M.4, was put down farther in rear and also
connected to M.1 and M.3.   However, by the end of
January, 1916, the second shaft was down 82 feet in blue
clay and the drive about to be started.   There was no
interference by the enemy, although sounds were heard which
were attributed to surface work, and by the end of April
the drive reached its objective.   In the actual event, however, no mines were fired from these galleries, which were
outside the area of the attack.

Five months later a scare arose.   An N.C.O., captured
by the Germans on the Somme, made a statement to
the effect that offensive mining was being carried on at
Ducksbill.   Here the newly-formed Pioneer Company
No. 22 had several shafts 20 metres deep.   This news was
somewhat disconcerting.   Defensive galleries were at once
started to protect our shafts, the most vulnerable part of the
mining system.

In addition to the mines, a great amount of work was
done in providing mined dugouts along the front.   In
fact, every headquarters down to battalions had underground protection provided for them.   Numerous subways were also made, some 15,000 feet of gallery being
provided.

Of all the numerous mined dugouts along this part of the front, the most famous was the one at Hill 63. It was constructed by the 1st Australian Tunnelling Company, who gave it a picturesque native name, Wallangarra. It was not a single dugout, but a series of chambers with connecting galleries, exits and entrances. But its chief claim to notoriety was not due to any special feature of its construction or accommodation. It was something quite unusual—in war time at least—something which savoured of a civic demonstration, such as the opening of a new bridge or building. The dugout was to be officially declared open, and the Army Commander was to perform the opening ceremony !

If the striped awning and carpet, which provide the hall-mark of dignity at functions in this country, were missing, at least they were represented in principle by the archway of tree branches erected over the entrance, and the liberal application of sawdust underfoot. Little bunches of gaily coloured bunting relieved the sombre green in the triumphal arch. Nor was the sawdust a symbol only —it was a necessity—a liberal application was essential to mop up the water and conceal the mud on the floor of the entrance.

A band helped to enliven the proceedings, and with the presence of no less than twenty generals and their staffs ensured that the function was not lacking in dignity. If not a red-letter day, this was indeed a " Red Hat " day. Quite a goodly number of officers and men from the neighbouring hutment camps helped to swell the attendance, while numerous lorries and other vehicles were temporarily neglected while their drivers satisfied their curiosity.

Fortunately the ceremony passed off without any molesta tion from the enemy. Had a searching gun got busy, then promotion would have been accelerated.

XVI

Mention has already been made of German mines, two of which destroyed our deep galleries. During the early part of 1917, the Germans fired a series of heavy mines in the Wytschaete area, some of which were behind his front line. These craters were consolidated immediately. Others were heavy camouflets, and as these did not break to surface we could not locate their positions accurately. At the same time, craters were blown at important road crossings in the back areas. Heavy shelling of our front —and especially supposed shaft-heads—accompanied these blows. It was at this time also that delay-action mines were exploding in the Bapaume area, details of which appear in another chapter.

It was thought at the time that these mines were fired for tactical purposes, but it now seems probable that the Germans had secured some information of our deep mines in November, 1916, when one of our men, tiring of the view from our trenches, or perhaps determined to study the dispute from both sides, proceeded across No Man's Land, hastened en route by a burst or two of machine-gun fire from his forsaken comrades. Probably the unprecedented delay in firing the mines helped to discredit his information.

A German publication previously quoted * (*Der Ehrenbuch der deutschen Pioniere*, Major Paul Heinrici) states that they located our gallery at Spanbroekmolen, fired an overcharged mine at a depth of over 40 metres (more than 130 feet)—i.e. deeper than our gallery—and that our attack to destroy his galleries failed. After this they blew their shallow level.

True it is that the Germans did wreck a branch gallery of the Spanbroekmolen mine ; nevertheless a charge of 91,000 lb. of ammonal was fired under the main objective on the 7th June. It seems evident then that with these mines the Germans were probing for our charges—a somewhat hopeless project, as success depended on mere chance.

The enemy also sought to destroy our shaft heads by portable charges. A raiding party entered our trenches, but failed to locate the shafts. They had been railed off and marked : " Deep Well. Keep out." This simple

* See page 234.

ruse was sufficient to protect them from the marauding enemy and his portable charges.

XVII

It will have been noted that, although some of the charges were placed in position only on the eve of the attack, the majority had actually been *en situ* for a considerable period—in some cases, over a year ! This fact was unprecedented in mining warfare—and the inordinately long waiting period was a nightmare to the responsible Tunnelling Officers. The constant and anxious task of keeping the mines intact was far more nerve-racking than actual mining, with all its risks. Less and still less continuity registered each time the leads were tested, indicating deterioration. Would they last out—or would the all-pervading dampness penetrate the insulation and cause a short circuit ? Had the chambers collapsed, and so fractured the tins, allowing the charge to be saturated and become useless ? Would a chance enemy blow wreck a gallery ? These, and a hundred other such thoughts, tormented the Tunnellers and tended to bestow grey hairs on those in charge.

As the days passed, slowly it seemed, tension increased ; nerves frayed almost to breaking point ; officers dreaded testing the leads, fearing that the tell-tale pointer on the dial of the tester might indicate a break of continuity, knowing full well how much depended on firing the mines. And so the days dragged on.

Above ground unmistakable signs were not wanting to indicate that " the day " was not long to be delayed. More and more guns and troops crowded into the area, and filled to overflowing the dugouts which the miners had prepared for them.

The stage was set for a gigantic mining offensive, in conjunction with a general action—without parallel in military history. At midnight on the 6th–7th June, 1917, nineteen huge mines were ready for firing.

Plumer, ready exactly to the day he had given Haig a month earlier, had finally fixed zero for 3.10 a.m. on the

Q

7th.   The Tunnelling Staff had known the date for that
month.   For some companies, whose programme was
incomplete, these were days of feverish activity.   To the
others, whose mines had been laid a year previously, the
time dragged in appalling fashion ; minutes seemed hours,
and hours days.   There may have been some nerveless or
fatigued Tunnellers who lay down to sleep in that pleasant
midsummer night, but they must have been few in number.
This was their Day.   In casual warfare they had gained
the mastery over the enemy, on the Somme and at Arras
they had played a small yet important part in great battles.
But at Messines their contribution was *vital*.   If the
mines failed, not even the heavy artillery concentration
nor the careful staff preparations could avoid frightful
casualties.

   Midnight passed ; nervous fingers grasped sensitive
instruments, testing leads which had already been tested
a hundred times.   The first hours of the new day passed
slowly and solemnly.   The preliminary bombardment,
which has thrashed the air for days with its thunder, has
now died away.   Over the battle-field there is comparative
silence—an ominous silence, like that preceding a tropical
storm.   Only fretfully it is broken—sometimes by the
frightened cry of bird or beast, unable to understand the
unwonted stillness : occasionally a Very light lazily climbs
into the air, hissing sullenly, explodes, and momentarily
sheds its ghostly light over the scene of desolation below ;
now a machine-gun rattles out a short indiscriminate burst ;
nervous sentries, particularly from the German side, blaze
away at real or imaginary terrors ; an aeroplane skims low
over our line, to be lost immediately in the grey half-light
of dawn.

   Hundreds of pairs of eyes constantly gaze at watches.
In the forward trenches the assaulting troops are gathered.
How would you describe them ?   Those pictures painted
by the newspapers of the day—of men laughing, cheering,
and shouting " Remember Belgium "—bore no resem-
blance to reality.   No one who has not undergone the
experience can ever know how slowly the minutes before
zero can pass.

Deep in the security of underground power houses, the very engines seem aware of their own importance ; their murmuring hum accentuated by the stillness about them, it seems as if they are striving to extreme capacity, giving of their utmost to provide that vital spark so necessary and soon to be needed.

Only a few moments to go. 3.5 a.m. At the firing posts stand officers; their pale faces show unmistakable signs of the strain of suspense. 3.6 a.m. Innumerable watches are consulted. 3.7 a.m. A hasty wipe of clammy hands. 3.8 a.m. Watches held to the ear. 3.9 a.m. Hands tremble slightly as fingers close around switch and exploder handle : complete silence, broken only by laboured breathing. Eyes staring at synchronized watches. Three hours . . . nine minutes . . . fifty-nine seconds . . . ZERO !

The supreme moment at last ! With almost the same grim feeling as a soldier plunges his bayonet into the belly of his enemy, the Tunnellers banged in switches and slammed home plungers. Instantaneously the leads carry the message of destruction to the charged mines, hundreds of yards away. The long hibernation was ended.

In a flash the monsters of destruction lurking below the ground were goaded into wakefulness. With a stupendous paroxysm they shook themselves free, convulsing the earth for miles around. The awaiting infantry felt the shocks and heard the rumble of an earthquake. Gazing towards the German line, they witnessed an unforgettable sight. It seemed as if the Messines Ridge got up and shook itself. All along its flank belched rows of mushroom-shaped masses of debris, flung high into the air. Gradually the masses commenced to disintegrate, as the released gases forced their way through the centres in pillars of flames. As if in echo, the earth trembled again like a fallen leaf agitated by a peevish wind. Then along the enemy line rolled dense columns of smoke, tumbling into weird formations as they mounted into the sky, at length opening like a row of giant umbrellas, spreading a dark pall over the yawning, cavernous craters below.

The heights of Messines rocked and trembled. The reverberations of explosions to north and south rumbled

threatening, echoing and re-echoing. This was a man-
made earthquake, a spectacle out-majestied only by Nature
in her most ungovernable moods. Even as the troops
scrambled over the parapet, with their faces to the east,
the civilian populace of Lille, twelve miles away, was
tumbling panic stricken into the streets, crying out that
an earthquake had overtaken them.

XVIII

Following the first wave of the attack, parties of
Tunnellers went over to investigate the enemy's mines.
These were difficult to locate, but a few shafts were found.
One was a deep concrete-lined shaft ; this must have
caused a lot of trouble to the sinkers, for it was very much
out of plumb.

In the St. Eloi craters several deep inclines were found,
one being 100 feet deep. Also at Petit Bois shafts and
galleries were found, and in Messines itself German mine
plans were found. A study of these shows that months
after our mines had been placed the Germans had made
half-hearted efforts to locate them.

The crater at Ontario Farm was most unusual, as owing
to the saturated nature of the ground, scarcely any lips

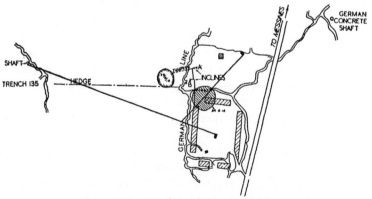

GERMAN INCLINES (A AND B) AT PETIT BOIS.

were formed. For a long time after the blow the crater resembled a seething cauldron, the semi-liquid mud bubbling like some gigantic porridge pot on the boil.

The Tunnellers received great assistance from the A.E. & M.M. & B. Coy, who put in numerous electrical plants for lighting, pumping and haulage, both in the mines and dugouts. They also put in the leads to at least one charge.

XIX

The chief features of the Messines mines were (*a*) the extremely heavy charges used, the aggregate amounting to nearly five hundred tons of high explosives ; (*b*) the inordinate lapse of time between placing and firing some of the mines, due to the cancellation of the 1916 offensive after the original scheme had been partly completed ; (*c*) the number of charges placed, twenty-three in all ; (*d*) the depth of the shafts and the length of some of the galleries ; and (*e*) the length of front covered, about ten miles. All these features combined to form what was unquestionably the greatest military mining offensive in the history of warfare.

In the absence of previous experience of the effect of firing, simultaneously, so many large charges, every precaution was taken to protect our own troops from injury. Special instructions were issued forbidding anyone to be within two hundred yards of any mine at the time of firing. It was feared that damaged walls, trees and even parapets of trenches in the vicinity would be shaken down. These, and the bottoms of craters were to be avoided. Tunnelled dugouts and subways within a radius of four hundred yards of a charge were to be evacuated at the moment of firing.

These precautions proved adequate, though in one division some little confusion was caused by the circulation of reports that large enemy mines had been fired in our support lines. Subsequently these reports were proved to be false, no craters being found in our lines. No doubt the configuration of the line, with its numerous salients and re-entrants, viewed in the uncertain light of early dawn, gave rise to these reports. To men standing in one of our salients, mines in a German salient would appear to be behind them. This can be understood easily when one remembers that, to an observer standing on Westminster Bridge, St. Paul's appears to be on the south side of the river, whereas in reality it is on the north side. The illusion is accounted for by the fact that, at Westminster, the Thames flows almost due north.

If the effect of the mines on our own men was almost overpowering, the condition of the enemy may be imagined. Long stretches of his first and second line were utterly destroyed, together with every living creature in them ; strong points and machine-gun nests simply disappeared off the map. Not until our infantry passed beyond the first enemy line did they encounter resistance worthy of the name. The German garrison of the Ridge seemed to be stupefied ; groups of men who a few months earlier— and a few weeks later—would have fought it out to the last, now lifted their hands in uncomprehending despair. Hundreds of Germans simply ceased to exist : no trace of their bodies was found, or is ever likely to be found. Yet the great achievement of the mines was not the heavy casualties which they inflicted, but the effect upon the survivors. (Nevertheless one mine is reported to have killed 1,000 men of the 40th Jägers and the 4th Bavarians.) Brigadier-General Charteris, the Director of Intelligence at G.H.Q., himself examined many of the German officer prisoners. They reported that the mines " so upset their men's nerves that they offered no resistance." *

The opinion of Ludendorff himself is perhaps even more valuable ; in his " Memoirs " he writes : " We should have succeeded in retaining the position but for the exceptionally powerful mines used by the British, which paved the way for their attack. . . . The result of these successful mining operations was that the enemy broke through on June 7th. . . . The moral effect of the explosions was simply staggering."

It is not an unimportant lesson—that moral effect is

* See *At G.H.Q.*

at least as decisive as material damage. Even had the mines failed to kill a single German, they would still have paved the way to victory. Even noise can spread terror —the first use of primitive artillery was to make a noise, to frighten the horses of the knights.

The battle of Messines was a limited siege operation, and all its objectives were attained within a few hours. At a comparatively small cost, more than 7,000 prisoners were captured, and the German losses in killed and wounded were very heavy. For the remaining months of the War the Tunnellers worked hard and unceasingly, but June 7th, 1917, was their Crowning Glory. Essential as their further labours were, they savoured of anti-climax. Haig and Plumer generously paid tribute to the value and valour of their work. It is disputed that Wellington ever said that Waterloo was won on the playing fields of Eton, but it is certain that the Battle of Messines was won in the bowels of the earth.

CHAPTER XI

I

AFTER Messines, the Fifth Army took over the Boesinghe–Hill 60 front, and preparations were started at once for what is officially termed the Third Battle of Ypres—more popularly known as Passchendaele. Of the five Tunnelling Companies already in the army area, 177th had been two years at Railway Wood— a difficult sector, wet, and so impervious to sound that headings approaching each other could not be heard when only 6 feet apart. It was here that a listener reported the enemy so near that he could hear them talking so plainly that he distinguished the words " Gott strafe England." Eventually the sounds heard were traced to dripping water !

Caisson shafts had been sunk to 100 feet deep from the surface. These were started from the 20 feet level, previously driven ; there was also an intermediate level so that the defence was fairly complete.

The 2nd Canadian Tunnelling Company had been at Armagh Wood—Tor Top since first coming into the line early in 1916, and had suffered heavy losses when the Germans overran the 3rd Canadian Division in a local attack.

Time was limited, and a large amount of work, some already commenced, required to be finished, so that four more companies were drafted to the battle area. There seemed little possibility of an enemy mining offensive of any seriousness, so that miners were withdrawn from Railway Wood and Tor Top, listening patrols only being maintained, and in July there were ten and a half companies at work on the preparations for the coming offensive.

Work now became more general, but the companies

were chiefly employed on dugout work for battle head-quarters, both for brigades and battalions, which previous experience had proved to be invaluable. Underground dressing stations, subways, O.P's cable trenches, and shelters for troops were all included in the programme of work.

Progress was slow and work difficult on account of the nature of the ground. At selected dugout sites hundreds of trial borings were made, proving the ground to vary considerably within a few yards. The water-bearing layers of sand had to be penetrated before reaching the blue clay, the clay itself proving treacherous and requiring very careful handling to prevent caving. Many of the dugouts were wet. It may be of interest to note here that the Germans made no attempts to construct underground shelters in the Ypres area, but pinned their faith to rein-forced concrete " pill boxes." (These " pill boxes," by the way, were not popular with the German troops, particu-larly during a bombardment.) They had a few dugouts in Sanctuary Wood, and a long subway under Menin Road, leading into Hooge ; and, of course, the Polygon Butte at Zonnebeke was honeycombed with underground passages and chambers.

Most of our dugout sites were in exposed positions and were subjected to heavy and continuous shelling, both high explosive and gas, which greatly interfered with the disposal and concealing of spoil. In addition, all roads and approaches were constantly raked by artillery fire, especially by night, making the delivery of materials most difficult. To the credit of the A.S.C. sections with the Tunnelling Companies, it must be said that they did splendid work under very trying conditions. Getting the men from forward billets in the canal bank or the ramparts at Ypres to their work without loss was also a difficult problem. Some companies allowed the men to make their own way in parties of twos and threes, by their own favourite route, so long as they relieved their mates on time—and they kept their part of the bargain. Nevertheless, losses were heavy, amounting to ten per cent. of effective strength.

II

The moral effect of the Messines mines cannot be gainsaid. We have the evidence of Ludendorff's own words that "the moral effect was simply staggering"—and he might have added lasting and far reaching. The enemy was now doubly keen to observe any traces of mining. The inadvertent exposure of blue clay spoil at Lancashire Farm brought on an almost incessant torrent of shells on to the area. Convinced that we were mining from here, the Germans reduced their front line garrison to a minimum and finally evacuated the position. On 13th and 14th June the enemy exploded a series of mines at Railway Wood, and two at Tor Top. The German wireless broadcast at the time claimed that "these mines played havoc with the English defences." Evidently the moral effect of the Messines mines was felt in Berlin, and this last effort was probably intended to convince the home front that their own men could blow mines also. Actually the mines did no damage to our position above or below ground. In fact, they were so innocuous that the exact position of the craters could be ascertained only by examining aeroplane photographs of the area. It was then found that he had destroyed his *own* line and crater posts near Bellewaarde Farm !

At Boesinghe, the opposing armies glared at each other (through periscopes) across the Yser Canal. Here the 173rd Tunnelling Company made a number of chambers in the canal bank for the storage of bridging material ; the bridges were to be erected immediately after zero on the day of the attack.

Perhaps becoming somewhat suspicious, the Germans decided to investigate what was going on in our lines, and sent over a raiding party. To their horror and dismay, they saw what they thought to be mine shafts—the storage chambers. One fleeting glance was sufficient, and they hurried back to their own lines to warn their comrades that they were sitting on the edge of a volcano. Messines was still fresh in their memory, so they betook themselves well out of harm's way to a new position some five hundred

I.W.M. Photo

AUSTRALIAN TUNNELLERS CONSTRUCTING DUGOUT

yards from the canal bank.   It was difficult to drive the
Germans out of their trenches, as the Allies found to their
cost, but it was not very often throughout the whole of
the War that we were able to *frighten* them out.   On these
few occasions the governing factor was the fear of mines
—surely a significant feature.

Bridge approaches had to be made through the canal
banks for two pontoon bridges.   Instead of cutting them
by manual labour, gaps were blown by charges of explosive
in cylinders placed in boreholes drilled by the Wombat
Drill, this saving time and labour.   184th Tunnelling
Company was allotted to the Tank Corps and made numerous tank crossings over the canal and tank jump crossings
over streams and ditches, in addition to approach roads.

253rd Tunnelling Company sent one section to each
Corps of the Fifth Army to work with the Tramways Companies, laying and maintaining light railway tracks to battery
positions from lorry stands.   In many of the dugout
systems, electric light plant was installed and maintained
by the Australian Electrical and Mechanical Mining and
Boring Company.

The Fifth Army attack opened on the 31st July, 1917.
The Germans were awaiting it, but in one sector they were
taken by surprise.   The heap of spoil from the Lancashire
Farm series of dugouts had grown to an enormous size.
The Germans drew the only apparent inference—mining.
Knowing our conservative methods, the Germans were
convinced that, as at Messines, our attack would be pre-
ceeded by mines, the firing of which would be the signal
for their artillery to open fire.   But there were no mines ;
consequently their barrage was late in falling, which was
a decided advantage to the attacking troops—who swarmed
over and captured the enemy's position all along the front,
with the result that his mines at Railway Wood and Tor
Top fell into our possession.

III

Generally speaking, the German was a good miner and
did excellent work in a thorough and efficient manner.   He

was very tenacious, and at crater fighting he had no superior. When a crater was made, no matter on what part of the front, a party was always at hand to rush forward and seize the near lip, fortify it, and sap back to the front trench. In the early days, at least, these parties were equipped with steel shields. Placed on the flanks, they afforded ample protection for snipers, who successfully prevented any interference with the consolidating party.

The Germans also made extensive use of boring, both hand or manual and power machines being used. The early models suffered from the same defect as our first blowers—they were far too noisy. A boring machine used in the vicinity of Hill 60 made such a row that it even provoked the phlegmatic Teutons to mirth. When the machine started working they began to laugh, and it was audibly suggested that, even if the British were not blown, they would at least be frightened by the noise of the machine !

Timbering was always very well done in the German galleries. It surprised us to find how lavish the enemy was in its use. Even in hard chalk all galleries were close timbered. It is not generally known why this was done— it was unnecessary to support the roof and sides, the normal functions of timbering. The explanation is to be found in the following extract from old German Mining Regulations, captured at Fricourt in July, 1916. " Work in galleries with frames at intervals can be heard farther than in galleries that are completely cased in."

It may have prevented efficient listening also, as an extract from a mining officer's diary, dated 1.5.16, also captured at Fricourt, reads : " It is not at all clear how the enemy, at a considerable depth (35 metres) can work his way past our workings without being noticed." This is an unsolicited testimonial to the efficiency of the British Tunneller !

One decisive advantage rested with the British through-out the War—our rate of progress, our speed of driving galleries, whether in chalk or clay, was far superior to that of our opponents. This information was first gained in June, 1915, by 174th Company at Houplines, and was confirmed many times afterwards. The practice of each shift of marking its progress on the timbers gave us the speed per foot driven. It proved that the German rate was only two-thirds that of our own. It enabled us, with confidence, to listen to the approach of an hostile gallery towards Hill 60 mine in the full assurance that it would not intercept our gallery before zero day.

Further, as a rule we were quicker to get into our galleries after a blow, either our own or the enemy's, than were the Germans. This enabled us to " nip round the blow," and in about thirty-six hours, or less, after we had been blown. We would then be in an even stronger position than previously. This can be partially accounted for by the fact that every charge fired destroys a small length of the firer's own gallery. Often we would drive out beyond the face of our original gallery for days before we heard the Germans coming in to clean up their side of the blow. It was by this method that we were able to drive the enemy back to the middle of No Man's Land and pin him there, even after he had blown our front line.

Thus his advantage of an early start was countered by the speed and determination of our miners. All along the front could be found evidence of this. That we did not profit to the full extent is accounted for by the fact that on most fronts we were restricted to a policy of defensive mining. That is to say, we were content to stave off enemy underground offensives, and to keep him at a respectable distance from our line, and were not permitted to follow up and exploit our success. It cannot be doubted that in purely offensive mining we were superior to the Germans. Messines clearly proves this.

We identified over fifty Mining, Pioneer Mining, and Miscellaneous Mining Companies along the front. These formations were smaller than ours, usually about two hundred and fifty to four hundred strong, with only a few officers. It frequently happened that some of the officers were not mining men—they were in command largely for disciplinary purposes. This may perhaps explain the rather mechanical nature of some of the German mining warfare.

The German was a clean, hard-fighting opponent in this strange underground battle which raged continuously for three years. The Tunnellers respected him highly—until he invented booby traps.

IV

There was now no serious mining activity north of the Lys or south of Hill 70 ; thus, as after the Somme attack, the activities of the Tunnelling Companies were diverted to more general work. Parties of Tunnellers followed each successive attack in the weary Passchendaele series to reconnoitre enemy dugouts and shelters, while large numbers were employed in road repairs, pipe laying, digging cable trenches, salving tanks that had become bogged, booby trapping and similar tasks.

For months, far into the winter, the advance dragged doggedly on towards Passchendaele Ridge, the Germans contesting every inch of the water-logged, shell-riven ground, which had now become a veritable Serbonian quagmire, over which it was impossible to pass except on duck-board tracks, plank roads, or light railways, of which miles were laid by the Tunnellers.

In places mined dugouts were put in to provide winter accommodation, and hundreds of elephant shelters were erected ; pill boxes were pumped out, drained, cleaned and made habitable by blocking up the entrances and cutting new ones the other side, i.e. making them about turn, while in less exposed and less advanced positions, numerous hutment camps were erected ; round each hut a sandbag barrier was erected as a protection from the incessant bombing. Day and night enemy planes pounded the Salient, especially the vicinity of Ypres and the canal, which no doubt offered a good target even at night.

In a letter from the Commander-in-Chief to the Engineer-in-Chief the following minute occurs :

" Please convey my hearty congratulations to the Tunnelling and Electrical Mining Companies on the splendid work which they accomplished in connection with the operations of the Fifth Army on 31st July, 1917. That so large a programme of work was completed in such a short time and in spite of great difficulties, reflects the greatest credit on all ranks, and shows with what spirit and energy everyone must have worked."

(Intd.) D. H.,

7th Sept., 1917.

Nevertheless, to Tunnellers—as to other arms engaged —Passchendaele lacked the thrills of Messines ! Infantry, tanks, artillery, engineers—all complained that the terrain was quite hopeless from their point of view. Yet the battle dragged on for three weary months. The only consolation —a poor one—is that the enemy was just as uncomfortable and nerve-strained as we were.

CHAPTER XII

THE MARCH RETREAT, 1918

I

THE year 1917 was a disappointing one. Begun with such high hopes, it had ended in gloom. The early British success at Arras had been followed by the French failure on the Aisne, the brilliance of Messines dimmed by the misty swamps of Passchendaele, and the tank break-through at Cambrai hopelessly outweighed by the Italian debacle at Caporetto. To crown the misfortunes of the Allies, Russia had plunged into the long-expected revolution and had passed out of the War.

The German policy for 1918 was an obvious one—taking advantage of the defection of Russia, a million men could be transferred to the Western front, thereby giving Germany a numerical advantage there for the first time since 1914 ; these new armies must be hurled against the exhausted British and French troops before the Americans could lend effective aid. The necessary plans were executed with true German efficiency ; three separate attacks were planned ; for these, the first was doomed by circumstances rather than forethought to be the greatest.

It opened on 21st March, 1918. Its primary object was to drive a wedge into the weakest part of the front, the junction of the French and British Armies. The next step would be to roll up the British flank to the north, leaving a wide gap through which masses of troops would pour to victory.

The attack was launched on a front of over sixty miles, from the Scarpe to the Oise. The Third Army was holding a front of more than twenty miles from north of the Scarpe to a point near Gouzeaucourt. It had been some time in this area and the line had been continuously strengthened.

The line was intersected, at more or less regular intervals, by the Scarpe, Cojeul, and Sensée rivers and by the Canal du Nord.

After months of floundering in the mud between Ypres and Passchendaele, the Fifth Army, towards the end of 1917, was withdrawn. Its units went into the line again on the right of the Third Army, taking over some new ground from the French. Actually they held a front of over forty miles from Gouzeaucourt to Barisis—a quiet sector, but, owing to its length, only thinly held because of lack of troops. It was something of a paradox that at the moment when the German army was strongest, the British was weakest. Most units were far below strength —the necessary reinforcements were either retained in England as a consequence of the mutual distrust existing between Haig and Mr. Lloyd George, or were irreplaceably buried in the swamps of Passchendaele.

The greater part of the line lay between two canal systems running in a general north and south direction. In front and not very far off, were the St. Quentin Canal and Oise just above La Fére, while behind and further away ran the Canal du Nord and the Crozat Canal.

II

This, perhaps the most colossal of all battles on the Western Front, has been refought—on paper—many times since 1918, and most readers will be acquainted with its main features. Here, of course, it is only proposed to follow the work of the Tunnellers. Battle stations had been selected and prepared, and in several cases practice in manning them had been carried out. Signs were not lacking that an attack was imminent. R.A.F. reports were confirmed by prisoners and deserters. A prisoner captured near St. Quentin gave 20th or 21st March as the probable date. On another part of the front a number of small balloons, liberated by the Germans, drifted across to our lines. Attached to these were illustrated pamphlets setting

R

forth the advantage of surrendering to the Germans.   This seed fell upon stony ground !

At about 4.30 a.m. on 21st March, a withering barrage, in which gas shells were freely used, crashed down upon the front ; it continued, with varying intensity, for several hours.   Then, plunging into a sea of thick mist which had been intensified into a fog by the smoke and gas from the bursting shells, the enemy advanced.

Meeting with stiff resistance at first, especially from the Third Army, which generally occupied highly fortified positions, the enemy suffered heavy losses.   But his superior numbers enabled him soon to overrun the front line trench system.   Most of the Tunnelling Companies became involved in the fighting, especially those sections working in advanced areas, and sustained heavy casualties.   Long-established conditions changed in a day.   The Tunnellers, who had been accustomed to long periods in settled billets or camps, found themselves involved in another phase of their varied career, a war of movement.   Day after day found them hurriedly evacuating camp ; continually marching and counter-marching ; digging and holding posts ; beating off attacks and counter-attacking ; bombing and machine-gunning and executing all the tactical manœuvres usually regarded as the prerogative of infantry.   In addition, a number of road craters were blown, and bridges and other works destroyed or prepared for demolition. Large dumps of stores, ammunition and materials were jettisoned, sacrificed in a holocaust of destruction lest they should fall into enemy hands.   These tasks were willingly undertaken, and served to bring out the best spirit of all ranks.

Once again the detailed stories of the individual companies will be considered from north to south of the battle area.   In the Bullecourt Sector, 174th Company suffered severely—one section losing two officers and thirty-seven other ranks.   They were working on machine-gun emplacements, and with them was a fatigue party of about thirty machine-gunners.   The whole party, under Second-Lieutenant Macdonald, acted as infantry when the assault developed, and were last seen holding a piece of line near

Railway Reserve. During the next week this Company dug and wired over 9,000 yards of trench and cleared out caves at Monchy-au-Bois.

The Hermies Catacombs, caves capable of holding some hundreds of men, were entered by two inclines. Off the western entrance was a power plant for lighting the caves and pumping drinking water from a well to a water point in the eastern entrance. 175th Company prepared each entrance for demolition by placing charges of two tons of ammonal. These were fired by an N.C.O. of the Company after the infantry had evacuated the village.

A charge of 600 lbs. of Blastine was placed by the New Zealand Tunnelling Company in an old German dugout under the Cambrai Road. This charge was fired by the 15th Division, while the Germans were advancing. The New Zealanders also mined the railway and the Blangy-Fampoux and the Blangy-Feuchy Roads.

252nd Company blew a crater in No Man's Land on the main Cambrai Road at a place called Scott's Farm, 200 yards from the German wire. Two other charges were placed at Boursies and handed over to Field Companies. Two more were placed in galleries driven off a dugout beneath the Cambrai Road. These charges were not fired, as the N.C.O. detailed to fire them was badly wounded for a second time. He had previously blown in a well after receiving his first wound.

Unable to carry out some of the tasks allotted to it, owing to the rapid advance of the enemy, the 2nd Australian Tunnelling Company nevertheless did good work in saving the bulk of its stores, tools and equipment in face of heavy transport difficulties.

On the fourth day of the retirement it was instructed to mine the main Albert-Bapaume Road. A section of 179th Company, which was in touch with the Australians, offered to save time and labour by placing the mines in old dugouts and mine galleries, with which they were familiar, having mined this sector prior to the July, 1916, attack. Although great difficulty was experienced in getting explosives, these mines were placed and fired, cratering the road in three places.

The Third Army Mine School was working on the Army Reserve Line under the C.R.E. Defence Zone. After the attack, the personnel returned to their units, as it was unlikely they would be used again as a school.

III

There were eight Tunnelling Companies in the Fifth Army area. Of this number, six were concentrated in the vicinity of the Péronne bridgehead, a very important strategic position about midway along the VII and XIX Corps fronts, though somewhat to the rear. The severity of the barrage put down by the enemy left no doubt as to his intensions, and soon after it began most of the Companies " stood to." 172nd Company was working on a new line, Lanchy to Bray St. Christophe, and also a switch line Douilly-Matigny in the XIX Corps area. On receiving orders from Corps, " Man Battle Stations," the sections took up their allotted positions, which they held until relieved by infantry. The parties detailed for bridge demolitions also took up their stations.

No. 1 Section dug in near Villecholes. About midday a strong force of the enemy was seen advancing from Maissemy. This section advanced in company with 12th Notts and Derby Regiment and dug in on a new line some 300 yards in advance. In the evening 900 yards of concertina wire were laid. The following day the work was completed on the two trench lines mentioned above, but these could not be held owing to the collapse of the flanks. By this time the enemy was in force at St. Simon, but the bridge across the Somme was destroyed. Another bridge at Ollezy was also destroyed in face of heavy shell fire.

173rd Company was at work on the " Green " Line, making machine-gun posts and dugouts, detachments of 171st Labour Company and 15th Entrenching Battalion assisting. The Company received orders to withdraw and eventually fell back to Wiencourt. 253rd Company was then also at Wiencourt, where they found billets in a prisoners of war camp opposite the R.E. dump. Here both companies took part in a most unusual incident. French troops were coming up to relieve the battered British battalions, but, owing to a rumour that the enemy cavalry had broken through, there occurred a remarkable stampede of troops, wagons and motor lorries along the Guillaucourt-Marcelcave Road. 173rd Company " stood to," and officers were despatched to reconnoitre forward roads. In the meantime a piano was brought to the road-side and a Tunneller officer who was something of a musician thumped out popular airs. Even the martial strains of the Marseillaise were not sufficiently compelling to prevent our French allies quitting the stage.

253rd Company also tried to stop the panic. Its measures were more severely practical. The O.C. and officers turned out, and instead of a piano brought out some lorries, which they placed across the road. The Company " stood to " in Wiencourt Dump, and a picquet was placed on the road to stop all troops. This had the desired effect. Order was restored within an hour, and the Company retired to billets.

About this time reports were current of cases of Germans, dressed as British officers, mixing with our troops and spreading false reports of enemy successes and ordering our troops to retire. In the confusion which prevailed it would not have been a difficult matter for enemy agents to do this. Perhaps the stampede referred to above was caused in this way. There seems to have been no other reason for it.

In the following days 173rd Company carried out a number of demolitions of bridges over the Somme at Frise, Cerisy and Sailly-Lorette. They also blew up bridges over the Avre and Luce and an ammunition dump, and burned the dump at Wiencourt.

All this time the enemy gradually but surely had forced us back, and was now drawing nearer and nearer to Amiens. Soon he would be within striking distance of the town itself. Should Amiens fall a smashing blow would be dealt to the Allied cause, the moral effect of which would do incalculable harm, apart from the loss of a very important rail junction. And yet Amiens was secondary among

Ludendorff's aims, but its capture would made easier the rolling up of the British flank.

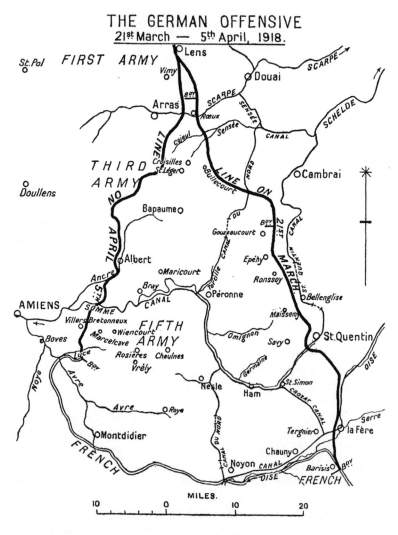

The situation had become very grave. The continual combat, always against superior odds, had depleted sadly our fighting units—divisions had dwindled to a mere handful of troops, battalions to a few dozen weary men, worn out with fighting and marching on short rations and little or no rest. Exhausted men sat or fell by the wayside ; there they slept, careless of their fate.

Reserves of fresh troops were no longer available. Here and there tattered remnants and stragglers were collected and welded into composite units together with lines of communication troops. It was into such a unit, collected and placed in position by General Grant, Chief Engineer of the Fifth Army, and later known as Carey's Force, that 253rd Company became absorbed.

Carey's Force was one of many such forces hastily collected—though nevertheless foreseen—and thrown into positions as stop gaps. It consisted of about two thousand troops, and was posted along a front of eight miles between Mericourt l'Abbé on the Ancre and Aubercourt on the Luce. This line ran in front of Marcelcave, and in this section 253rd Company was posted on March 26th and prepared defensive posts. The following day a series of adjustments went on, during which the Company front was altered several times in the vicinity of the Cemetery. These moves considerably interfered with the preparation of the posts.

A warning was received that the enemy had reached La Motte. Early on the 28th, the 61st Division arrived to attack La Motte. By noon the assault began, but met with no success. Then, after a sharp bombardment of Marcelcave, during which Company H.Q. received two direct hits, the Germans launched a counter-attack and, pressing forward, gained the village about dusk. Owing to the blackness of the night and a drenching rain, the Company became scattered, but later a post was established on the road behind Marcelcave, and contact made with troops on the left flank. In order to strengthen the position, the commanding officer, Major Currie, went to the cross roads and succeeded in collecting about two hundred and fifty men. These he used as supports and, placing them in position, they soon dug in. Currie then took a small party into Demuin, on the south side of the Luce, and salved a quantity of ammunition and rations, which were brought to the troops, the village being shelled at the time.

At 4 a.m. on March 30th, all available officers and men of the Company took up a position on the road near Hangard.   An attack developed almost at once, and the troops on the right were compelled to retire.   A patrol sent into Démuin had a brush with a few of the enemy, who retired after the exchange of a few shots.   This patrol remained there while a large party was sent to clear the village.

Troops were seen to be falling back from behind Marcel-cave, and an attempt was made to support them, but ultimately the whole party had to be withdrawn, falling back on to other troops, where a stand was made.   During these movements the various units became hopelessly mixed, and any sort of cohesion was impossible.   Troops in support refused to leave their position and go forward, saying they were " acting under the orders of their own Battalion Commanders."

253rd Company became so scattered that small groups of men attached themselves to any unit, however fragmentrary, in their vicinity.   A disjointed battle developed and continued until dusk, when reliefs began to arrive.   The Company were ordered to Boves, a rendezvous being arranged at Cambos Farm, and here the survivors eventually gathered, the Company having suffered one hundred casualties during the fighting.

177th Company also was working on the " Green " Line, building machine-gun posts and dugouts for crews. Their line ran from Manancourt through Nurlu and Templeux to Trincourt.   Normal work was carried on until noon on the 22nd—an indication that the advance had not been quite so rapid in this sector.   By this time the infantry were falling back on the " Green " Line.   Every assistance was given the infantry to locate the dugouts.

Three bridges over the Somme at Halle and four between Cléry and Omiécourt, and also a trestle bridge west of Cléry, were prepared for demolition.   On the 23rd the 17th Entrenching Battalion retired across the Halle bridge at 6.30 p.m., reporting that it was in touch with the enemy. Soon after a force of Germans was seen 200 yards west of Halle, and the charges were successfully fired.   At one bridge an anti-aircraft lorry had fallen partly through. It was fired, setting alight the bridge and destroying several spans.

The remnants of the 9th Division were crossing the Cléry-Omiécourt bridge under heavy machine-gun fire from the enemy ; the only remaining bridge, that over the canal, was destroyed at 9 p.m. The girders were cut near the north pier and dropped into the canal. A pair of lock gates were rendered useless, and the long trestle bridge west of Cléry was set on fire. Lieutenant Cartwright and a party, who had been left at Bray, destroyed the pumping station.

Sections of 178th Company were at Fins, Gouzeacourt Wood and Heudicourt, all these places coming under a heavy bombardment, gas shells being freely used. All sections " stood to " in their box-respirators, Nos. 3 and 4 taking up previously allotted positions east of Heudicourt. These two sections remained in the trenches all day under shell fire. The Company Medical Officer, Captain Harlow, R.A.M.C., remained with them, treating the infantry wounded coming down from the line.

For the next day or so the Company did nothing but fall back. Then a party was dispatched to carry out demolitions of bridges over the Tortille River between Moislains and Péronne, and seven bridges were destroyed. All our transport and guns were safely across before the charge exploded.

At Ribémont orders were received to prepare for demolition all bridges over the River Ancre between Méaulte and Mericourt-l'Abbé. Of the ten bridges, four were prepared and handed over to Field Companies. Later the Company prepared a number of road mines and bridge demolition, and the Somme canal at Lamotte-Brebière was prepared for flooding the south side of the river by cutting sluices in the bank.

The commanding officers report read : " The Company has been remarkably fortunate during the retreat. Owing to the fine resistance offered by the 9th Division, the enemy never broke through, and it was possible to retreat at normal pace, without fighting."

After Ronssoy had been captured, 180th Company manned the "Brown" Line between St. Emilie and Ronssoy and held it for four hours. Several parties of the enemy approaching the position were repulsed, and casualties estimated at about two hundred were inflicted on them. A Lewis gun, salved from a nearby battery position, did particularly good work and greatly assisted in beating off the attackers. Later the Tunnellers were relieved by infantry and withdrew to Hamelet.

On the 23rd Péronne was evacuated, and when the enemy was close to the town the bridges were destroyed. At this time the town was deserted and in flames and being heavily shelled. On the 26th four bridges on the Cappy Road and a large double road bridge at Bray were destroyed.

The Company Commander, Major Johnston, then discovered that the double railway bridge at Bray was not completely demolished—by special arrangement of G.H.Q. the destruction of railway bridges had been left to the French, who let us down rather badly. Securing the small quantity of explosive remaining at Bray, and with the aid of four men from the 7th/8th Royal Inniskilling Fusiliers, he was able to render the bridge impassable to cavalry. At 7 p.m. the same day Sailly Lorette was evacuated, and the outposts withdrawn. The party from 180th Company who were standing by the bridges waited four hours to allow any stragglers to get through before they blew up the four bridges. During the retreat this unit destroyed twenty-one bridges, two camps, a large R.E. dump and many billets.

The sections of 182nd Company were spread over a wide area, and it was with difficulty that they were collected. All available men were ordered to proceed to Fargnier and to work forward from there in an easterly direction. At Fargnier they got in touch with the 2nd/4th Royal Fusiliers, and proceeding through a heavy barrage they reinforced the garrisons holding out in Nos. 1 and 2 Keeps.

No. 2 Section, under Captain Godson, went forward to assist a machine-gun post east of the Cemetery. It was decided to improve the position here by extending along Fermin Alley, held by the enemy. A bombing party was formed and the enemy driven back to our wire, where a post was established. The enemy made several attacks, but on each occasion he was driven off, two well-placed Lewis guns giving valuable assistance and inflicting heavy losses.

Considerable trouble was caused by a German machine-gun placed in some housetops. The Forward Observation Officer of the Royal Horse Artillery spotted this gun, and a few well directed salvos succeeded in silencing it for a time.

While the commanding officer of the Company, Major Mulqueen, was making a reconnaissance of the houses east of the church, a machine-gun opened fire on the party. It seemed that the enemy was working towards the centre of the village. Both field gun and 6 inch howitzer fire, directed on to the spot, soon silenced the machine-gun and no further trouble was experienced from that quarter. About midnight Fargnier was evacuated.

On 24th March the Company dug a line of posts about 1,000 yards east of Babœuf for the 18th Division, after which they marched to Varesnos.

The following day the enemy heavily shelled the bridge over the canal on the Noyon-Varesnos Road, and the Company was ordered forward to build a foot bridge in case the main bridge should be destroyed. One of the Company officers writes of this incident as follows : " The Tunnellers formed up in perfect order and marched back to the bridge, the men singing popular airs, while the scattered and broken infantry of all kinds hurried past in the opposite direction." It was found impossible, however, to construct the bridge for lack of material. The party, therefore, was taken across the main bridge and dug a line of posts on the south side of the Oise north and east of Varesnos. This party was spotted and came in for some shelling, but no attempt was made by the Germans to advance towards the bridge.

Later the same day the Company was ordered " to dig in and hold till further orders " a position on the south of the Oise to the west of Bretigny. On reaching the position, patrols were sent out on each flank, but except for some retiring French soldiers, they failed to find touch

with any other troops.   The night was very dark and the
Tunnellers felt completely isolated, and though they kept
perfectly cool, they were indeed relieved when orders were
received to withdraw.

IV

The attack had been in progress about five days when
the situation became very precarious.   Our supply of fresh
reserves was almost completely exhausted.   In consequence
two emergency battalions were formed from the XIX Corps
R.E. Troops.   The 173rd and 258th Tunnelling Companies, 5th Field Squadron and four Army Troops Companies provided the personnel for these units.

All the fit men from the above were drafted to No. 1
Battalion, which was to be a fighting unit, commanded by
Major Buchanan, R.E., of the 5th Field Squadron.   Many
of the men were without equipment, but this was overcome by borrowing from No. 2 Battalion.

The older and unfit men formed No. 2 Battalion, under
Major Lowry, R.E., commanding officer of 173rd Company,
and were intended for demolition work.   It is not proposed
to follow the movements of the whole battalion, but only
of " A " and " B " Companies, which were composed of
officers and men from 173rd and 258th Tunnelling Companies respectively.   " A " Company was commanded by
Captain Jack, R.E., and assembled at Bayonvillers, where
H.Q. was established, and was ordered to Vrély.   Here it was
to assist the 15th Entrenching Battalion, but failed to locate
it in the confusion.   In the meantime Major Mair, G.S.O.2
of the 24th Division, ordered the Company to take up
line on the right of " B " Company, in front of Vrély and
600 yards west of Méharicourt, and to dig in and hold on.
Subsequently it was placed in support to " B " Company
and a fire trench dug.

The 20th Entrenching Battalion, on the left, sent out
a patrol, and reported seeing a strong enemy patrol in
Méharicourt, where no doubt the enemy was concentrating
for an attack.   It developed the following morning.
Under a barrage of field guns, machine-guns and trench-

mortars the enemy attacked down the valley from Méharicourt. "B" Company and the troops on their left were forced back, leaving both "A" Company's flanks exposed. Seeing this, the enemy established machine-guns to enfilade the position, and "A" Company also had to retire, a movement carried out in good order. By this time the reserves had retired, for no apparent reason, but when the reserve trench was reached a counter-attack was organized. Assisted by a company of the Notts and Derby Pioneers, the Tunnellers cleared the Germans from the front line. In their haste to leave, the Germans left behind five machine-guns.

In spite of accidental shelling of our line by our own artillery, the situation was restored and touch established with troops on the left, though the right flank was still uncertain. "A" Company returned to support again, while a detachment of Notts and Derby Pioneers took over the front line, with the 20th Entrenching Battalion in reserve.

At midnight on 27th–28th March, the troops were seen retiring from the front line, and also the supports, the commanding officer considering that he could no longer hold the line and must withdraw. This movement exposed "A" Company's right, but the 20th Entrenching Battalion sent out a platoon to protect it. The enemy then put down a heavy machine-gun barrage, accompanied by H.E. and shrapnel, followed by a strong infantry attack ; the Company was forced to fall back south-west of Vrély. Here it got into touch with the 15th Entrenching Battalion and went into action in front of Le Quesnel. An enemy attack was beaten off, but he renewed the attack with greater force and our troops fell back on to Beaucourt. The next day "A" moved to Boves, where it rejoined 173rd Tunnelling Company.

It will be seen that "A" Company—comprising the greater portion of 173rd Tunnelling Company—had fought as infantry for several successive days. They had successfully carried out one of the most difficult of all military operations—a rear-guard action. They had stood up to enemy attacks of all kinds without flinching, had never

lost their nerve, had suffered severe casualties, but had
never fallen back without orders.　It is almost comic to
record that, three years previously, the men of this company
had sent a deputation to their commanding officer, protesting
that drill of any kind was not included in their contract !

"B" Company of the emergency battalion was formed
from 258th Tunnelling Company, under Captain Gilchrist,
R.E., of that Company, and included four other officers and
one hundred and ninety-two other ranks.　In the evening of
25th March, 1918, the day the battalion was formed,
"B" Company was exercised in manual drill and infantry
movement—surely a little late in the day for such exercises !
But the following day the men were engaged in work at
which they had few equals—digging in.　A line was dug
in front of Risieres, and a junction was made with the 24th
Division on the left.　Scarcely had a line of posts been
completed than an enemy patrol was located in Méharicourt,
immediately in advance of the Company's front.　The
Company was now holding about five hundred yards of the
front line on the right flank of the 8th Division, the 20th
Entrenching Battalion having taken over the posts previously dug.　An attempted enemy advance was effectively
dealt with by rifle fire.

Just before dusk on the 26th, the troops on the right
retired, leaving "B" Company's flank "in the air," so a
few posts were thrown out to protect it.　These posts
were at fairly wide intervals, and a ration party, stumbling
between two posts, were surprised to find themselves confronted by two German officers !　On being called upon
to surrender, two of the party, Sappers Quinn and Marshall,
decided to make a dash for liberty.　A fusillade of bully
beef tins (loaded) surprised the Germans, while the two
men turned and fled, making good their escape, but not
before one had been wounded.　Later the second man
was also wounded.　The third man remained a prisoner.
It is not known how the Germans appreciated our
rations !

A party of the enemy collected in some disused gun-
pits about eighty yards away.　Some of them advanced
towards our trenches, indicating an apparent willingness

to surrender.   On being fired upon, however, they immediately returned the fire and retired.   Well directed rifle fire from the left flank dislodged the party from the gun-pits. During the night all the posts were linked up into a continuous line.

The next day (27th) heavy artillery fire was directed on to the front and parts of the line gave way ; " B " Company fell back on to Vrély.   Later a counter-attack drove the enemy back to his old position.   The Sherwood Foresters took up the front line position, while " B " Company filled a gap in the support line, linking up with " A " Company and the 20th Entrenching Battalion.   The morning of the next day saw a repetition of the previous day's tactics— heavy shelling of the front line, and a consequent retreat to the supports.   Continued enemy pressure forced the whole line to retire through Vrély.   This movement was well executed, the troops moving back in open order.   A stand was made behind Vrély, and again, with the assistance of some stragglers, who threw in their lot with the Company, on a ridge farther back.   Both positions were soon abandoned and " B " Company eventually reached Moreuil.

By this time the men were beginning to show signs of the strain of continual marching, digging and fighting without adequate rest, so they were billeted for the night. Then, proceeding to Jumel, the rallying point for the 8th Division, the G.O.C. of that division expressed the opinion that " the Tunnelling Companies had done exceedingly well."   By this time adequate reserves were arriving on the scene of action ; so, having successfully completed the tasks for which they were formed, the two R.E. Battalions were disbanded, the surviving troops returning to their respective units.

v

No. 2 R.E. Battalion, also formed on the 25th March, 1918, was under the command of Major Lowry, O.C. 173rd Tunnelling Company.   Assembling at Wiencourt, its chief functions were to prepare and carry out demolitions, bridging, or any other urgent R.E. work.   Its activities covered a large area between Péronne and Amiens. Certain bridges over the Somme west of Péronne, and those over the Luce from Démuin, inclusive, westward, were prepared for destruction, together with four bridges at Villers Bretonneux. Most of these bridges were blown up between the 26th and 29th March. Several R.E. dumps were also destroyed.

As stated above, the two emergency battalions were broken up on 31st March, 1918. But the same day two other R.E. groups were formed. Each group consisted of one Tunnelling Company and two or three Army Troops Companies. The two Tunnelling Companies concerned were 173rd and 258th, and in each case the O.C. Tunnelling Company was commanding the Group—Majors Lowry and Pope respectively.

Their chief work was to prepare and carry out demolitions of bridges. The necessity for this wholesale destruction of bridges is not far to seek—one glance at the map will suffice. To the east of Amiens a number of tributaries join the Somme. On the north bank there are the Hallue and the Ancre, while on the south is the Avre with its two tributaries, the Noye and the Luce. These streams flow from five points of the compass, N., N.E., E., S.E., and S., and following the valley of each, except the Somme and the Luce, is a railway line, all converging on Amiens, the immediate goal of the enemy. While no railway line follows the course of the Somme River, there is another form of transport, a canal, while south of the river and parallel to its general direction are the road to St. Quentin and the railway line to Ham.

For us time was of great importance. The longer the enemy could be held off, the less likely he was of achieving his objective. Therefore, as we were forced to yield ground, the final work of delay was to destroy the bridges in the face of the advancing enemy, thereby holding up his advance until such time as he was able to construct temporary structures to take the place of those destroyed.

The reason for this work being allotted to the Tunnellers was that they were accustomed to the use of high explosives. So the bridges across the Avre from Castel northwards, and those over the Noye from Ailly-sur-Noye northwards, both inclusive, were prepared for demolition.

At Boves No. 2 Group erected a pontoon bridge, and carried out work on the Gentelles switch line, while on the night of 3rd–4th April a series of traversed posts was dug east of Villers Bretonneux. In the morning they were forced to leave their billet on account of heavy shelling.

No. 1 Group prepared the bridges across the Celle, from Vers to Amiens. By this time, however, French reinforcements were arriving on the scene, the work handed over, the R.E. Groups were disbanded.

VI

It will have been seen that during this epic battle the Tunnellers had acted in every capacity except that of Tunnellers. Their conduct won them new laurels : those called upon to man trenches, to advance against the enemy, or to fight rear-guard actions had done a man's job with coolness, determination and courage. They had suffered severe casualties—in some cases amounting to more than a third of their effectives. Yet, when a perilous task was involved—the destruction of a bridge under enemy fire —there never was need to call for volunteers ; each man simply took his turn—the Tunnellers' creed includes the phrase, " all in a day's work."

Yet, in spite of the tragedies and excitements of the battle, it was something of an anti-climax after the glories of Messines. Though they might be so adaptable as to serve as emergency infantry or field engineers, Tunnellers were Tunnellers. In the long run it does not pay to use up your specialist corps—they are not easy to replace.

The Fifth Army was greatly undermanned, and was continually crying for more labour for the construction of forward strong points and rear defence. For such essential tasks the Tunnellers were withdrawn from their proper sphere. The game of " if " is never unpleasant and often illuminating. Suppose the Tunnellers of the Fifth Army

S

had tunnelled ?   If the effect of the Messines mines had been so shattering in blowing half-empty trenches, what would have been the effect of a similar series of mines, blown at the moment of assault on 21st March, under trenches packed with troops awaiting the nervous signal to scramble over the parapet ?   In an assault the first five minutes are often decisive.

CHAPTER XIII

I

WHEN Ludendorff loosed his legions against the
Fifth Army on the Somme, he had, with true
military prudence, more than one auxiliary plan
in his pocket should the first one fail. Despite the
apparently spectacular success of the Somme attack, it had
failed, and Ludendorff knew it : he had not broken the
British and French armies asunder—he had not even
captured the vital railway junction of Amiens. Consequently he turned to the nearest of his alternatives—for
his plan was to batter the British Army to impotence before
overwhelming the French.

Nevertheless, he had raided his reserves in a desperate
attempt to exploit his success on the Somme, and his
offence in the Lys Valley was considerably abbreviated as
compared with the original scheme. But his chances of
victory were considerable. A great part of the front was
held by divisions which had been terribly mauled in the
fighting on the Somme ; an important sector was held by
the Portuguese—men who had no real interest in the War.
Here, too, the rewards of success would be overwhelming.
On the Somme front an advance of forty miles meant little ;
on the Lys a similar advance would put the Channel ports
at his mercy, and would cripple the British Army. On
the Somme our line could be resilient : here it must stand
firm.

II

On the southern edge of the area selected for attack
was the village of Givenchy. This had throughout the

War been a centre of active mining, as described in Chapter VII. The whole battle sector was thoroughly organized for mining, and our defensive schemes functioned so well that the enemy was definitely held in check.

Following the events on this front described earlier, there ensued a period during which listening and pumping were systematically carried out, the former by electrical sets established at central listening stations underground and supplemented by patrols ; the latter by electrical pumps, thereby economizing in man power. Indeed, with the capture of the enemy's mines at Railway Wood and Hill 70, no more than two companies shared the front from the Lys to Hill 70—a sector of about twelve miles in length—a front which had remained stationary since the commencement of mining. Between the Lys and the La Bassée Canal 251st Company, with the assistance of the newly arrived Portuguese Mining Company (which was placed in the charge of Captain D. Ivor Evans, M.C.), mounted guard, while 170th Company was south of the canal, where a continuous underground lateral of about four miles in length, in front of our trenches, extended south to Hulluch ; this connected several systems and made for further economy in miners.

Givenchy was a key position of vital importance. Its loss would jeopardize the few remaining coal mines of Northern France still in the hands of the Allies. Should the output from them cease or be reduced an added burden would be thrust upon our already overtaxed and harassed shipping ; and our mining resources at home, already suffering from the loss of so many good miners serving with the forces overseas, would be hard put to make up the deficiency of coal required both by the army in the field and the French civilian population. For this, and other reasons, a further strengthening of the Givenchy defences was undertaken.

To ensure access to our mines in the event of the enemy overrunning our first line and gaining possession of the shaft heads, a long tunnel, Bunny Hutch Subway, was driven back from the mine system until it came to surface on the rear slope of Givenchy Ridge near Moat Farm, well behind our support line. Off this tunnel the mining officers' dugout was made. It had a spiral stairway exit leading up into Caledonian Road, the communicating trench, while further forward of this an incline shaft, Piccadilly, provided the chief connection with the surface. But the *pièce de résistance* was just behind our support line, which ran along the crest of the ridge. Here a strong and extensive dugout system, capable of holding two battalions if necessary, was constructed, having a minimum head-cover of 40 feet, a thickness capable of withstanding the severest bombardment. It connected two strong points, Givenchy Keep and Marie Redoubt, some three hundred yards apart, to each of which shafts gave access. Three wide exits driven at an easy incline permitted rapid entry of the garrison into the support line direct in case of necessity, while three vertical steel-lined shafts, used in making the dugouts, provided good ventilation and con-tained the pumping equipment necessary to keep the system free from water. A borehole down to the chalk ensured a plentiful supply of good fresh water, while tiers of bunks provided good sleeping accommodation for the infantry garrison. A power house at Pont Fixe supplied power for lighting and pumping, the equipment for which was installed and run by the ubiquitous A. E. & M. M. & B. Company.

A feature of the shafts was the large specially reinforced concrete " hood " over each of them, as much as 100 tons of concrete as well as hundreds of steel railway rails being used in one " hood " alone.

Of the numerous machine-gun pill boxes constructed in this area, one had no less than 200 tons of reinforced concrete put into it before it was considered strong enough. It had been foreseen that they would probably have to undergo an extremely heavy and persistent bombardment, hence the lavish use of concrete.

During the early part of 1918, events elsewhere necessi-tated other preparations for resisting an attack being put in hand without delay. In anticipation of a possible break through north of Givenchy, a detachment of 251st Company made a reconnaissance of ammunition dumps, with a view to their demolition, and also mined cross roads and culverts behind the Portuguese Corps. Whatever

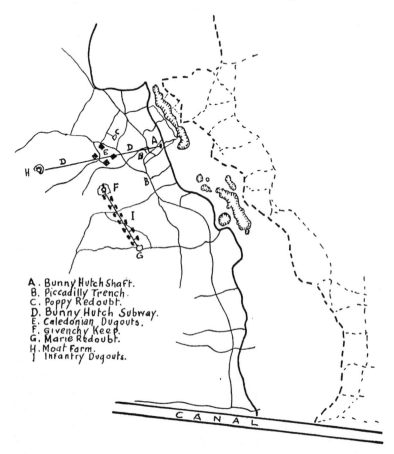

A. Bunny Hutch Shaft.
B. Piccadilly Trench.
C. Poppy Redoubt.
D. Bunny Hutch Subway.
E. Caledonian Dugouts.
F. Givenchy Keep.
G. Marie Redoubt.
H. Moat Farm.
I. Infantry Dugouts.

enemy attack might develop, no point was better prepared for its reception than was Givenchy.

III

The moment of attack was acutely chosen. Arrangements had been made to relieve the Portuguese, who were considered unreliable in an attack, but for the moment one

Portuguese division held a wide front.   Only a few hours before it would have been relieved, the blow descended with shattering effect.

Shortly after 4 on the morning of 9th April, a severe bombardment opened on a wide front—from the Lys to south of the La Bassée Canal, a stretch of ten miles, held by the Portuguese Corps on the north and our own I Corps on their right ; the 55th Division held the flank at Givenchy. The trench system was heavily pounded with shells of all sizes, and the artillery was augmented by numerous trench-mortar batteries, while roads and gun positions and back areas generally came in for a lot of gas shelling.   After slackening, the bombardment was resumed with redoubled severity about 8 o'clock, especially in the neighbourhood of Givenchy.   An hour later the enemy infantry advanced to the attack.   Although the attack had been expected for some time, the Portuguese front disintegrated so rapidly that demolition charges, already in position, were not fired. Had they been, the probability is that the enemy would not have penetrated so far or so rapidly as he did.   In fact, so little resistance was offered by the Portuguese that members of a party from 251st Company which had gone up to complete mining the culverts in their areas were never seen again.

At Givenchy events moved rapidly.   The thick mist which had enveloped the area of the attack was intensified by the smoke of bursting shells and clouds of dust.   Under its ægis the enemy came forward in two streams on either side of Givenchy.   By 9.30 they occupied the ruins of Givenchy church and established a machine-gun post there. Battalion H.Q. was attacked and Moat Farm practically surrounded.   Small parties of our infantry in saps, though isolated, still tenaciously held out.   Machine-gunners fought their guns while some of the crews drew their revolvers and shot down the enemy who had actually entered the rear compartment of their pill boxes.   Enemy patrols penetrated as far as Windy Corner, and a few men got as far as Lone Farm.

The timely precaution of blocking up solid with sandbags all shaft pent houses prevented the enemy entering and thereby gaining access to Bunny Hatch subway, in which many of our infantry sought shelter during the bombardment.

The protection afforded by the fortified entrances to Caledonian dugouts and the numerous strong points and pill boxes enabled our troops effectively to break up the attack and prevent it developing, thus robbing the enemy of the opportunity of exploiting the advantage gained from the protecting mist. But the mist no longer favoured the attackers. It cleared suddenly, exposing in the open large parties of the enemy. These were caught in a merciless fire from our machine-guns, the few who escaped being dealt with by the infantry. By evening the situation at Givenchy was restored completely, and we occupied all trenches held by us prior to the attack, although to the north the Germans had penetrated our position a considerable distance.

Soon after the bombardment began, the relief shift left 251st Company H.Q. at the Chicory Factory for Givenchy, and as the vicinity of the billets was being shelled, the remainder of the Company " stood to arms " As the morning wore on the situation gradually worsened. No instructions had reached the Company from Corps Headquarters, nor at this time could contact be made with Corps—all telephone lines were out of action. The O.C., Major Church, D.S.O., M.C., who had just taken over the Company, decided in the circumstances to move. Selecting the most essential stores from the accumulation of years, they were loaded speedily into lorries and sent off before the roads through Béthune, already being shelled with incendiary and H.E. shells, should be blocked by fallen masonry from the ruined houses or by shell craters.

The relief failed to reach Givenchy, and Captain Auret, M.C., was sent to find them and take charge. Avoiding the roads which were being searched by artillery fire, Auret made his way across country to Cambrin, but failed to find his men. Again striking across the open, he threaded his way past vacated battery positions, now being freely " peppered " with mustard gas ; at last he reached Harley Street dugouts, where he found about a dozen men, whom he ordered back to H.Q. Proceeding to the power station near Pont Fixe, the Australians running the plant informed him that it had been absolutely impossible to maintain the power lines intact (they had been laid in an open trench), and that the mines and dugouts would soon flood and become untenable. Learning that none of the morning relief had reached the trenches, Auret returned to report.

Tired out and ill from the effects of gas, Auret flung himself on his bunk to rest. His respite was brief. An hour after his return he was ordered again up the line to report at once to H.Q. 164th Brigade. From Brigade he went to Battalion H.Q. with authority to collect a working party to cover the exposed power cables, after which he was to be attached to the garrison in the trenches until further instructions.

It was with difficulty that a party was turned out, a party worn out by a day's strenuous fighting ; it seemed cruel to order them, in their exhausted condition, to undertake so arduous a task, but there was no alternative. Fortunately, the shelling had now ceased, and while the Australian electricians were mending the broken cables, the sound parts were covered up.

Then, going to Caledonian Dugouts, where Lieutenants Wood, Bendall, Gibbons and forty other ranks had already been on duty thirty-six hours, and had assisted the infantry in the fighting throughout the day, Auret assumed command and rearranged their disposition. A few men were detailed for listening and pumping in the mines ; two N.C.O.'s and a dozen men posted to Givenchy Keep ; Lieutenant Bendall and three men to the foot of Piccadilly Shaft, while Lieutenant Wood and twenty men converted No. 4 mine sap into a fire trench, which they manned. This party remained constantly on duty in the line until relieved on 17th April.

By 3 o'clock in the afternoon (9th April), a report reached Company H.Q. that Sergeant Newell and twenty men of the relief shift had taken up and were holding a position in the Sailly-Labourse—Tuning Fork line. They had found it impossible to reach Givenchy, but, determined to take a hand in things, they threw in their lot with the infantry. Later, Captain D. Ivor Evans, M.C., together with five other officers, thirty N.C.O.'s and one hundred and eighty men, proceeded to take up a defensive position between Essar and the Lawe Canal. Coming under the orders of the 166th Infantry Brigade, they remained in this locality for a week, holding trenches by day and digging support lines by night, during which time they suffered casualties both in officers and men.

On 17th April, after a period of nine days in the line, the party at Givenchy was relieved by Captain Walker, M.C., Lieutenants Rees and Marsland and thirty-nine other ranks. Owing to the situation prevailing at the time, and the strong possibility of a further German onslaught, the Tunnellers were told off to special stations to assist the infantry in resisting the threatened attack. Their positions were as follows : Lieutenant Marsland, one N.C.O. and three other ranks at Moat Farm entrance to Bunny Hutch Subway. Lieutenant Rees and a party of twenty men at No. 4 shaft pent-house and the sap leading thereto. (This was rather an exposed position, but it was excellently sited to cover the north side of Caledonian Road pent-house and Moat Farm entrance.) One N.C.O. and four men in Givenchy Keep dugout system to act as guides and maintain liaison between the garrison in Givenchy Keep and Mairie Redoubt. Colonel Evans, 1st Black Watch, approved of these dispositions on the evening of 17th April.

The Tunnellers then went about their lawful occupations of pumping, listening and maintenance in the mines, dugouts and subways.

IV

Since 9th April almost incessant shelling had been directed on Givenchy, particularly on strong points like Moat Farm and Givenchy Keep, the exact location of which, no doubt, the enemy had noted during his brief occupation. They had resisted very well, although numerous direct hits had been registered on them. Scarcely a vestige of habitable trench remained.

On 18th April, after a bombardment of unprecedented severity which lasted eight hours, during which reserve and battery positions received a continual drench of gas shelling, the enemy launched a second attack on Givenchy. Again he succeeded in overrunning the first defences, and got possession of the shaft top at Moat Farm dugouts.   A counter-attack was launched, in which the Tunnellers assisted the infantry, and relieved the pressure on the garrison in Caledonian Road pent-house.   The senior infantry officer was killed and a second attack was led by Captain Walker, R.E.   During this attack Walker was wounded severely in the leg by machine-gun fire.   He managed to crawl back to Bunny Hatch Subway, and from there he continued to direct operations, and continually urged NO surrender !   The Tunnellers were now the only defenders of the Moat Farm entrance.   Beaten back from the entrance by bombs, they built a barricade farther back.

By early afternoon the subway had become congested with wounded, estimated at about two hundred.   The enemy had gained possession of the entrances, and threatened to spray down gas unless the garrison surrendered.   The hopelessness of the situation was further aggravated by the fact that supplies of bombs and ammunition had given out.   In order to save the wounded further unnecessary suffering therefore, no further resistance was offered, and all the troops in the subway, including the survivors of two companies of the 1st Black Watch of the 1st Division were taken prisoner.   They were ordered by the Germans, upon pain of death, to evacuate the subway via No. 3 shaft—and their order of going was arranged for them.   N.C.O.'s were to proceed first, followed by other ranks.   In spite of the threat of death, three sappers secreted themselves behind pumps, tools and sandbags, eluded their captors, and so escaped.

Captain Walker was on a stretcher and Sergeants Newell and Menadue constituted themselves his bearers.   As he could not be evacuated through the spiral stairway in No. 3 shaft, he was to be taken out via Moat Farm entrance, which he had so well defended.   Accompanied by Sapper Turner and another sapper, they set off for Germany—

at least so their captors thought ! On approaching the
entrance at Moat Farm, Sergeant Menadue went forward
quietly to reconnoitre. There were two sentries at the
entrance, both of whom he dealt with effectively. When
the remainder of the party reached the surface they
" changed direction " and made for Pont Fixe and not
captivity.

Such incidents as these illustrate why the British Army
is hard to beat. N.C.O.'s and men, when thrown on their
own initiative, are seldom at a loss as to the action appropriate to the occasion, and they act quickly, without consulting the drill book. For his exemplary conduct
Menadue was awarded the D.C.M. As a result of his
wound, however, Captain Walker's leg had to be amputated.

It is, of course, obvious that a dozen minor dramas were
being played consecutively at many scattered points. It is,
however, well worth while to hold up the main narrative
for a moment to record the exploit of Sapper Turner and
Sapper Stewart. These men were the sole survivors of
the party of No. 4 Pent-house. From the first attack they
hung on bravely in their isolated position till 1 p.m. in
the afternoon. Knowing full well their chance of relief
was slight, and what would be their fate if they fell into the
hands of the enemy, Turner maintained an incessant rifle
fire while Stewart kept him supplied with a loaded rifle.
How many rounds he fired is not known—nor the condition
of his shoulder. What we do know is that the gallantry
and devotion to duty of these two sappers, isolated in a
shaft head, with the enemy all round, holding out so
long against such odds, is well worthy of admiration.

Of the party of sappers at Givenchy Keep, only one
succeeded in surviving the ordeal in which they had put
up a " good show." Yet the situation was becoming
clearer ; reinforcements were arriving, and on the following
day the 1st Northants and 1st Black Watch successfully
drove the enemy out of Bunny Hutch, Scottish Trench,
Ware Road, New Cut and Piccadilly.

The Tunnellers displayed a magnificent spirit throughout the remaining days of the battle. When a call for
volunteers was made, miners came forward eagerly, offering

their service before knowing what they may be called upon to do. The knowledge that they were required to guide the troops in a counter attack only increased their willingness to place their special knowledge of the locality at the disposal of the newly-arrived infantry, unfamiliar with this part of the line. Lance-Corporal Jose and four other ranks acted as guides, and of this party two were reported missing after the attack.

Of the three officers and thirty-nine other ranks who went into the line on the 17th, one officer and six other ranks returned to Company H.Q., the remainder being killed or captured.

v

Actually, the contribution of the Tunnellers was far more important than is apparent at first sight. They played a worthy part during the battle, responding to the calls of the emergency in such fashion as would have amazed those staff officers who in 1914 deprecated their enlistment because of their lack of discipline. They had fought well and hard, and their thorough knowledge of the ground—they had been stationary in the sector, whereas the infantry were continuously moved—was of the utmost utility. Yet the best work of the Tunnellers was done before the battle commenced, in the fortification of the Givenchy Ridge.

The ideas of British G.H.Q. on the subject of fortification differed vastly from those of the German command. In one famous edict the British staff had decided against the use of deep dugouts ; although these afforded safe shelter, it was argued, there would be a tendency to use them too freely : our men, obsessed by their safety, would be reluctant to come out into the open to meet or develop an attack. It was perhaps fortunate for *moral* that this derogatory opinion was not circulated to the troops ! The Germans were not slow to leave their dugouts at the proper moment, and presumably our courage was equal to theirs.

In the last year of the War, however, ideas began to change : as usual, the moment was too late ; not nearly

enough labour was available to put the whole of our front
in a proper defensive state. Givenchy was one of the
lucky sectors, and here the Tunnellers were given almost
a free hand. We have seen the network of dugouts,
tunnels and concrete shelters which they constructed, and
the great part they played in the defence of the village and
its environs. Givenchy was one of the two key points of
the German attack : had it fallen then the German advance
would have extended southwards with disastrous results.
But Givenchy held firmly, a corner bastion on which all
enemy assaults broke. The credit for this gallant defence
is rightly given to the 55th Division of Lancashire Terri-
torials, and the veterans of the 1st Division, who in those
days of strain built up a famous reputation for dogged
pluck. They, however, would be the first to acknowledge
the tremendous asset of the fortifications of Givenchy.
Other divisions, equally gallant and well led, faced the
assault further north from the usual defences of the British
line : they fought bravely, but were forced back. Givenchy
was a strong point equivalent to the German villages on
the Somme ; Tunnellers were never too proud to learn,
and had taken the best German ideas and improved upon
them. Modern fortifications manned by brave men are
immensely difficult to capture ; thus Givenchy held, and
the chances of a decisive German victory vanished.

VI

Had there been a Givenchy on the northern flank of
the Lys battle-field, a very different story might have been
told. There, however, our front rapidly crumbled.
Whereas earlier in the War we had been ridiculously
obstinate in hanging on to useless ground, now it seemed
that we were ready to yield ground all too freely—so much
so that Haig penned his famous " backs to the wall "
appeal to the weary soldiers of the northern armies. The
German advance was startling : Armentières, that permanent fixture in the British line, was hastily evacuated ;

even Merville, once a centre for rest cures, fell into enemy hands.

In the Ypres salient the position was critical. We

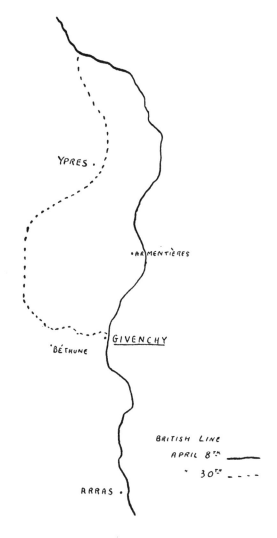

had obstinately fought our way to a precarious foothold on the Passchendaele Ridge, but it was always intensely difficult to hold—and now its southern flank was in great danger.   Plumer cheerfully gave one of the bitterest orders of the War, yet one long overdue—the order to withdraw to our original positions, and in some parts even behind them.   The new salient was abandoned : the old one remained.

The last troops to leave the dearly purchased salient were small parties of Tunnellers, who had remained to destroy the culverts and crossings over the Steenbeek and the other smaller beeks, and to crater the Menin Road.   This was done without molestation from the enemy ; in fact it was not until the late afternoon of 12th April that his scouts were seen approaching our new position.

The final stage of the evacuation was not without its touch of drama.   Two officers of one party had prepared the last charge to destroy a culvert near St. Julien.   Everything was in readiness, and the fuse was about to be ignited. " Just a moment," said one, as he walked back over the culvert, turned and strutted majestically across like a drum-major on a ceremonial parade—thereby staking his claim to be the last British officer to leave the salient.   Not to be outdone, the other officer performed the ritual.   This was repeated several times till at last they compromised, and crossed together, sharing the distinction.   Honour was satisfied.

VII

On withdrawing from the salient, 171st, 184th, 255th and the 3rd Canadian Tunnelling Companies rendezvoused at Boeschepe.   From this vantage point a wonderful panoramic view spread itself before them.   On one hand the country-side looked fresh, beautiful and verdant, the tree-lined roads like emerald green tapes, easily discernible winding amid the corn and hop fields from village to village, the inhabitants of which still remained, ignorant of the fact that all was not well in the battle zone.   This was the obverse.

The immediate view of the reverse was not dissimilar. But what a contrast a few miles to the eastward !   Here the canker of war had bitten deeply into and ravaged the country-side, leaving in its train a trail of ruin and destruction. Not content with the devastation already wrought, it was even now striving to fling out and fasten its parasitic tentacles further into this fair land.

In their thousands the Germans were pouring over the Messines Ridge, sweeping aside all opposition, until they were pounding on the portals of peaceful Bailleul. The ancient town was soon deserted. A parting " shot " was taken by an official photographer, over a hastily built barricade, as the enemy advanced up the Armentières Road. Merris and Merville fell. Even the heights of Mount Kemmel, towering loftily above the Flanders plain, were in the enemy's hands. All day long woebegone crowds of civilian refugees streamed down the roads leading away from these towns, fleeing as from a noisome pestilence, a motley of old and young, middle-aged men being conspicuous by their absence. All, even the small children, carried some treasured possession. Rickety wagons, piled high with domestic belongings hastily salved, upon which sometimes could be seen perched precariously the remnants of a passing generation, drawn by oddly assorted teams of domestic animals—even dogs were drawn into service— attached by improvized harness to strange vehicles, hand-carts and wheelbarrows, jostled one another in their anxiety to escape. Pedestrians filled any road space available in the traffic jam and overflowed into the fields at the roadside. Occasionally shells from long range guns fell near, adding greatly to the distress of the already harassed fugitives, while aeroplanes swooped low overhead. It was indeed a pathetic spectacle. Yet withal the fugitives bore their persecution with commendable fortitude. As the crowd surged along one sometimes recognized buxom wenches who, but a short while previously, had dispensed copious libations to all and sundry at the " Au Pot au Lait," or " Au Bon Coin," or some such local hostelry.

The enemy advanced so rapidly that Boeschepe soon fell within range of his guns. It became untenable, and less exposed camps were found for Tunnellers. The situation became precarious. The four companies already mentioned were joined by 173rd, 183rd and 258th

T

Tunnelling Companies, rushed up from the south for work on the St. Omer line of fortifications, often contemplated but now, for the protection of the Channel ports, desperately urgent : thus seven companies were spread out along a front of over twenty miles from Reninghelst to St. Omer, digging and wiring trenches—a task at which they excelled. At first they were the only organized troops facing the advancing enemy. Indeed, at several points along the line, with the exception of isolated parties of stragglers, for the most part unarmed, they were the *only* troops available capable of offering any resistance, and were eager to show their prowess. In fact, on the afternoon of the first day's digging, they came under machine-gun and light trench-mortar fire, and had to man the trenches before being relieved—in some cases by French troops.

With much chopping and changing they remained in this area until June, 1918, doing all manner of work. Many miles of trenches were dug and wired, in addition to an enormous amount of work on rear communications, bridges, roads, tracks, causeways, scrub cutting, machine-gun pill boxes, shelters, command posts, in addition to supervising labour. The 3rd Canadian Tunnelling Company placed demolition charges in the abutments of bridges over the canal de Neuf-Fosse at Campagne, Wardrecques, Arques, between St. Omer and Aire.

Here the war was being waged in country well behind the original trench lines. With the exception of a few skirmishes between cavalry patrols in 1914, it had not been disturbed by fighting, nor had the usual workaday life been interrupted until now. Unable to drive off their livestock with them, farmers liberated them before vacating their farms. Consequently, droves of cattle and pigs roamed at large and became a great source of trouble. Although every effort was made to drive them back to safety, many were unable to cross the open trenches. At intervals crossing places were left for them, but numbers became " wired in " in No Man's Land and eventually had to be destroyed. Such are the sidelights of war.

VIII

The Battle of the Lys died down. Once again Ludendorff had achieved an apparent success—but no more. To
be effective, it was essential that his drive should extend to
the south, there to join hands with the great salient before
Amiens. But in the south was Givenchy, perhaps the most
strongly fortified point on the British line, gallantly
garrisoned. Useless to push out his salient farther while
Givenchy remained, a dangerous re-entrant, so Ludendorff
called off the battle, and transferred the scene of action to
the Aisne front. He did not know it then, but his great
victories on the Somme and the Lys had cost him the War.

Military historians rightly point to Givenchy as the
key to the Lys battle. The Germans knew something
about the art of fortifying villages, as their work on the
Somme has shown. But at Givenchy they had to give us
best, and more than one of their commanders has paid
tribute to the work of the Tunnellers in the creation of
this vital and impregnable position.

CHAPTER XIV

THE TURN OF THE TIDE

I

LUDENDORFF'S gamble had failed. He had battered the British, he had driven two great salients into their line, but he had not beaten them or won a decisive victory. Yet once again he tried : this time a furious assault broke on the French front on the Chemin des Dames front, and four British divisions which had been sent thither by Foch for a " rest " were almost annihilated. Yet once again initial success was elusive ; again the victory was more apparent than real—another great salient, but no decision. The time was almost ripe for the initiative to pass into the hands of the Allied Command. Foch by this time was Generalissimo, and there was no special credit in prophesying that he would order offensive action at the earliest possible moment.

In spite of the absence of tunnelling, the Tunnellers were never busier. In the space of a few weeks they changed their occupations a dozen times. We have seen them fighting as infantry on the Somme and Lys, following up gallant work by yeoman service as field engineers. Three companies then found themselves in the unfamiliar rôle of firemen. Béthune, at the height of the Lys battle, was set on fire by incendiary shells ; more than a dozen fires were burning in different parts of the town at the same time. A harassed town-major, devoid of all normal assistance, had an inspiration ; he called out a section of 170th Tunnelling Company who soon had the outbreaks under control. 172nd Company had had a similar experience at Amiens a fortnight earlier, and the 2nd Australian Company performed a similar duty at Péronne.

But before the inevitable counter-attack could be

launched, a vast amount of preparation was essential. At first, indeed, the Tunnellers' work was defensive, for after the battle of the Lys it was by no means certain that a further retirement might not be necessary. As a precautionary measure, therefore, a detailed reconnaissance was commenced, covering an area south of a line Pointe de Gravelines—St. Omer—Anvin—St. Pol—Frévent—Doullens—Flixecourt—Mollines-Vidame. It was divided into four sectors, each being in charge of a captain and two subalterns from Tunnelling Companies in the First, Second, Third and Fourth Armies.

Provided with special passes from G.H.Q., permitting free movement, and mounted on motor cycles, they patrolled their allotted areas, selecting suitable sites such as road crossings, cuttings and embankments on roads and railways, bridges over navigable waterways, stores, plant—in fact, anything the destruction of which would impede the enemy's advance came within the scope of the scheme. Full particulars of each proposed demolition were forwarded to G.H.Q.

At first sight this seems nothing more than an ordinary precaution, but on closer examination it throws into relief the fact that we were prepared, in 1918, to abandon the Channel ports, as far as and including Boulogne, and still fight on.

A moment's reflection will serve to emphasize the significance of such an expedient to the Allies, and Great Britain in particular. At this time the enemy possessed guns credited with a range of forty-five miles. This would bring Canterbury within the possibility of damage from shell fire. Fortunately, the turn of the tide in the autumn of 1918 rendered the completion of the scheme unnecessary. Had it been necessary to put this " Z " scheme into operation, no doubt the Tunnellers would have been called upon to do it—and very few of them would have survived.

One officer who had been working for a week in the vicinity of Calais, and had almost completed his task, returned to check some details in connection with an important bridge over a canal. He had not been long at work when a tender drew up near the bridge : a party of linesmen got out, one of whom swarmed up a telegraph pole and made a connection. In a few moments a telephone was in operation, much to the amusement of the Tunnelling Officer, who sensed the import of the proceedings, the furtive glances in his direction giving the show away completely. Very soon the " flying squad " appeared on the scene, and the luckless but innocent prisoner was duly marched off, at once to appear before a very imposing " tribunal " ! His G.H.Q. pass was scornfully disdained as a forgery. He was detained at the pleasure of the court. Wires buzzed. The pompous dignity of the court was somewhat ruffled by an admonition from G.H.Q. for questioning the authority of their edicts.

The previous day a very bad description of the said Tunnelling Officer, from which it would have been impossible to recognize him, had been circulated in Army Orders. He must have chortled as he read a none too flattering description of himself. Yet, in the early days of the War, men had been shot as spies on more flimsy evidence.

II

Before we could turn our minds to counter-attack, the ground which we now occupied had to be consolidated, both battle position and rear zone. These preparations involved an enormous amount of labour, in which the Tunnellers had a very large share. In addition to digging and wiring many miles of trenches, they repaired and re-made miles of roads and other communications, as well as supervising the work of numerous labour units, native as well as European. All along the front, mined dugouts and machine-gun posts were constructed by the hundred. In places where the ground was unsuitable for underground protection, a standard type of concrete pill-box was made. Reinforced concrete machine-gun posts, with underground accommodation for crews, were erected in ruined buildings at strategic points. Great attention was paid to concealing these posts by the use of suitable camouflage. The camouflage artists became so expert that, even at close range, it was difficult to distinguish the real from the unreal. Indeed, a horse grazing in a pasture field began to nibble at camouflage covering a mined machine-gun post. On another occasion a too-curious animal approached too near a half-completed gun pit and tumbled into it. He had to remain for several days in unusual surroundings while a special exit was dug for him. During his temporary confinement he received food and water at the hands of the Tunnellers, and when liberated commenced to graze as though nothing had happened.

In the area forward of Vimy Ridge, numerous small caves were located and explored and, where found suitable, were cleaned out and made habitable. Here also numerous dugouts were made for headquarters of all formations, even down to platoons.

Along the First Army front, existing dugouts, the mining systems, and the numerous subways at Givenchy, Cambrin—Auchy, Hairpin, etc., were maintained and put into a state of defence. Machine-gun and trench-mortar emplacements were built in inclines leading up to surface from the subways. Traverses, into which loophole plates were built, were erected in most subways as a defence against enemy raids. It was during this period, when 185th Company was driving several subways, that, at Lance Subway, on Reservoir Hill, they set up a remarkable record. No less than 62 feet of subway were driven in twenty-four hours. This record was established by hand labour only, no mechanical appliance of any sort being used.

Then, when the defensive work was well under way, selected parties of Tunnellers were given a special course of instruction in the proper methods to be adopted in investigating newly won ground, and the removal and destruction of enemy traps, mines, and demolition charges. " Booby-trapping," as the Tunnellers called it, required a quick eye and keen observation, caution and ready deduction.

It is astonishing how quickly, after a little experience, one acquired a flair to " sense " danger. That the Tunnellers soon became expert " booby-trappers " is proved by the small losses they sustained in comparison with the enormous amount of explosives they removed.

Intensive courses were instituted also for the personnel of Tunnelling Companies in infantry training. These preparations could have but one meaning—a counter-attack.

Thwarted in the field, disturbed by the internal political and economical situation, alarmed by the steady inflow of American reinforcements into France, and dismayed at the failure of the ruthless submarine campaign, to the Germans the next move ought to have been obvious. Nevertheless, the British onslaught on August 8th caught the enemy napping. After Messines, this was perhaps the most perfectly planned attack of the War. Even more than its heavy material gains, it revealed the declining *moral* of the Germans ; when confronted with reports of the battle, no wonder that Ludendorff referred to 8th August as the " Black Day of the German Army."

In this action, as in the succession of widely-spread hammer blows which followed, the Tunnellers played an active part. Their newly allotted share in the tactical scheme was immediately and successfully put into operation. Scouting parties of Tunnellers accompanied the infantry and searched trenches, dugouts, etc., for traps and mines, placing warning signs at suspected points. Following the scouts came working parties, who immediately began to remove the mines. Special attention was given to the examination of dugouts, particularly those likely to be used for accommodating our own troops.

Albert had received special treatment by the Germans before they were driven out. Here 180th Tunnelling Company did exceptionally good work under conditions trying enough to deter all but the most stout-hearted. Machine-gunned, bombarded with H.E. and gas shells, they worked away undeterred amidst the gas-drenched ruins of demolished Albert. The strenuous manual labour involved was difficult enough, but the difficulty was increased enormously by the necessity of wearing gas masks. The glass eyepieces of the goggles are opaque enough at the best of times, but, when still further dimmed by heat after continuous use, the wearer's vision is greatly diminished. Thus handicapped, dealing with explosive charges, mines, and booby traps becomes a very risky business indeed. In such work any obscurity of vision is almost a vital drawback. For two days this Company worked under such appalling conditions, during which time they removed thirty-two unexploded charges and over one hundred land mines.

Later the same Company cut away the broken railway bridge at Albert, and removed dams from the Ancre to lower the inundations. All the other Companies in the Fourth Army did similar work at various times. Generally speaking, all the Tunnelling Companies were similarly engaged right up to the end of the War, their work falling under the following headings :

Communications, road, bridges, and railways—the main-tenance and repair of which involved them in an enormous amount of work.

Wells and water supply—locating, cleaning and repairing wells and pumping plant.

Mines, traps and demolition charges and tank mines, the removal of hundreds of thousands of pounds of high explosives.

In many instances the scouting parties which were operating in conjunction with the infantry found them-selves right in the van of the advance. Thus it was that they secured numerous prisoners. Most of the prisoners were taken from dugouts, which they refused to leave until they are assured that *Nach Berlin* was *not* the direction of their next move.

A party from 185th Company, under Lieutenant Garment, were so far ahead of our infantry that they were actually the first British troops to enter Douai—on 17th October. They had gone in to reconnoitre the Grande Place, which was thought to be mined. Garment had the satisfaction of hauling down the German flag from the Prefecture, which had been used as H.Q. The departing German troops must have been in a very great hurry indeed when they forgot to take their flag back to Germany with them.

During the advance, 175th Company was engaged in the erection of two bridges over the River Ancre, removing detonators from road mines, etc. Search was also in progress for traps and mines. Wells and water points, the locating, cleaning and repairing of which is a very important duty during an advance, also claimed their attention.

During this work Sergeant Booth, by his coolness and daring, prevented the destruction of a bridge across the River Ancre in Aveluy Wood. Proceeding well in advance of the infantry, he reached the bridge. A brief search soon revealed the demolition charge, which he rendered harmless, saving the bridge from destruction.

All the Companies in the Third, Fourth and Fifth Armies were employed on similar work. As the advance continued, the Tunnellers not engaged on " traps " and mines were employed on communications, the repair and maintenance of which was a tremendous task, more particularly in the devastated areas. Roads had to be cleared of all manner of obstructions ; trenches and road craters had to be filled in ; trees, wire, bricks and debris (the result of years of bombardment often amounting to half a small village strewn along a main road), all had to be moved before wheeled traffic could pass. Rivers and canals had to be cleared of dams, fallen bridges, and other obstructions, inundations drained, damaged lock gates removed and repaired. Railway lines were in an appalling state of devastation, with bridges down, formation destroyed, metals broken or twisted into fantastic shapes by mines and shell fire—there was scarcely an undamaged set of points and crossings in hundreds of miles of railways, so thoroughly had the work of demolition been carried out.

To remove the wreckage of destroyed bridges, small charges were used to reduce masses of twisted girders to manageable sizes. Oxy-acetylene plant was also used for cutting girders. When cut, the girders were hauled out of the river bed by lorries ; even tanks were sometimes pressed into this service.

When the debris had been removed, the Tunnellers accomplished a *volti subito*. Hitherto most of their work had been *de*structive ; now it was to be *con*structive.

Bridges had to be erected to replace those destroyed. Hundreds of bridges of various types, improvised and stock, were erected all along the advance. Trestle, Inglis and Hopkins bridges of various lengths were speedily erected over the Canal de l'Escaut, the Lys, the Scheldt, the Canal du Nord, and numerous other places. These bridges, though hastily constructed, were none the less serviceable. In fact, a bridge built by the 3rd Australian Tunnelling Company at Moudit—built under heavy shell fire and frequently damaged—is still in use at the time of writing.

III

Perhaps the most spectacular work done by any Tunnelling Company was the erection of the Havrincourt Bridge by the New Zealand Tunnelling Company.

In September, 1918, our advance had reached the Canal du Nord, and before the Germans had retired they destroyed the original bridge which carried the Hermies— Havrincourt Road across the canal. A new bridge was essential, and General Harvey, who was at that time Chief Engineer, VI Corps, was allotted the New Zealanders for the task.

The original site was visited by Captain Hopkins, Bridging Officer at G.H.Q., and designer of a type of bridge bearing his name, and Captain Holmes, A/O.C., New Zealand Tunnelling Company, who found the old position unsuitable, as it was on the crest of a ridge, and under direct observation from the direction of Bourlon Wood. A more favourable site, some hundred yards south of the road, was selected, but, as the canal was virtually our front line, this position came in for a fair amount of enemy shelling.

The gaping ditch of the now waterless canal, whose sides " Y-ed " out to 180 feet across the top, some 90 feet above the bottom, presented a formidable obstacle to bridge, even to expert builders under peaceful conditions, and only one of the New Zealanders had had previous experience in this work. True, one officer and a few non-commissioned officers had spent some days at the bridging park at Rosel, erecting and taking down sections of various types of portable bridges, under the guidance of the R.E. in charge, and there their knowledge ended.

Early on September 27th the bridging material began to arrive on lorries, but owing to the conjested state of the roads and the difficulty of unloading under shell fire, it was late at night before the last of the convoy got away. Work was carried out in reliefs, for which the Company divided into two shifts, one coming at dawn and working till midday, the other coming on and then working till dark in order to get the job finished as soon as possible. To facilitate the work further, the much reduced 565th and 577th Army Troops Companies were attached to the New Zealanders.

The longest " stock size " bridge was 120 feet, and here the gap to bridge was 180 feet, but, as this type of bridge is so designed that all its members are interchangeable, two bridges were built up into one complete unit of 240 feet. In addition, a counterbalance of twenty tons of railway rails was loaded on the shore section.

The whole structure was ready to launch on the afternoon of 1st October, and was advanced till one bay overhung the abutment rollers ; then, as there was not time to launch before darkness set in, work was stopped for the day. The following day the span was 110 feet out from the abutment bearings when a halt was made to change the tackle.

Here disaster almost overtook the whole scheme. A keen lookout had to be kept constantly for the slightest sign of weakness or defect in any of the members. The failure of one faulty girder would, in theory, wreck the whole structure, the members being inderdependent and interchangeable. To the consternation of those in charge a fault did appear—one member began to buckle. There was no other alternative but to accept the risk, a very considerable risk indeed, of complete collapse. As effectively as possible, temporary struts were put in and the faulty member removed and replaced.

On 3rd October, launching continued successfully until

HAVRINCOURT BRIDGE

there remained but 8 feet to go : then one of the winches jammed—the barrel could hold no more rope ! As it happened, there was room to erect a crib and to jack up the end of the bridge and free the winch. No sooner had work been resumed than the other winch also jammed. Again the end had to be jacked up and the winch cleared, after which, in the failing light, the bridge was safely hauled on to the abutment and launching successfully completed.

The next day the decking was put on, and the superfluous 60 feet removed from the launching end. In the short time of eight days the bridge was opened for traffic, complete with footway and handrails.

The Commander-in-Chief took a personal interest in this work, which he twice visited, and on its completion sent a message of appreciation to the New Zealanders " for the excellent work done by the company during the erection of the Havrincourt bridge."

IV

One intriguing incident cannot pass without notice— if only to illustrate further the versatility of the Tunnellers. For observation in flat country both sides made extensive use of captive kite balloons. These, defenceless as they were, formed an easy prey for venturesome enemy airmen willing to run the barrage of anti-aircraft shells. One harassed Balloon Company commander at Vis-en-Artois called in the services of the Tunnellers. An old balloon was loaded with 525 lb. of ammonal and raised to an altitude of 2,500 feet, where it floated, inviting attack. Presently, along came a plane displaying the black cross on its wing tips, and made for the balloon. A burst of machine-gun fire, and the plane came nearer. When the plane appeared to be about 100 feet above the balloon, there was a tremendous explosion—impelled by electric charge from the ground. A dense cloud of smoke filled the air. Burning debris seemed to be thrown all round the plane. Faintly through it the plane could be seen rocking

about in the air eddies.   Dark smoke appeared, for about
thirty seconds, on one side of the plane.   There were no
other signs of damage, however, and the pilot regained
control :   he turned for home, no doubt having had one
of the shocks of his life.   He returned the following day,
however, and attacked other balloons in the same neighbourhood.   Some days later, two other balloon baskets
were loaded with a quantity of ammonal and shrapnel.
These, however, were not attacked.

Yet the stratagem did claim at least one victim, for
Ober-Lieutenant von Eschwege was killed as a result of
a deliberately exploded balloon.

In connection with these experiments, an interesting fact
was brought home   The firing cables, attached to their
balloons, became so heavily charged with static electricity
that it was feared the charges would be exploded
prematurely.

V

The succession of heavy blows on all parts of his front,
coupled with his own declining *moral*, impelled an enemy
retreat, punctuated with many desperate rear-guard actions.
The work of the Tunnellers in dealing with delayed mines
and booby traps vastly increased.

By far the greater number of mines and traps were found
in the Third Army area.   This is accounted for by the fact
that the enemy's retirement on this front was carried out
fairly slowly.   On the Fourth Army area, few mines were
found, owing to the rapid withdrawal of the enemy.   But
road repair work was particularly heavy, as the Germans
had neglected most of them—particularly the secondary
roads.

Our own anti-tank mines, of which there were numerous
fields, had to be removed.   There was no evidence to
show that any of these fields had caused the enemy any
damage, except at one place where a few dead horses and
broken limbers were found.   Two of them were wired off
and notice boards erected.   An old mine field running
east of the Ronssoy—Epéhy road at Lempire, consisting

of trench-mortar shells, delayed our tank advance until a Tunnelling officer went forward and removed the contact pins and cleared a passage through.

As was natural, the scouting parties of Tunnellers, anxious to break new ground, often became detached from the infantry, and waged private warfare with the German rear-guards. At Peizière, two officers and a sapper met with considerable opposition from a well-placed machine-gun post. The occupants of the post, no doubt feeling quite secure with their superior weapons, delayed their withdrawal too long and found themselves captured. The small party had actually stalked the post. The sentry fled down to warn the garrison, followed by the small party of Britishers. What happened next is not clear. This we do know ; the garrison of the post consisted of two officers and nineteen other ranks, all of whom were made prisoners.

256th Company was responsible for the patrol and repair of the railway line from Trones Wood to Ytres and Fins. Six tons of explosives were removed from that short section of line. The subsequent advance in this area demanded unusual methods.

Where the ground was suitable, the Germans made extensive use of deep dugouts, subways and tunnels. One of the most elaborate of these was discovered on 30th September, 1918. It was nearly one mile in length, and extended from near Bellenglise to Magny la Fosse. Numerous entrances gave access along the tunnel, and ventilation was supplied by several vertical shafts to surface. Leading off it were thirty-five living chambers, providing good and safe accommodation for a large number of troops. It also contained two magazines for explosives, and an engine-room with two lighting sets.

The search party knew well, from previous experience, that traps and demolition charges would be secreted in the tunnel. It seemed obvious also that the charges would be connected to the lighting sets. In order to examine the tunnel the search party might be tempted to start up the engine, close the switches and so explode the charges. But a more intriguing alternative was adopted.

Permission was granted to have the German engineers, who had been in charge of the plant and were now prisoners, returned to the tunnel to be questioned about the circuits and the positions of the mines. At first they roundly denied any knowledge of charges connected to the switch board. For some time they persisted in denial. "Very well," said the Tunnellers, " You must remain in the tunnel while the engine is started and all the circuits on the switchboard closed." This moral suasion had the effect desired. The Germans indicated the circuit and the charges. The leads were cut and the detonators removed from the charges. All troops were cleared from the tunnel and sentries posted to prevent anyone entering. The engine was started. One by one the switches were closed—a very tense job. No explosion occurred and the whole tunnel was lighted throughout.

This enabled the search for traps to be carried out speedily. Well over four tons of purdite were removed —sufficient to destroy the tunnel utterly—and numerous traps. The latter were mostly stick bombs and 5·9 shells placed behind the timbers in such a manner as to be easily detonated by pressure on the timber.

The removal of these explosives was not the type of work which could be done hastily, yet it must of necessity be done as carefully and quickly as possible. The removal of delay-action mines some days after they had been timed to explode called for cool and determined action. That there were bound to be charges so well concealed as to defy detection was a foregone conclusion. They did occur. The wonder is that so many were detected and so few losses occurred from this.

The Tunnellers had strange experiences and came upon strange things whilst " booby-trapping." After the Hindenburg Line had been stormed and captured to the east of Hagicourt there was still another formidable barrier to be stormed—the St. Quentin Canal. Just south of Bellicourt the canal enters a tunnel which extends north-wards to a point opposite Le Catelet.

This tunnel had been extensively used by the Germans. A string of twenty-four barges was moored in the tunnel ;

these had been converted into living quarters for troops. Engine rooms contained plant for lighting purposes and numerous tunnels, dugouts, chambers, etc., had been constructed in the solid ground above the canal tunnel. This much we knew, from a prisoner, before we reached the tunnel.

The 5th Australian Division were the first troops to visit the tunnel, followed soon after by a party of 182nd Tunnelling Company. They found the ground above the tunnel honeycombed with shafts, tunnels, galleries, dug-outs, chambers, stairways, etc. One gallery led to the cellar of a house in Bellicourt! Indeed, it was so strongly fortified that a few resolute troops could have held it almost against all comers. In their search the Tunnellers came upon a chamber leading off a stairway. The stench here was so bad that the N.C.O. in charge ordered the men to don their gas masks—an order they readily obeyed! In the chamber they found an underground kitchen fitted with a number of coppers, not unlike those set in the wash-houses of pre-War houses in this country. One of these contained human limbs, and on top reposed a skull. Near by were tins of grease and a number of corpses. At this time, of course, the " corpse factory " legend was still current, and it was immediately assumed that we had stumbled upon a branch establishment! The sensational news spread rapidly, and men of all arms off duty crowded to view the gruesome sight. At one time there was quite a queue of sensation-seeking rubbernecks !

The headquarters of the 5th Australian Division was informed, so that immediate investigation might be made in view of its potential use as propaganda. The investiga-tion, however, damped the ardour of those who harboured sensational thoughts. After examination of the chamber and of prisoners, the responsible officers reported that the chamber was a field cook-house ; that a shell had been burst just as the men were lining up for rations, and— by one of those freak cataclysms so frequently the object of comment at the front—a number of human limbs had been tossed by diabolic accident into one of the coppers.

But sensation dies hard. To this day, in spite of the

U

British official admission that the corpse factory story was a propaganda fake, there are still dozens of British and Australian soldiers who are firmly convinced that they saw it.

VI

The Allies were now steadily but surely advancing to victory. The delaying tactics adopted by the enemy were not proving insuperable, though roads and bridges were everywhere destroyed. But not all. The enemy delayed too long at Landrecies, and was not able to complete all destruction intended. A party of nine sappers in charge of two N.C.O.s of 182nd Company were advancing with the first wave of the infantry, and approached to within 400 yards of the western outskirts of the town. Here the infantry halted, while the Tunnellers moved on towards the main road bridge and canal lock. Just as they reached the bridge the superstructure was blown by the Germans. Immediately the debris had fallen, the Tunnellers rushed across the lock gates and attacked the demolition party and the machine-gunners covering them. Although outnumbered by about two to one, the Tunnellers inflicted several casualties and captured fourteen prisoners and one machine-gun. This surprise onslaught prevented further damage being done to the abutments of the main swing bridge and the masonry of the lock. Ten demolition charges were removed from the vicinity. It was then a comparatively easy task to bridge the lock, a span of only 17 feet, for the passage of tanks. What the infantry did during these operations is not stated, nor it is quite clear why they allowed the Tunnellers to go forward when it was obviously their job to clear the hostile troops from the vicinity of the bridge *before* the Tunnellers advanced.

Charges were also removed from a wooden bridge, before it could be destroyed by the enemy. It was then strengthened by the sappers and rendered serviceable for traffic.

On one occasion, when 177th Company was well forward constructing a bridge over the Phonelle they had a very unpleasant experience. Work had been in progress for some little time and the bridge was taking shape, when the Germans thought the moment had arrived for a counter-attack. Very soon the Tunnellers found themselves in the very van of battle. Discarding their bridging tools for rifles, they once more took part in defending the line, as they frequently did during trench warfare. Having repulsed the attack, they completed the construction of their bridge.

There was one classic occasion when at the Tambour, in 1916, 178th Company took a great share in repulsing a raid. The Divisional General was so thrilled at the fighting qualities of the Tunnellers that his Orders recorded : " An enemy raid at the Tambour was repulsed by the Tunnellers, *assisted by the infantry*."

When one remembers the lack of military training of most of the Tunnellers, and how, at least in the early days, they were relieved of their ammunition lest they should be a greater danger to their fellows than to the enemy, it seems incredible that such an order should come to light.

In addition to finding mines at such obvious places as cross roads, they were discovered in the most unlikely places. Behind the brickwork of a lock wall was a favourite place for a charge. Possibly the most " low down " place for a charge to be placed was a church tower—not even a church is sacred to the god of war.

At Le Cateau a charge of 500 lbs. was removed from the clock tower of the Hotel de Ville. But the *pièce de résistance* was a parcel of over half a ton of high explosive which had been placed in the church tower. Both these charges were removed by No. 1 section of 182nd Company.

At the station at Felleries were three train loads of German ammunition, containing about fifty thousand shells. Almost every shell had to be examined separately and carefully. Many were found to contain delay-action fuzes. These were so well camouflaged to resemble ordinary fuzes that the greatest care had to be exercised in making the search. Several boxes containing " 1917 German Long Delay-Action Fuzes " and acid were found near by. This seems to indicate that time was insufficient for the German

demolition party to complete its work. Several fuzes had
been inserted, for our men found them in trench-mortar
bombs, in separate trucks.

    In order to get an adequate idea of the work done by
the Tunnellers in removing mines and traps, it must be
remembered than an enormous area had to be searched in a
limited time, and that the examination of the ground takes
time and calls for cool-headed action. If the work were
rushed, accidents were bound to occur, both to the searchers
and the infantry. If the work were delayed, then the
retreating enemy would have ample time to carry out more
complete demolitions and add to the difficulties of our
advance. Much work must have been done which yielded
no results, yet a total of over 3,000,000 *lbs. of explosives*
was removed, a little over 500,000 lbs. being British
charges. The removal of traps and charges calls for cool
courage of the highest order, especially in dealing with
delay-action mines. On roads alone many weeks of work
were done, often under shell fire. Hundreds of miles
were cleared, repaired and made fit for traffic, in addition
to deviation tracks and sleeper roads across devastated
areas in each Army area. The aggregate of road repairs
easily exceeds one thousand miles.

                              VII

    The end was in sight. The Germans were now fighting
no more than rear-guard actions, and a retreat at least to
the Meuse appeared inevitable. Soon sensational rumours
penetrated the lines : Germany was in revolution ; the
Kaiser had abdicated ; an armistice was being arranged.
While the terms were being discussed, the Inspector of
Mines dispatched his assistant from G.H.Q.—on Sunday
night, 10th November—to the British Mission attached
to Marshal Foch. Here he was handed all the available
information regarding delay-action mines laid by the
Germans. This information was the first of any sort
divulged by the Germans. Post haste it was circulated
to all the Tunnelling Companies.

THE TURN OF THE TIDE

The following day, as all the world knows, an Armistice was signed at eleven o'clock in the forenoon of 11th November, 1918. To most troops this was the cessation of hostilities—with the Tunnellers the state of war continued : they still had to face war risks in one of its most dastardly forms—the delay-action mine.   Nor is this mere hyperbole.

It was soon found that the information given by the Germans concerning the delay-action mines was not very accurate, though it assisted to some extent.   It is not suggested that this information was deliberately misleading. The information we had showed the scheme on paper, but the mines were not always to be found at the exact location indicated in the scheme, not within, say, 50 feet.   When this was discovered, German officers were detailed to assist the Tunnellers in locating the mines, while further information was supplied through the British Mission.   Many of these mines exploded before they could be located, but hundreds were removed and, considering the hazardous nature of the work, casualties were slight.   That any should have occurred at all is most regrettable : a casualty in times of peace is, for some reason, far more appalling than a dozen in times of war.

On 15th November, 1918, 180th Tunnelling Company was at Épéhy, which had been occupied by us since 20th September.   Part of their work was to examine the railway line from Épéhy south of St. Emilie.   This was being done by No. 3 Section when two mines were located.   Work to permit the removal of one of the mines was at once put in hand.   The tamping had been almost completely removed and the charge could be seen : then, without the slightest warning, there was a tremendous explosion.   Second-Lieutenant P. Barclay, R.E., and six other ranks were killed outright, while three sappers were wounded, one of whom died in hospital later.   The second charge was unwillingly removed—by German prisoners !

For many weeks work of this kind continued, with the inevitable sequence of casualties.   Other Tunnellers were busily engaged on the more mundane but decidedly healthier tasks of road making and bridge building.   And, if only to maintain the Tunnellers' reputation for versatility,

the 3rd Canadian Tunnelling Company undertook the repair
of the city waterworks at Roubaix !

VIII

Yet, from the moment the Armistice was signed, it was
obvious that very many of the surviving Tunnellers would
soon be home.   Most of them were coal miners, and the
industry was crying out for their return.   As a consequence,
hundreds of Tunnellers were hurried home in the same
swift and dramatic fashion as they had first been rushed out
to France !

Small cadres of companies remained on duty, however,
to attend to any oddments of undiscovered mines—and
prepared to expand to full strength once again should the
Armistice not develop into a Peace.   But the days of
excitement were over ; the easy life in billets was anti-
climax after the excitement of Messines or the thrills of
booby-trapping.   The short but glorious career of the
Tunnelling Companies was ended.

And, since we recorded the names of the first Tunnellers,
it is only just to chronicle the last—Captain D. Richards,
M.C., of 173rd Tunnelling Company, was the last to leave
France.

CHAPTER XV

I

THE horse has been faithfully described as the "friend of man." Long before he was used as a beast of burden, so scientists tell us, he was regarded as a source of food. Even to-day he is used for human consumption in some countries. Nowadays it may be said he is the "miners' friend," for many thousands of horses are employed underground, the world over, especially in coal mines, drawing the tubs to and from the workings to the main haulage ways. During their work in the Arras Caves, the New Zealand Tunnelling Company used a horse to draw trams of spoil along a light railway laid along the galleries.

But the Tunnellers' friends were much more humble creatures. It has long been known that small animals and birds are more quickly affected by poisonous gases than human beings. The reason for this is that their pulse rate, their breathing, is much more rapid than that of humans ; consequently they feel the effect of poisonous atmosphere, breathed into the lungs, much sooner.

Even in the middle ages this was well known, and pigeons and rats were frequently used in mines for noxious gas detection. Later smaller birds and animals were used, such as canaries and mice.

Even these modest creatures played a very important rôle in the Great War. They were an R.E. store item, and were supplied on indent, just as were rations, tools, etc. This procedure had its difficulties. On one occasion six white mice were indented for. Six were duly handed over, but on arrival at Company H. it was found that the cage contained twenty-seven mice ! It is not known if

this " surplus to requirements " involved any serious
difficulties in filling up ration indents.

As soon as possible after a mine had been fired by either
side, a party, led by an officer, and equipped with self-
contained breathing apparatus, and carrying a small cage
with a mouse or a canary in it, would descend to assist the
men caught below, and also to ascertain what damage had
been done to the galleries. In one company a certain
canary became a regular " old soldier." On entering the
mine he would topple off his perch immediately, and pretend
to be dead. On being taken out of the mine he would
" recover " at once and hop about the cage and chirp
merrily as though he enjoyed his joke !

One considerate Company Commander used to keep a
full record of his canaries. After a canary had been gassed
three times, he classed it as " P.B.," and promoted him to
the headquarters dugout, where his only duty was to sing
to the Commanding Officer.

Gas would hang about a blown end for days. At one
time the end would be quite free from gas, and a few
minutes later it would come welling through the broken
ground, liberated perhaps from some cavity when atmo-
spheric pressure was lowered, as indicated by a falling
barometer. In such cases a canary or mouse would be
kept near the face, and his condition observed from time
to time. If he showed signs of distress, the miners would
withdraw from the face until the foul air had been displaced
by a more vigorous working of the air pump. Sometimes
the miners, well knowing the risk they ran, would place
the cage close to the end of the air pipe so that the mouse
was in good air all the time. So placed, he would be
utterly useless as a gas detector—but his life would be
safe. Some Australians did this at Hill 60. An officer
who pointed out the danger of keeping the mouse near the
air pipe was told : " Why, all the air that —— mouse
eats won't hurt us ! "

At Calonne, a Scots miner, on seeing a canary topple
off its perch, said : " Och ! thon bir-r-d has nae guts ! "
Soon after Scotty was brought out—on a stretcher. Luckily
he was revived with oxygen.

It was the custom to keep the canary at the entrance of the tunnelling officers' dugout, where he would have all the air possible, and any sun that was going. A staff officer passing along a trench, and seeing the canary, was heard to remark : " These Tunnellers are sentimental chaps—they bring their pets into the trenches with them."

There is a sad story about a canary who deserted. He escaped, or was liberated by some kindly disposed person, and fled to a bush in No Man's Land. A sniper was called upon to dispatch the renegade. He failed, and the bird flitted across to the German wire. Then the trench-mortars were told off to deal with the situation. After their first round no more could be seen of the truant. A lot of fuss to make about a canary, apparently, but there is more in it than meets the eye. The reason was that mining was being carried on at that particular spot unknown (we hoped) to the Germans. Had they spotted the canary the secret would have been revealed.

Canaries were a never failing excuse for a visit to Paris, until some meddling busybody discovered that the local breed was equally as good as the Paris model. However, before the discovery was made, the adjutant of a company with a considerable knowledge of the Givenchy front was " sent " off to Paris for canaries. On reporting to the A.P.M. (renowned far and wide for his popularity), he was asked the nature of his business. " I have come for some birds, sir." " You'll find plenty of those here ! " the A.P.M. replied. The adjutant quickly led the wandering thoughts of the A.P.M. back to the path of duty, and explained that he required canary birds for detecting mine gases.

It took some few days to collect the canaries ; then the adjutant set off on his return journey via Rouen, where he had to remain overnight. He arrived early at the station next morning, feeling a little self-conscious with his unusual " baggage," hoping to have a compartment to himself. Placing the cage upon the rack, he spread out his kit as freely as possible to give the impression that most of the seats had been taken. Standing at the door of the compartment, he managed to scare away several wouldbe occupants.   At last a peppery old dugout, Colonel Blimp, came along and, not to be deterred, entered.   With this the adjutant retreated to the opposite corner of the compartment and entrenched himself behind the latest issue of *La Vie Parisienne.*   Not to be outdone, the Colonel took cover behind a copy of *The Times,* several days old.

A few reconnoitring glances from each corner, and silence reigned.   No one else entered the compartment.   The atmosphere was tense.   Presently the train began to draw out of the station slowly.   A canary chirped.   *The Times* rustled.   More chirping.   *The Times* quivered ominously. *La Vie* trembled.   The two men glared at each other over the tops of their literature.   The birds twittered.   The adjutant felt that some explanation was necessary, so he said : " Canaries, sir ! "   " What ? " snorted the Colonel, huge veins standing out on his forehead.   " Canaries . . . for the mines, sir," said the adjutant.   " Good God ! What is the British Army coming to ? " was all the exasperated Colonel could get out before collapsing into his corner.

Somewhat later he recovered.   By way of making amends he eventually produced the largest flask ever seen on the Western Front.   It was the size of a small petrol can.   The adjutant, being a Scot, was in his element. Before very long the two were on the best of terms.   Ere the journey ended—and the flask emptied—they were boon companions, about to begin playing " Clap hands."

II

In this, the greatest war of all time, where millions of troops, many thousands of guns, and thousands of tons of high explosives were employed ; where hundreds of villages and large towns were literally blown out of existence, who would have imagined that such a seemingly trivial and apparently insignificant matter as the length of a canary's claws could be of any importance ?   And yet they were very important indeed.   Care had to be taken to have them properly pedicured.   Were they neglected and allowed to become too long, the value of the birds as gas detectors would be reduced considerably. On being exposed to noxious gases the birds would, in their endeavour to withstand the gas and resist death, lock their claws round the perch and remain in a sitting position. In such a case, the miner carrying the bird would proceed farther into the gas-laden atmosphere than he would have done had the bird fallen from the perch. Perhaps he would collapse. Others would rush to his assistance, with the result that several men would be gassed—where none need have been affected had the bird's claws been cut.

A gunner F.O.O., passing the entrance of a tunnellers' dugout on his way out of the lines, saw a canary hanging there. Whether he thought it would help to brighten up his quarters in the wagon lines, or whether he was moved by humanitarian grounds is not known. We do know he took the bird away. Soon the Tunnellers were hard on his tracks. It took some little time to convince him he had " removed " an R.E. store, the loss of which might have been responsible for the loss of lives.

The services rendered to the Tunnellers in particular, and to the Army in general, by the " wee, sleekit, cow'rin', tim'rous beastie " and the canary, have not been allowed to pass unnoticed and unhonoured. In that most beautiful of all War Shrines, in Edinburgh Castle, they have a place of honour and a lasting memorial. There, graved in the stone of one of the columns, in a laurel wreath surround, are " The Tunnellers' Friends."

CONCLUSION

I

A S Captain Grieve was himself a Tunnelling Officer, with four years's service in France to his credit, the peroration to the story of the Tunnellers is written by his collaborator.

The infantryman of the World War was surely the supreme judge of courage, and he never refused honour to the Tunnellers. Generally, men are not afraid of death, but only of the manner of dying. No one envied the Tunneller his comparative security from enemy bombardment, deep in his burrow, usually far out in front of our front line. Everyone could easily visualize the special terrors which awaited him *at every second* of his duty—the collapse of a gallery, due to the wrath of Nature or enemy, and the subsequent waiting for death in its most horrible form, gasping for air until death came as a relief. The infantryman, accustomed to communal operations, always gave especial credit to individual courage ; hence he allocated no mean praise to airmen and tunnellers.

Few who have no experience of military mining can visualize the prevailing conditions. Only once did I go below, and was mighty thankful when my duty never called on me to do it again. The low galleries alone were enough to terrify an ordinary man—mere burrows, apparently about to collapse at any moment. Danger was always near—or it *appeared* to be always near, which is just as exacting to the nerves. The idea of hand-to-hand combats in these military drain-pipes appeared to be preposterous : yet dozens of men actually faced this startling experience. I came to the conclusion that tunnelling demanded a different brand of courage to that which I possessed, and not even the calm unheeding nonchalance of the Tunnellers themselves could inculcate underground confidence within me.

This book is a record of unusual courage and endeavour. It will recall vivid recollections to many thousands of men —not only Tunnellers, but the tens of thousands of " attached infantry " who at one time or another became temporary Tunnellers themselves. If we have told our story justly, it ought to have a far wider appeal—to all those who delight in human courage and endurance, to all those who can sense the drama of the battle against Nature and the enemy, to all those who appreciate a difficult job well done.

II

Probably one of the first impressions of the general reader will be a sense of irritation against the British method of " muddling through." In spite of their drama and courage, those episodes of 1915 make lamentable reading. We, the premier mining nation of the world, to make such scant and spasmodic use of our specialists ! We, the premier mining nation of the world, to allow the enemy to strike the first underground blows—even the Turks were ahead of us ! It is not enough to deride the official attitude to tunnelling in its early days.

The lack of appreciation on the part of most military men on the subject of tunnelling and its potentialities was at that time profound. Perusing the vast mass of reports, orders and other papers on which this book is largely based, I chanced upon one record of correspondence which is almost too good to be true. It reads :

To V Corps, H.Q.
    Can you please say if you have made use of any ammonal, and if so, whether the results are satisfactory ?
                    (Sgd.)   Lieut.-Col.
                            A.A. and Q.M.G.,

To Camp Commandant, V Corps.
    For report, please.
                    (Sgd.)   Lieut.-Col.
                        A.A. and Q.M.G., V. Corps.

To A.A. and Q.M.G., V. Corps.
   This is not understood. For what purpose is ammonal used, please ?
Is it a drug or an explosive ?
(Sgd.)   Lieut.-Col.
Camp Commandant, V. Corps.

To Camp Commandant, V Corps.
   Perhaps the Medical Officer attached to Corps H.Q. will be able to
give you all required information.
(Sgd.)   Lieut.-Col.
A.A. and Q.M.G., V Corps.

To A.A. and Q.M.G., V Corps.
   In accordance with your Minute 4. I have consulted the M.O. in
command at V Corps, H.Q. He informs me that ammonal is a compound
drug extensively used in America as a sensual sedative in cases of abnormal
sexual excitement. So far as I am able to ascertain, this drug is not a
medical issue to Corps H.Q. Under the circumstances, I regret that I
am unable to report as to the results of the uses of ammonal being satisfactory or not, and at the present moment the M.O. states that no cases
have occurred among the V Corps H.Q. personnel indicating the necessity
for administering the drug.
(Sgd.)   Lieut-.Col.
Camp Commandant, V Corps.

   The Tunnelling organization began its career in typical
British fashion—ill-apppreciated and ill-equipped.   Its
" technical " apparatus was mostly borrowed—water bottles
from the French as crude listening instruments, to be
superseded by listening sticks as used by the Metropolitan Water Board for tracing leaking water mains !
We have seen how any new officer who bought his own
instruments received an uproarious welcome.   A considerable part of the early equipment was purchased by Tunneller
officers themselves.   Yet this Cinderella service, again in
typical British fashion, was before the end of the War the
most thoroughly efficient of all arms, had fought the enemy
to a standstill on his own ground, and was appropriately
appreciated by the high command, both British and German !
   The lesson of this is to the future.   The work of the
Tunnellers has the effect of saving life in wartime : the
Messines Ridge, for example, must have cost at least four
times the actual casualties had it been attacked by frontal
assault without the mines.   The effect will still prevail

in a future war, if any. Consequently, it is not too much to urge that the lessons of the last underground war should not be forgotten.

There is a tendency to-day to think in terms of mechanized and highly mobile units. On the Continent, however, the greater reliance is still placed on the army of mass. What, then, are the possibilities in the case of the outbreak of war? Imagine, purely for the sake of argument, the circumstances of 1914 repeated. There would be almost immediate frontier clashes, and raids by the mechanized forces into enemy territory. The first fortnight of the War, in fact, would be infinitely more lively and eventful than the same period of the last. But by that time the armed masses would have been mobilized. With the mechanized land and air forces now acting as auxiliaries instead of principals, the masses would march to battle. *And the side which got the worst of the first serious encounter would immediately dig itself in.* Then, as in 1914, there must of necessity follow a reversion to siege tactics; and in siege tactics the Tunneller is vastly important.

Since 1918, mining has made many technical advances, some of which could easily be adapted to military purposes. Courses of mining instruction should be part of the essential training of every officer of the Royal Engineers. It would be absurd to press for the formation of regular Tunnelling Companies, *but is there any reason why Territorial Tunnelling Companies should not be enlisted?* There are enough young miners out of work to man the necessary minimum a dozen times over. Nor could the formation of such companies be classed as militant or provocative, as in the case with other arms. The question of increased armaments does not arise : the real point is, that while you have armaments at all you should have the most efficient armaments you can get.

One parallel point, too. The next war, should we ever be foolish enough to permit its coming, will be an underground war—air forces will see to that. From the very first second of the war the urgent demand will be for underground shelter—not merely on London, but in every town and village in the British Isles. Who is going to construct the necessary dugouts ?　Why not enlist the necessary specialists *now* into a tunnelling reserve of Royal Engineers ?　Why not employ out-of-work miners on such tasks *now* ?　There is no hint of offensive warfare in the suggestion ; it is purely defensive.　So long as there are militant air forces, so long shall we need adequate *and immediate* protection.　When air forces are abolished then the dugouts could be demolished.　We should have lost nothing.　There is a serious school of thought—and its adherents include tens of thousands of unemployed—which considers that it is better for men to dig holes and fill fill them up again rather than remain compulsorarily idle, existing on the mis-called " dole."

III

The very magnitude of the tasks of the Tunnellers is enough to stagger the imagination.　The Tunnellers were a specialist corps—and yet General Harvey had under his command more British troops than Wellington could deploy at Waterloo !　We have read the stupendous figures of the sizes of charges placed in the mines, and compared them with the puny efforts of previous wars. Compare the 8,000 lbs. of Petersburg with the 1,000,000 lbs. of Messines !

If you walk along the old front line to-day, you will be amazed at the manner in which the scars of war have been effaced.　Villages rebuilt, fields retilled—only the woods still bear the marks of war upon them, for you cannot grow new trees in a generation.　But here and there you will come across little lakes which are not marked on a war-time map—near Messines particularly.　These are the old mine craters, now full of water and bordered by reeds and rushes, a perfect-fitting feature of the landscape. In their present peace it is almost impossible to visualize the fury of their formation, the earth heaving skywards, the angry hovering clouds, the men who simply disappeared from the earth's surface—and the other men who watched their terrible handiwork.

IV

One of the features of this book, too, must be the revelation of the remarkable versatility of the Tunnellers. We have seen them in a dozen different capacities, from infantry to bridge-builders, earning high praise from their commanders. I chanced across one unusual incident : Captain W. B. R. King was able, by a piece of deduction that would have done credit to Dr. Thorndyke, to prove that the Germans were transporting war material via Holland. Captain King and Lieutenant-Colonel Sir T. W. Edgeworth David were examining some of the famous " pill boxes " of the Ypres and Vimy fronts, and in the concrete used in their construction found pieces of one of the rarest rocks in the world. This was a very peculiar kind of basalt, which occurs only at Niedermendig, on the Rhine above Cologne. The obvious method of transport from this area was via the neutral Dutch waterway system, where it was described as civil material for Belgium. The proof that it was used for military purposes was forwarded to the Dutch government, and the illicit traffic was immediately stopped.

V

The military student will, I think, find his attention attracted and held by more than one of the detailed incidents in the story of the Tunnellers. He will already be familiar, of course, with the triumph of Messines—although few books describing the battle give sufficient weight to the material *and moral* effects of the unprecedented series of mines. But other points have almost escaped comment— the complete absence of mining at Loos, for example ; here was an area admirably suited to the Tunneller's craft —yet the ground was only handed over to him *after* the battle was lost. Nor will he fail to remark the potentialities of mining at Gallipoli, where a trifling advance would have

x

meant so much. With a couple of thousand tunnellers available, the peninsula might have been ours.

I imagine, too, that the description of the preparations for the Battle of the Somme will occasion some hard thinking. I now learn that I need have faced comparatively little danger on July 1st, 1916 ; that instead of that death-crawl across the wide No Man's Land, the men of my division might have reached a spot within a mere thirty yards of the German trenches by means of perfectly safe Russian saps. Why no one took the trouble to tell us of this before the battle I am at a loss to understand.

And yet, I fancy, thoughtful students will find their retrospective thoughts after reading this book concentrated on one episode—not the Somme, or Vimy, or Messines, or the personal epics of tunnelling and booby trapping, but on the defence of Givenchy. The greater part of the credit has been given, quite rightly, to the heroic infantry who defended it, but they would be the first to acknowledge their immense debt to the Tunnellers. As an ordinary sector of the British line, Givenchy might easily have gone the way of the rest. Fortified as it was by every device of tunnelling, it was an impregnable stronghold. Its vital importance can be visualized in a series of " ifs." If Givenchy had fallen, then Ludendorff's right hand punch would have connected with his left. Nine-tenths of the British front would have been broken ; with so wide a base for further attack, the Channel ports must surely have been captured. This does not necessarily mean that we would have lost the War, but it does definitely mean that we could never have won it in 1918.

VI

The men who did these mighty works, who fought in the bowels of the earth, who defied Nature's fitful moods, who loosed thunderbolts that Jove might have envied, who laughed at death and the continuous threat of death, who matched their wits against the enemy's in that nerve-racking business of booby trapping, whose lives depended upon the length of a canary's claws—where are these men to-day ?

The officers, mostly mining engineers, are scattered all over the world. The addresses of the first few hundred orders for this book read like a gazeteer of the British Empire. The rank and file—or their survivors—are still with us, most of them in our own islands. The piece of coal burning in your hearth may have been hewn by a man who once fought to the death with a German in a pygmy underground gallery. And, when you ride through the distressed areas of Northumberland or South Wales or elsewhere, observe those men squatting on their heels by the road-side ; it is sheer habit, for they have done no mining for years ; later you will see them in pathetic queues outside the Employment Exchange—men who have almost lost hope ; among them are the men of Messines and Givenchy, the men who gambled with death for their country.

Their work brought little glory—and less publicity. It was seldom spectacular and always dangerous ; consequently it did not appeal to very many newspaper correspondents. Their work was for their fellows—by their own perilous toil to economize in the ghastly expenditure of lives. Sapper Hackett, V.C., epitomized the Tunneller's creed when at the moment of death he proclaimed : " I am a Tunneller. I must look after my mate."

As I have said, the infantry took off their hats to the Tunnellers, and that is the highest praise in the world. Haig, after he had failed to use them at Loos, learned to appreciate their work at its proper worth. After witnessing one of their versatile efforts, Haig remarked : " They are the best unit in the whole army ; there is nothing they cannot do." Time after time he sent written evidence of his esteem, and at the moment of victory he penned them a special message with his own hand.

" A large number of men are now being withdrawn from Tunnelling Companies for urgent work at home.

" Before they leave the country I wish to convey to the Controllers of Mines and to all ranks of Tunnelling Companies, both Imperial and Overseas, my very keen appreciation of the fine work that has been done by the Tunnelling Companies throughout the last four years.

" At their own special work, Mine Warfare, they have demonstrated their complete superiority over the Germans, and whether in the patient defensive mining, in the magnificent success at Messines, or in the preparation for the offensive of the Somme, Arras and Ypres, they have shown the highest qualities both as Military Engineers and as fighting troops.

" Their work in the very dangerous task of removing enemy traps and delay-action charges, on subways, dugouts, bridging, roads and the variety of other services on which they have been engaged, has been on a level with their work on the mines.

" They have earned the thanks of the whole Army for their contribution to the defeat of the enemy. Their fighting spirit and technical efficiency has enhanced the reputation of the whole Corps of Royal Engineers, and of the Engineers of the Overseas Forces.

" I should like to include in the appreciation the work done by the Army Mine Schools and by the Australian Electrical and Mechanical Mining and Boring Company.

" D. HAIG, F.M.,

Commander-in-Chief,

British Armies in France.

" General Headquarters,
December 4th, 1918."

INDEX

(Units indexed separately at end)

A

Achi Baba, 78.
Ægean, 78.
Aeroplane Trench, 122.
Ailly-sur-Noye, 273.
Aire, 290.
Aisne, 144, 256, 291.
Alabaster, Capt. E. O., 66.
Albert, 66, 259, 296, 297.
Allenby, General, 64.
Amiens, 66, 261, 272, 273, 275, 291.
Ancre River, 113, 118, 124, 134, 263, 265, 272, 297, 298.
Annequin, 191, 195.
Anvin, 293.
Anzac, 77, 85, 86.
Artois, 156.
Arques, 290.
Armagh Wood, 58, 248.
Armentières, 59, 64, 108, 140, 156, 289.
Armistice, 153, 309, 310.
Arras, 108, 139, 140, 141, 143, 149, 154, 156, 157, 159, 161, 205, 256, 324.
Arras—Bapaume Road, 157.
Arras—Cambrai Road, 157, 158, 259.
Arras Caves, 154, 156, 157, 158, 159, 311.
Arras Citadel, 159.
Aubercourt, 263.
Aubers Ridge, 60, 69.
Auchy, 295.
Auret, Capt., M.C., 280, 281.
Au Ritz, 99.
Aveluy Wood, 298.
Avre, River, 261, 272.

B

Babœuf, 267.
Bailey, Lieut. C. E., 104, 105.
Bailleul, 72, 289.

Bapaume, 145, 146, 149, 157, 259.
Bapaume Town Hall, 145, 146.
Barclay, 2nd Lieut. L. A., 36, 56.
Barclay, Lieut. P., R.E., 309.
Barisis, 257.
Bayonvillers, 268.
Bazentin Ridge, 130.
Beasley, Capt., 91, 93.
Beaucourt, 269.
Beaumont Hamel, 116, 117, 132, 135.
Bedson, Sapper, 222.
Begg, Private, 84.
Bell, Lieut. F., 68.
Bellenglise, 303.
Bellewaarde Farm, 250.
Bellicourt, 304.
Bendall, Lieut., 281.
Berles, 99.
Berlin, 250.
Berlin Tunnel, 210, 211, 212, 213, 214.
Bernard, 2nd Lieut., 84.
Berthonval sector, 142, 153.
Béthune Concession, 191, 192.
Béthune—La Bassée Road, 169.
Beugnatre, 146.
Birdcage, 237.
Bishop, Lance Corporal, 56.
Bishop, Private, 56.
Blangy, 259.
Bliss, Capt. P. W., R.E., 61.
Bluff, The, 65, 98, 108, 140, 175, 176, 177, 178, 179, 180, 181, 182, 183, 184, 185, 186, 187, 188, 189, 190, 207, 210, 214, 216, 225, 231.
Boeschepe, 288, 289.
Boesinghe, 248, 250.
Bois Carre, 216.
Bois Francais, 122.
Bois Quarante, 208.
Booby-traps, 147, 148, 295, 302, 303, 304, 310, 324.
Bordall, Lieut., 56, 57.
Boulogne, 293.

Bourlon Wood, 299.
Boves, 264, 269, 273.
Boyes, Lieut., 80.
Brattice, 57.
Bray, 65, 265, 266.
Bray St. Christophe, 260.
Bretigny, 267.
Brickstacks, 30, 45, 49, 50, 67, 87.
Brigade Mining Sections, 29, 66.
Brisco, 2nd Lieut., 177, 178, 179.
Brown, Capt. T., 196, 197.
Brown, 2nd Lieut., 93, 94.
Brown, Private, 84.
Buchanan, Major, 268.
Buckingham, Capt. W. E., R.E., 68.
Bulgar Point, 122, 123.
Bullecourt, 144, 258.
Bullen, Capt. F., 72.
Burnside borer, 123, 177.

C

Caddy, Lieut. J. P., 86.
Caisson, 64.
Calais, 293.
Caledonian Dugouts, 280, 281.
Caledonian Road, 277, 282, 283.
Calonne, 150, 160, 312.
Cambos Farm, 264.
Cambrai, 256, 259.
Cambrin, 50, 106, 280.
Canadian Government, 161.
Canal du Nord, 257, 299.
Canterbury, 293.
Caporetto, 256.
Cappy, 266.
Carency, 139.
Carency Sugar Factory, 139.
Carey's Force, 263.
Carnoy, 65, 116, 123.
Cartwright, Lieut., 265.
Cash, Capt. J. N., R.E., 68.
Casino Point, 122, 123, 125, 126.
Cassel, Lieut., 48.
Castel, 272.
Caterpillar, 52, 64, 211.
Celle, River, 273.
Cerisy, 261.
Chalk Pits, 70, 109.
Chambers, Capt., 85.
Chanticlere, 108.
Chapeau de Gendarme, 97.
Chapigny, 104.
Charteris, Brig.-Gen., 246.

Chatham, 24, 35, 37.
Chemin des Dames, 143, 161, 205, 292.
Chicken Run, 63.
Chicory Factory, 280.
Chord, 88.
Chrinchon Stream, 159.
Church, Major, D.S.O., M.C., 280.
Cité St. Elie, 88, 150.
Clarke, Lieut., 174, 214.
"Clay Kicking," 25, 30, 32, 33, 34,
    35, 37, 39, 43, 182, 220, 225.
Cléry, 264, 265.
Clifford, Lance-Corporal, 59.
Cloutman, Lieut., 43.
Cojeul, River, 257.
Cologne, 321.
Cordonnerie Farm, 59, 91.
Coulthard, Major R. W., 108.
Courtney's Post, 78.
Cowan, Major S. H., R.E., 58.
Craters :
    "A" Crater, 183, 184, 185, 186.
    "B" Crater, 178, 180, 181, 182,
        183, 184, 185, 186.
    "C" Crater, 186, 188.
    "D" Crater, 186, 188, 190.
    "E" Crater, 186, 188, 190.
    No. 2 Crater, 215.
    No. 3 Crater, 215.
    No. 4 Crater, 216.
    No. 5 Crater, 216.
    Broadbridge, 141.
    Broadmarsh, 154.
    Cassel, 218.
    Cawley's, 81.
    Cöln, 217, 218.
    Crosbie, 141.
    Football, 141.
    Grange, 141.
    Irish, 141.
    Kennedy, 141.
    Lichfield, 162.
    Lochnagar, 120.
    Longfellow, 154.
    Love, 141.
    Momber, 141.
    Montreal, 141.
    Ontario Farm, 244.
    Red Dragon, 166, 167.
    Warlingham, 168.
    Zivy, 162.
Crimean War, 100, 135.
Cropper, Lieut., 64 ; Capt., 72 ;
    Major, 216.

Crozat Canal, 257.
Cuinchy, 30, 44, 45, 46, 49, 64.
Currie, Major E. B., 88, 263.

D

Dale-Logan, Lieut.-Col., R.A.M.C., 75, 196.
Danford, Major B. V. W., R.E., 44, 75.
Daniels, Lieut., 57.
Dardanelles, 78, 108.
David, Major T. W., 109, 236 ; Lieut.-Col. Sir T. W., 321.
Davis, Capt. A. W., 87, 108, 212.
Dean, Sgt.-Major, 81, 82.
Delay Action Mines, 146, 148, 302, 304, 309, 324.
Démuin, 263, 264, 272.
Dennis, Private P., 82.
Dick-Cleland, Lieut., R.E., 55.
Dixon, Capt. E. J. Q. (" Birdy "), 164.
Dixon, 2nd Lieut., 192.
Docherty, Sapper, 91, 93.
Douai, 70, 297.
Douai Plain, 139.
Double Crassier, 88, 94, 95, 96.
Doullens, 293.
Duck's Bill, 110.
Duck's Bill (Givenchy), 163.
Duigan, Major J. E., 108.

E

Eaton, Lieut. A. E., 97, 98.
Edmonds, Col. J. E., R.E. (now Brig.-Gen. Sir James, C.B., C.M.G.), 73.
Edwards, Capt., 85.
Ellison, Corporal, 59.
Epéhy, 302, 309.
Ervillers, 146.
Eschwege, Ober-Lieutenant von, 302.
Essar, 282.
Evans, Col., 1st Black Watch, 282.
Evans, Capt. D. Ivor, M.C., 276, 282.

F

Factory Farm, 236, 237.
Falkenhayn, Gen., 113, 144.
Falmouth, 108.
Fampoux, 259.
Fargnier, 266, 267.
Fauquissart, 44, 109, 209.
Felleries, 307.

Festubert, 26, 163.
Feuchy, 259.
Fewtrell, Lieut.-Col., 108.
Fins, 265.
First Army Mine Rescue School, 75, 136, 138, 324.
Flame-thrower, 121, 122, 123, 126.
Flixecourt, 293.
Foch, Marshal, 292.
Fontaine-les-Cappy, 71.
Ford, Sergeant, 56.
Fosse 8, 191, 192, 193, 194, 195, 196, 197, 198.
Fosse 3, 192, 196.
Fosse 4, 192, 196.
Fosse 9, 192, 195, 196, 197.
Fosse 12, 192.
Fougasse, 165, 169.
Fowke, Maj.-Gen. G. H., 32, 34, 73, 209.
Frayling, Lieut., 236.
French Army, 40, 42, 48, 67, 69, 71, 116, 139, 140, 176.
Frévent, 293.
Freezing Process, 41.
Fricourt, 65, 66, 113, 116, 121, 122, 129, 252.
Frise, 261.
Fusilier Bluff, 80, 83.

G

Gallipoli, 77, 86, 165, 321.
Gard'ner, 2nd Lieut., 55.
Garment, Lieut., 297.
Gentelles, 273.
Gibbons, Lieut., 197.
Gibson, Private, 84.
Gilchrist, Capt., R.E., 270.
Givenchy, 26, 30, 31, 32, 34, 35, 36, 44, 45, 64, 140, 163, 166, 168, 275, 276, 277, 278, 279, 280, 281, 282, 283, 284, 285, 286, 291, 295, 322, 323.
Givenchy Keep, 277, 281, 282, 284.
Godson, Capt., 266.
Gomiecourt, 146.
Gouzeaucourt, 256, 257.
Gouzeaucourt Wood, 265.
Grace, 2nd Lieut. L. T., 91, 93, 94.
Grant, Gen., 263.
Great Eastern Tunnel, 132.
Greenhalgh, Lance-Corporal, 84.
Gridiron, 80, 81, 83, 85.

Griffiths, Major J. Norton, M.P., 25, 26, 30, 32, 34, 35, 36, 37, 38, 42, 45, 60, 61, 64, 74, 207, 208, 209.
Griffiths, Major D. M., R.E., 52.
Grimes, Private J., 82.
Guillaucourt, 261.
Gully Spur, 86.
Gurkha Bluff, 78.
Gwyther, Capt. J. R., 71.

H

Hackett, Sapper William, V.C., 166, 167, 323.
Haig, Field Marshal Sir Douglas, 143, 171, 199, 204, 206, 241, 255, 257, 286, 301, 323, 324.
Hairpin, 88, 295.
Hall, Private, 1st Black Watch, 57.
Halle, 264.
Hallue, River, 272.
Ham, 272.
Hamelet, 266.
Hangard, 264.
Hannay, Capt., 110.
Hansen, 2nd Lieut., 107.
Hargicourt, 304.
Hargraves, 2nd Lieut. E. P., 200.
Harlow, Capt., R.A.M.C., 265.
Harper, Sergeant, 57.
Hartley, Sapper, 105.
Harvey, Lieut.-Col. R. N., R.E. (later Maj.-Gen., C.B., C.M.G., D.S.O.), 32, 35, 61, 73, 75, 209, 299, 320.
Havrincourt Bridge, 299, 300, 301.
Hawthorn Redoubt, 117, 124.
Hawthorn Ridge, 117, 132.
Hazebrouck, 108.
Hebuterne, 116.
Heinrici, Major Paul, 234, 240.
Helles, 77, 78, 85, 86.
Heudicourt, 265.
Hepburn, Capt., 65, 176.
Hermies, 299.
Hermies Catacombs, 259.
Hesson, Pte., 56.
Hibbert, Lieut., 177.
Hickling, Capt. H. C. B., R.E., 71.
High Wood, 130, 131.
Hill 60, 39, 44, 51, 52, 53, 54, 60, 64, 98, 172, 173, 174, 175, 207, 209, 210, 211, 212, 213, 214, 248, 252, 253.
Hill 63, 51, 239.

Hill 70, 51, 109, 136, 171, 254, 276.
Hill, Lieut. L. C., 63.
Hill, Lieut. Stafford, 58.
Hindenburg Line, 135, 144, 149, 304.
Hindenburg Tunnel, 144.
Hodge, Corporal, 186.
Hog's Back, 73.
Hohenzollern Redoubt, 70, 72, 88, 150.
Holmes, Capt., 299.
Hollandscheschuur, 208.
Hollenscheschuur Salient, 216.
Hooge, 58, 70, 249.
Hopkins, Capt., 299.
Houplines, 44, 63, 252.
Hulluch, 70, 72, 88, 110, 150, 168, 276.
Hutchinson, Corporal, 57.

I

Imperial War Graves Commission, 162.
Inch Street, 119.
Inspector of Mines, 75, 124, 148.

J

Jack, Captain, R.E., 268.
Joffre, General, 112, 130, 143.
Johnston, Major, 266.
Jose, Lance Corporal, 285.
Jumel, 271.

K

Kaiser, 156.
Kemmel, 231, 289.
Kereves Dere, 78.
Kipling, Rudyard, 96.
King, Capt. W. B. R., 321.
Krithia Nullah, 79.
Krithia, Third Battle of, 79.
Kruisstraat, 208, 230, 231.
Kruisstraart Cabaret, 216, 230.

L

La Bassée, 163.
La Bassée Canal, 30, 36, 65, 87, 110, 150, 163, 164, 276, 278, 279.
La Boiselle, 65, 66, 72, 116, 119, 125.
Labyrinth, The, 108.
La Clytte, 72.
Lacy, 2nd Lieut. E. P., Westmorland and Cumberland Yeomanry, 50.
La Douve, River, 208, 232, 236.

La Drumez, 88.
La Fére, 144, 257.
La Mare, de Capt., 105.
La Motte, 263.
Lamotte-Brebière, 265.
Lancashire Farm, 251.
Lanchy, 260.
Landrecies, 306.
La Panne, 202.
La Petite Douve Farm, 208, 233.
La Philosophe, 68.
Laroque, 2nd Lieut., 179.
Laventie, 109, 110.
Law, Sapper, 104.
Lawe Canal, 282.
Lawrence, Dorothy, 66.
Laws, Capt. H. W., 79 ; Major, D.S.O., R.N.D., 85.
Le Cateau, 307.
Le Catlet, 304.
Leeming, Mr., 32, 35.
Lempire, 302.
Lens, 69, 70.
Le Plantin, 26.
Le Quesnel, 269.
Le Quesnoy, 169.
l'Escaut, Canal de, 299.
Lestrem, 58.
Lewis, Corporal, 197.
Liddell Hart, Capt., 206.
Lille, 156, 244.
Lloyd George, Mr., 257.
Lone Farm, 279.
Longstaff, Private, 62.
Loos, 70, 136, 321, 323.
Loringhoven, von Freytag-, General, 142.
Lowry, Major, R.E., 268, 271, 272.
Luce, River, 261, 262, 263, 272.
Ludendorff, Gen., 144, 246, 250, 262, 275, 291, 292, 296, 322.
Lys, 40, 208, 254, 275, 276, 279, 286, 291, 292, 293.
Lyster, Lieut., 180, 181.

M

Macdonald, 2nd Lieut., 258.
Macgill, Patrick, 47.
Macnamara, 2nd Lieut., 84.
Mad Point, 106.
Maedelstede Farm, 208, 223.
Magny la Fosse, 303.
Mairie Redoubt, 277, 282.

Maissemy, 260.
Mametz, 116, 129, 130.
Mametz, East, 122.
Mametz, West, 122.
Manancourt, 263.
Manning, Major, 194.
Marcelcave, 261, 262, 263, 264.
Maricourt, 65, 71, 113, 116.
Marshall, Sapper, 270.
Marsland, Lieut., 282.
McDougall, Corporal, 137.
McPherson, Lieut., 186.
McReady, Gen., 34.
Meaulte, 265.
Medlicott, Lance-Corporal, 153.
Meharicourt, 268, 269, 270.
Menadue, Sergeant, 283, 284.
Menin Road, 249.
Mericourt l'Abbé, 263, 265.
Merris, 289.
Merville, 286, 289.
Messines, 130, 139, 149, 250, 251, 273, 274, 321, 322, 323, 324.
Messines, Battle of, 61, 204–247, 296, 310, 320.
Messines—Wytschaete Ridge, 190, 199, 204, 205, 206, 289, 318.
Metropolitan Water Board, 48.
Miles, Foreman, 32.
Mines :
    G3, 121.
    G15, 121, 125.
    G19, 121.
    H1, 117.
    H2, 117.
    H3, 117, 118, 124, 132, 134.
    R1 (1), 133.
    R1 (2), 133.
    Bond Street, 164, 165.
    Bunny Hutch, 164.
    Duck's Bill, 164.
    " E " Sap Mines, 165.
    Hawthorn, 132.
    Hope Street, 164.
    Lochnagar, 72, 120–125.
    Orchard, 32, 56, 164.
    Red House, 164.
    Shaftesbury Avenue, 164.
    The Warren, 164.
    White House, 164.
Moat Farm, 276, 277, 278, 279, 282, 283, 284.
Moislains, 265.
Mollines-Vidame, 293.

Momber, Capt. E. M., R.E., 58.
Monchy-au-Bois, 259.
Montauban, 129.
Moreuil, 271.
Morris, 2nd Lieut., 94.
Morris, 2nd Lieut. A. E., 153.
Morse, Capt., 109.
Morton, Private, 84.
Mory, 146.
Mound, The, 46, 176.
Moudit, 299.
Muches, 156, 157.
Mudros, 83.
Mulqueen, Major, 267.
Munitions, French Minister of, 197.
Murray, Lieut., 186.

N

Nag's Nose, 218.
Neuf Fosse, Canal de, 290.
Neuve Chapelle, 44, 69, 88, 91, 104.
Neuville St. Vaast, 99, 154.
Newell, Sergeant, 281, 282, 283.
Niedermendig, 321.
Nieuport, 200, 201, 202.
Nivelle, Gen., 143, 199, 205, 206.
Nixon, Corporal, 85.
Noeux-les-Mines, 72, 88, 109, 191.
North, Major, 182, 183.
Noye, River, 272, 273.
Noyon, 143, 267.
Noyon Salient, 144.
Nurlu, 264.

O

O'Connel, Sapper J., 200, 201.
Oise, River, 256, 257, 267.
Ollezy, 260.
Omiecourt, 264, 265.
Orchard, The (Festubert), 26.
Ostend, 199.
Ovillers, 118.

P

Paris, 313.
Parker, Lance-Corporal, 80.
Passchendaele, 139, 201, 203, 248 to 255, 257.
Passchendaele Ridge, 254, 287.
Peckham, 88, 208, 225.
Péronne, 145, 260, 265, 266, 272, 292.
Péronne Road, 97.
Pétain, Gen., 206.
Peterhead Sap, 118, 134.

Petit Bois, 88, 208, 231.
Petit Bois, or S.P.13., 218 to 223, 244.
Phonelle, 306.
Picardy, 156.
Piccadilly, 277, 281, 282, 283, 284.
Piling, 42.
Pimple, The, 139, 141.
Pink Farm, 79.
Piraud, Capt., 66.
Ploegsteert, 44, 60, 210, 237.
Plumer, Gen., 204, 205, 206, 241, 288.
Pointe de Gravelines, 293.
Pollock, Capt., 109, 214.
Polygon Butte, 249.
Pont Fixe, 277, 281, 282, 283, 284.
Pope, Capt. A. W., 109.
Pope's Post, 78.
Preedy, Capt. R. E. (later Lieut.-Col., D.S.O., M.C.), 36, 45, 50, 56.
Proto Set, 91, 93, 133, 136, 137, 138.
Purfleet, 121.
Push Pipes, 131, 158.

Q

Quarries, 70, 88.
Queen Victoria Shaft, 214.
Quinn, Sapper, 270.
Quinn's Post, 77, 78.
Quinque Rue, 26, 28.

R

Railway Reserve, 259.
Railway Wood, 58, 248, 250, 251, 276.
Ravine, 180, 185, 216.
Rawlinson, Gen. Sir Henry, 25.
Redan, 72, 117, 132.
Red Lamp, 88, 94.
Rees, Lieut., 282.
Reims, 143.
Reninghelst, 290.
Reservoir Hill, 295.
Rhine, 321.
Ribemont, 265.
Richards, Capt. D., M.C., 310.
Richardson, Capt. T. C., R.E., 71.
Rivington, 118, 119.
Roberts, Capt., 197.
Roberts Trench, 134.
Robertson, Gen. Sir William, 34.
Robertson, Lieut., 195.
Robertson, Private, 84.
Roclincourt, 154.

Rogers, Major, 108.
Ronssoy, 266, 302.
Ronville, 154.
Ronville Tunnel, 158.
Rosel, 300.
Roubaix, 310.
Rouen, 66, 71, 109, 110.
Rought, Lieut. P., 62.
Rue de Bois, 64, 68.
Russell's Top, 86.
Russia, 256.
Russian Saps, 100, 115, 116, 118, 121, 127, 128, 132, 135, 154, 160, 169, 322.

S

Sailly-Labourse, 88, 281.
Sailly-Lorette, 261 to 266.
St. Eloi, 44, 46, 51, 61, 98, 115, 176, 207, 208, 209, 214, 244.
St. Emilie, 266, 309.
St. Marie Cappel, 87.
St. Omer, 32, 290, 293.
St. Quentin Canal, 257, 304.
St. Quentin, 144, 257, 272.
St. Sauveur's Tunnel, 157.
St. Simon, 260.
St. Pol, 293.
Sanctuary Wood, 48, 70, 249.
Sapignies, 146.
Sausage Valley, 120.
Saps :
    Arthurlie, 118.
    Balmoral Street, 121.
    Beet, 132, 133.
    Cat, 132, 134.
    Dinnet Street, 121.
    Excema, 132, 133, 134.
    First Avenue, 118, 134.
    Hunter Street, 132.
    Inverary, 118.
    John, 116, 132, 133, 134.
    Kerriemuir, 120.
    Mark, 132, 133, 134.
    Mary, 118.
    North Street, 132.
    Peterhead, 118, 134.
    Purfleet, 121.
    Rivington, 118, 119.
    South Street, 132.
    Waltney, 118.
    3, 4, and 5 Saps, 126.
    11 Sap, 123.

Saps—continued.
    12 Sap, 123.
    13 Sap, 122.
    14 (1) Sap, 122.
    15 Sap, 122.
    15 (1) Sap, 122.
    L.25 Sap, 122.
Scarp, River, 113, 139, 144, 159, 257.
Scheldt, River, 113, 299.
Schwarben Hohe, 120, 125.
Scott's Farm, 259.
Second Army Mine School, 109, 214.
Serre, 113, 116.
Shanks, Pte., 197.
Shotfiring, 121.
Shrewsbury Forest, 40.
Sign Post Lane, 110.
Smart, Lieut., 136, 137.
Smith, Sapper, 56.
Soissons, 143.
Somme, 65, 66, 71, 107, 113, 132, 135, 140, 143, 156, 159, 261, 272 to 275, 291, 322, 323, 324.
Souchez, 150.
Souchez River, 139, 150.
Souzanne, 71, 97.
Spanbroekmolen, 88, 208, 227 to 229, 240.
Spencer, Capt., 185.
Steenbeck, 288.
Stevenson, Lieut.-Col. A. G., R.E., 75.
Steward, Pte., 84.
Stewart, Sapper, 284.
Stokes, Lieut. R. G., 63.
Subways :
    Barricade, 154.
    Bentata, 154.
    Blue Bell, 153.
    Bulley, 150.
    Bunny Hutch, 280, 282, 283, 284.
    Cavalier, 153.
    Cobourg, 153.
    Douai, 154.
    Dudley, 150.
    First Avenue, 154.
    Gobron, 153.
    Goodman, 153.
    Grange, 153, 154, 161.
    Gum Boot, 150.
    Lane Tunnel, 169.
    Lance, 295.
    Marble Arch, 150.
    Mill Tunnel, 169.
    North, 150.

Subways—*continued*.
   Robertson Tunnel, 169.
   Rotten Row, 150.
   South, 150.
   Tottenham, 153.
   Vincent, 153.
   Zivy, 154.
   Sunken Road, 164.
   Surface Saps, F., D., H., K., J., 164.
Suvla, 85.
Syme, Lieut., 65, 177.

T

Tambour Duclos, 66, 72, 121, 125, 307.
Tank Corps, 251.
Templeton, 2nd Lieut. J. B., 110.
Templeux, 264.
Terdeghem, 58, 61.
Thiepval, 118, 132.
Third Army, 66, 75, 140, 256, 257, 298, 302.
Third Army Mine School, 260.
Thirlwell, Capt., 195, 196.
Thomas, Commandant, 66.
Torrin, Lieut., 56, 57.
Tor Top, 248, 250, 251.
Tortille, River, 265.
Tournai, 156.
Toutencourt, 72.
Trincourt, 264.
Trones Wood, 303.
Trounce, 2nd Lieut., 91, 93.
Trower, Capt. R. G., 72.
Trower, Lieut., 67.
Trueman, Sapper, 136.
Tubbing, 41, 42.
Turner, Sapper, 283, 284.
Tyndrum, 118.

U

Underground Reservoirs, 154.

V

Varesnes, 267.
Verdun, 113, 143, 206.
Vermelles, 68, 196.
Vers, 273.
Vineyard, 80, 81.
Villecholes, 260.
Villers Bretonneux, 272, 273.
Vimy Ridge, 99, 110, 139, 149, 150, 153, 161, 168, 321, 322.
Wérly, 268, 271.

W

Wardrecques, 290.
War Office, 25, 30, 31, 34, 35, 37, 38.
Walker, Capt., M.C., 282, 283, 284.
Walker, Johnnie, 187.
Waterloo, Battle of, 204, 247, 320.
Ward, 2nd Lieut., 138.
Weincourt, 260, 271.
Weincourt Dump, 261.
Wellesley, Capt. E. V. C., 52, 66.
Wellington, Duke of, 204, 247, 320.
Western Birdcage, 81.
Wheler, Lieut. A. S., 197.
Whidbone, Lieut. G., 57.
White, Lieut., R.E., 39.
White City, 132.
Whittaker, Sgt., 91, 93.
Wilkinson, Private, 80.
Williamson, Lieut., 176.
Williams, Major G. C., R.E., 44 ; Lieut.-Col., 75.
Wilson, Capt. T. W., 110.
Windy Corner, 163, 279.
Winchester, 110.
Wombat Drill, 251.
Wood, Lieut. A. S., 195.
Wood, Lieut., 281.
Woods, 2nd Lieut., 169, 170.
Wright, 2nd Lieut. S., 91, 93.
Wulverghem, 61, 98, 209.
Wytschaete, 149, 216, 223.
Wytschaete Wood, 224.

Y

Young, Sergeant, 105.
Ypres, 30, 43, 51, 108, 149, 176, 199, 249, 254, 257, 321, 324.
Ypres—Comines Canal, 175, 208.
Ypres—Comines Railway, 176.
Ypres Salient, 44, 46, 199, 254, 286-7.
Ypres, Third Battle of, 248.
" Y " Sap, 119, 125.
Yser Canal, 250.
Yser, River, 200, 201, 202.
Ytres, 303.
" Y " Wood, 97.

Z

Zeebrugge, 199.
Zonnebeke, 249.
Zouave Valley, 139, 153, 154, 155.
" Z " Scheme, 193.
Zwarteleen, 39, 46.

INDEX OF UNITS

ARMIES.

First, 30, 75, 109, 150, 293–5.
Second, 30, 75, 109, 228, 293.
Third, 66, 75, 140, 256, 257, 293, 298, 302.
Fourth, 113, 116, 199, 293, 298, 302.
Fifth, 248, 251–7, 260–3, 273–5, 298.

ARMY CORPS.

I., 32, 279.
III., 44, 118.
IV., 25, 44.
VI., 299.
VII., 260.
VIII., 83, 116, 126.
X., 66, 118.
XII., 71.
XIX., 260, 268.
Indian, 24, 26.
Portuguese, 275, 278, 279.
VII. (German), 26.

BRIGADES.

15th Brigade, 176.
164th Brigade, 281.
166th Brigade, 282.
Guards Brigade, 31.
Dehra Dun Brigade, 26.
Sirhind Brigade, 26.

DIVISIONS.

1st, 25, 50, 283–6.
2nd, 50.
7th, 44, 121, 130.
8th, 118, 270.
9th, 265.
15th, 259.

18th, 267.
19th, 120.
21st, 121.
24th, 268, 270.
28th, 39, 52, 176.
32nd, 118.
34th, 119.
36th, 118.
55th, 279, 286.
61st, 263.
5th Australian, 305.
Canadian, 72, 87, 108, 248.
1st Cavalry, 43.
2nd Cavalry, 40.
London, 142.
Royal Naval, 79.

REGIMENTS.

CAVALRY.
2nd Dragoon Guards, 44.
2nd King Edward's Horse, 25.
16th Lancers, 40.

ROYAL ENGINEERS.
29th Divisional Engineers, 79.
11th Field Company, 36.
1st Field Squadron, 43.
5th Field Squadron, 268.
Field Squadrons, 29.
1st Northumberland Field Company, 52.
2nd Wessex Field Company, 71.

TUNNELLING COMPANIES.
170th, 36, 49, 50, 56, 64, 72, 88, 150, 192, 194.
171st, 43, 52, 59, 64, 108, 176, 209, 210, 228, 230, 231, 233, 236, 237, 238, 288.
172nd, 46, 51, 55, 56, 57, 59, 60, 65, 98, 99, 108, 109, 140, 154, 160, 176, 177, 180, 181, 208, 209, 214, 215, 260, 292.

173rd, 44, 59, 64, 67, 88, 94, 109, 150, 250, 260, 261, 268, 269, 271, 272, 289, 310.
174th, 44, 59, 61, 62, 64, 65, 71, 116, 121, 134, 208, 209, 214, 237, 252, 258.
175th, 48, 58, 109, 177, 210, 211, 228, 230, 259, 298.
176th, 58, 64, 140, 143, 160, 163, 165.
177th, 61, 72, 87, 216, 248, 264, 306.
178th, 66, 67, 116, 121, 126, 131, 265, 307.
179th, 66, 116, 118, 259.
180th, 68, 70, 164, 266, 296, 309.
181st, 68, 88, 91, 99, 100, 110, 154.
182nd, 72, 87, 108, 142, 153, 160, 230, 266, 305, 306, 307.
183rd, 71, 116, 122, 289.
184th, 71, 97, 110, 140, 154, 157, 200, 202, 251, 288.
185th, 58, 72, 108, 140, 154, 297.
250th, 72, 88, 108, 216, 218, 223, 225, 227.
251st, 72, 106, 150, 168, 169, 276, 277 279, 280.
252nd, 71, 116, 118, 124, 132, 134, 135, 259.
253rd, 88, 150, 251, 260, 261, 263, 264.
254th, 88, 165.
255th, 88, 109, 150, 154, 164, 288.
256th, 110, 200, 303.
257th, 104, 110, 200.
258th, 109, 136, 268, 270, 271, 272, 289.
1st Australian, 109, 212, 239.
2nd Australian, 109, 187, 259, 292.
3rd Australian, 109, 110, 150, 171, 299.
New Zealand, 108, 110, 140, 154, 156, 157, 259, 299, 300, 311.
1st Canadian, 108, 182, 188, 214, 255.
2nd Canadian, 108, 181, 200, 248.
3rd Canadian, 87, 108, 172, 211, 212, 225, 227, 230, 232, 288, 290, 310.
Australian Mining Corps, 108.
VIII. Corps Mining Company, 79, 84.
Portuguese Mining Company, 276.

No. 1 R.E. Battalion, 268, 271.
No. 2 R.E. Battalion, 268, 271.

No. 1 R.E. Group, 272, 273.
No. 2 R.E. Group, 272, 273.

Army Troops Companies, 268.
565th Army Troops Company, 300.
577th Army Troops Company, 300.
Australian Electrical and Mechanical Mining and Boring Company, 109, 155, 245, 251, 277, 324.
171st Labour Company, 260.

INFANTRY.
13th Batt. A.I.F., 77.
1st Black Watch, 283, 284.
9th Cheshires, 120.
2/4th East Lancs., 169.
15th Entrenching Battalion, 260-8, 269.
17th Entrenching Battalion, 264.
20th Entrenching Battalion, 268, 269, 270, 271.
5th Gloucesters, 110.
2nd King's Own East Yorks, 39.
1st Monmouthshire Regt. (T.F.), 52.
3rd Monmouthshire Regt. (T.F.), 52.
1st Northants, 284.
12th Notts and Derby, 260.
12th Notts and Derby Pioneers, 269.
2/4th Royal Fusiliers, 266.
7/8th Royal Inniskilling Fusiliers, 266.
8th Royal Scots, 32.
2nd Royal Welch Fusiliers, 166.
Sherwood Foresters, 271.
8th South Staffs., 36.
8th South Wales Borderers, 36.
11th Welsh Regiment, 36.

FRENCH UNITS.

142nd French Territorial Regiment, 28.
6me. Gènie, 66.
15/3me. Gènie, 99.

GERMAN UNITS.

40th Bavarians, 246.
45th Bavarian Division, 234.
123rd Grenadier Regiment, 181.
124th Grenadier Regiment, 181.
40th Jagers, 246.
22nd Pioneers, 238.
163rd Regiment, 141.
XXXIII. Reserve Corps, 234.
17th Reserve Division, 141.
79th Reserve Infantry Brigade, 160.
86th Reserve Regiment, 142.

1225957R0

Printed in Great Britain by
Amazon.co.uk, Ltd.,
Marston Gate.